Pharmacy Practice and Tort Law

Pharmacy Practice and Tort Law

Fred G. Weissman, PharmD, JD
Associate Dean, Faculty/Student Affairs and Admissions
University of Southern California School of Pharmacy
Los Angeles, California

Jim Pinder, JD, MBA
Director of Academic Affairs
Assistant Professor, Pharmacy Law
Loma Linda University School of Pharmacy
Loma Linda, California

Mark R. Berns, JD
Attorney at Law
Beverly Hills, California

Mc Graw Hill Education

New York Chicago San Francisco Athens London Madrid Mexico City
Milan New Delhi Singapore Sydney Toronto

Pharmacy Practice and Tort Law

1 2 3 4 5 6 7 8 9 0 RHR/RHR 20 19 18 17 16

ISBN 978-1-259-64095-7
MHID 1-259-64095-7

This book was set in Stempel Schneidler Std by Cenveo® Publisher Services.

The editors were Michael Weitz and Peter J. Boyle.

The production supervisor was Richard Ruzycka.

Project management was provided by Sandhya Joshi, Cenveo Publisher Services.

The art manager was Armen Ovsepyan.

The designer was Eve Siegel.

RR Donnelley was the printer and binder.

This book was printed on acid-free paper.

Library of Congress Cataloging-in-Publication Data

Names: Weissman, Fred G., author. | Pinder, Jim, author. | Berns, Mark R., author.

Title: Pharmacy practice and tort law / Fred G. Weissman, Jim Pinder, Mark R. Berns.

Description: New York : McGraw-Hill, 2016. | Includes bibliographical references.

Identifiers: LCCN 2015044278 (print) | LCCN 2015044965 (ebook) | ISBN 9781259640957 (alk. paper) | ISBN 1259640957 (alk. paper) | ISBN 9781259640964 () | ISBN 1259640965 ()

Subjects: | MESH: Liability, Legal—United States. | Pharmaceutical Services—legislation & jurisprudence—United States.

Classification: LCC RA401.A1 (print) | LCC RA401.A1 (ebook) | NLM QV 733 AA1 | DDC 362.17/82–dc23

LC record available at http://lccn.loc.gov/2015044278

Contents

ABOUT THE AUTHORS

Fred G. Weissman

Fred G. Weissman presently serves as the associate dean for faculty/student affairs and admissions, and is an associate professor of pharmacy practice at the University of Southern California (USC) School of Pharmacy. Among the several courses Dr. Weissman teaches is the pharmacy law course. Dr. Weissman also teaches another law course entitled Medical Controversies and the Law in another department of the university. He has been recognized by his students as Teacher of the Year on five separate occasions over the last 20 years and was honored as the USC School of Pharmacy Alumnus of the Year in 2003. He has published numerous articles in a variety of pharmacy journals and has traveled both nationally and internationally to lecture on a variety of pharmacy-related subjects including issues dealing with both California and federal laws that impact the profession of pharmacy and health care in general. Dr. Weissman is a 1963 graduate from the USC School of Pharmacy and a 1989 graduate from Loyola Law School in Los Angeles.

Jim Pinder

Jim Pinder presently serves as assistant professor of pharmacy law in the Department of Pharmaceutical and Administrative Sciences and director of academic affairs at Loma Linda University School of Pharmacy. In addition to teaching pharmacy law, he also teaches an elective course, advanced pharmacy law. He has published in *California Pharmacist*, *Christianity and Pharmacy*, and *California Journal of Health-System Pharmacy*. He also presents at California state-wide conferences. Mr. Pinder is a 2004 graduate of the National University School of Business and Management and a 2008 graduate of William Howard Taft University Law School.

Mark R. Berns

Mark R. Berns is an attorney in Los Angeles, California, and a member of the State Bar of California. He is a graduate of the University of California, Los Angeles (UCLA) and the University of Southern California (USC) Gould School of Law. He has practiced in transactional and general civil litigation matters and has guest lectured for the pharmacy law and ethics course at the USC School of Pharmacy.

Preface

When studying pharmacy law as a pharmacy student, one encounters many abstract concepts. These concepts include duty of care, standard of practice, and learned intermediary doctrine. By rote memorization one can regurgitate these concepts and the applicable pharmacy laws or regulations on an exam. But for practicing pharmacy in the real world, a better way exists to internalize this information.

One thing many young adults remember are the stories they were told as children. The stories have meaning because they involve real people. The ending is often the best part. It tells us what happened! And if we were paying attention, we may recall the moral of the story.

One of the most successful ways of learning abstract pharmacy law concepts is through cases, or stories. We talk about the cast of characters, what happened to whom, which rules were allegedly broken, and what happened in the end. By the end of the case, or story, we will have a take-away message that will help students become better pharmacists.

This textbook begins with a history of tort law to orient students to the material being covered. Chapter 2 describes how to "brief" a case. This skill helps students break down a story into its component parts for dissection and internalization. In Chapter 3 the various torts are covered that are most relevant to the practice of pharmacy. The most important part of each chapter is at the end when the take-away message is discussed. What should students remember about this case? How does it apply to the current practice of pharmacy? A series of questions conclude each chapter that students and their instructor may wish to discuss.

Pharmacy law intimidates some students because it is so far removed from their primarily science backgrounds. This textbook is designed to help students make sense of tort law and apply it to their own experiences. It is hoped that the experiences of others, described in these cases, will help pharmacy students become competent professionals.

Disclaimer

The purpose of this textbook is to inform and not to advise. In case of being confronted with a legal issue, it is important that the reader consult an attorney familiar with the applicable statutes, regulations, and case law pertaining to the jurisdiction. The textbook was prepared and is organized to provide the reader with case law involving tort issues that are applicable to pharmacy-related situations. While the different tort law areas are discussed, it is important for the reader to recognize that each case presented represents a specific jurisdiction and decisions may have different outcomes in other jurisdictions. Thus, the main intent of this textbook is to provide the reader with an understanding of the different tort areas of law and how a specific tort principle is applied to the facts of a case.

CHAPTER 1

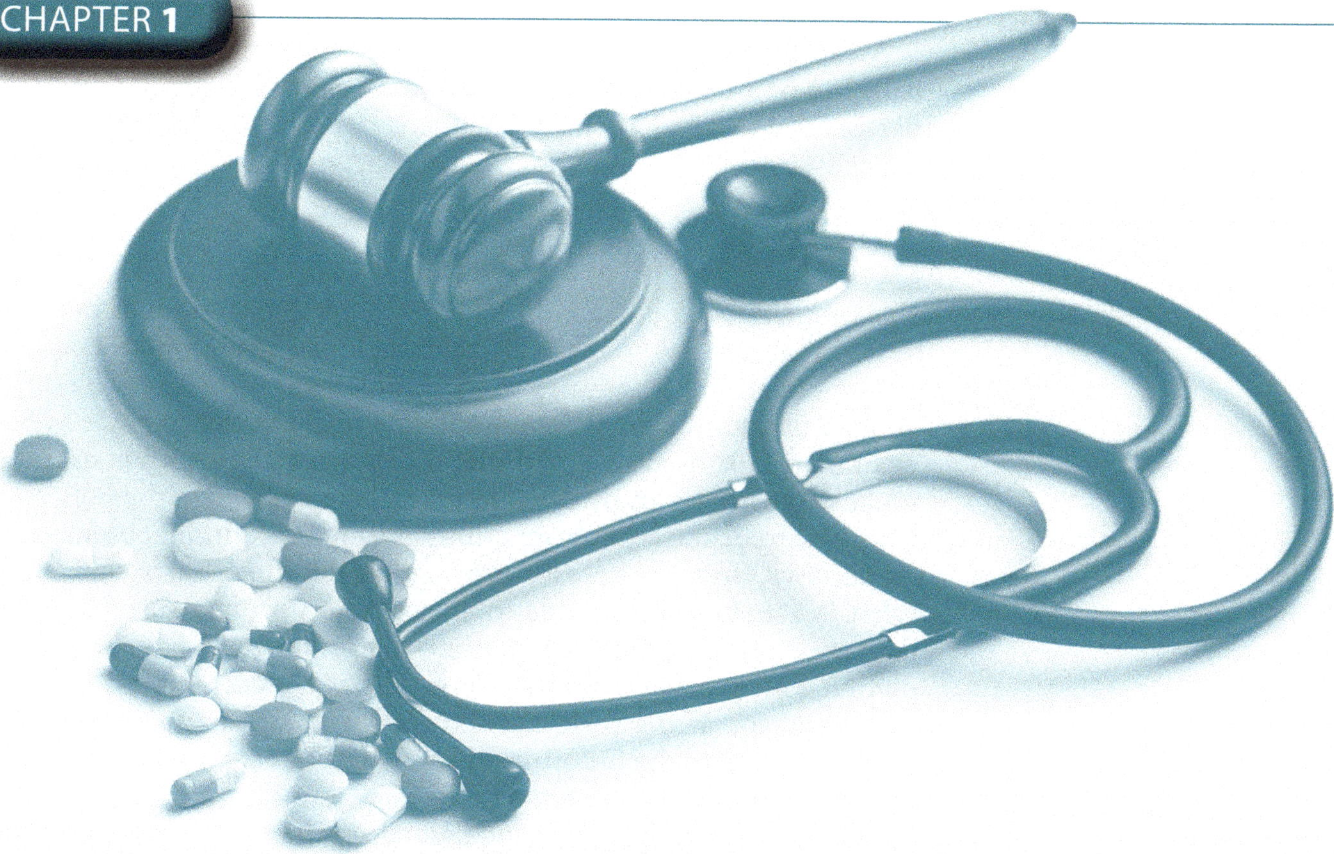

Introduction to Tort Law and Its Relevance to the Practice of Pharmacy

WHAT IS TORT LAW?

The area of tort law provides a person who has been harmed as the result of the wrongful acts of others the opportunity to bring a civil action for the harm or suffering caused. The person who has been injured or sustains pecuniary damages as the result of the wrongful act of another is referred to as the plaintiff, and the person causing the harm or damage is identified as the defendant or tortfeasor.

Three components must be satisfied in order for a tort action to exist:

1. The defendant had a legal duty to act in a given way toward the plaintiff.
2. The defendant breached that duty directed to the plaintiff.
3. The plaintiff suffered injury or harm as a direct result of the defendant's wrongful act.

A tort action is usually instituted by a plaintiff who is most often a person or an entity such as a business against a defendant who is a person and/or a given entity such as a corporation for the wrongful act caused.

HISTORICAL PERSPECTIVE ON TORT LAW

The origins of tort law are difficult to determine, and it has been suggested that tort law was poorly defined in the beginning.[1]

The underlying principles of tort law appear to have evolved from an examination of one's moral and civil obligations to society. Such examination is used to determine if one wronged another, and if so, what degree of harm or damage was done. However, the concept of torts was to be different from criminal action. A criminal breaks man-made laws, and a tortfeasor (wrongdoer) commits acts that violate what is generally acceptable to society. And if one caused sufficient damage, injury, or harm to another, his or her responsibility usually involved monetary compensation to the aggrieved party.

As long ago as the seventeenth century, it appeared that great concern was given to the unfortunate soul who was wronged. The English case of *Lambert v. Bessey* stated, "The law doth not so much regard the intent of the actor, as the loss and damage of the party suffering."[2] Thus, the wrongdoer became characterized as one who breached some civil duty owed to others and, as a result, would have to compensate the injured party a fair and equitable amount in order to make the injured party whole.

The word "tort" is derived from the Latin term "tortus," meaning twisted or crooked. The word came to mean simply "wrong," and then evolved to mean a "civil wrong."[3] By the twentieth century, tort law was established with specific areas of concern and defined legal boundaries so it would have its own unique character. It was intended not to infringe upon such legal areas as criminal actions, breach of contract matters, general property rights, government issues, and a host of other legal considerations. Although this legal isolation concept may work theoretically, in reality, the rules and principles of torts in some way touch every other legal category. Such interconnectivity of torts will become more apparent in the forthcoming chapters.

At the same time that tort law interfaces with other areas of law, it interfaces not only with one's day-to-day activities but also with the professions that one trains for and practices. The interface of tort law with professional pharmacy practice is the emphasis of this text. More specifically, this text will examine how the principles and rules of tort law become superimposed upon the profession and practice of pharmacy. Future chapters will look at the history and substance of major tort cases that have addressed whether or not a civil wrong occurred in specific scenarios relating to the practice of pharmacy.

AREAS OF TORT LAW

Tort law encompasses about 12 major topic areas, a number of which are further divided into subtopics. Some areas of tort law, such as battery or false imprisonment, are associated with an intent by an individual to cause harm. Other areas of tort law, most notably negligence, are not generally associated with intent, but with an accidental or careless act by an individual.

1. Intentional torts
   - Battery
   - Assault
   - False imprisonment
   - Intentional infliction of emotional distress (IIED)
2. Trespass to land
3. Trespass to chattels (eg, involves taking animals)
4. Conversion (taking another's property and using it like it was yours)
5. Negligence—what must be proven:
   - Duty (does a duty exist?)
   - Breach of duty (was there a breach of that duty?)
   - Causation (as a result of the breach of duty, was harm or damage caused?)
   - Actual causation
   - Proximate causation
   - Damages
6. Strict liability
7. Products liability
8. Misrepresentation (fraud or negligent misrepresentation)
9. Defamation (libel or slander)
10. Nuisance
11. Invasion of privacy
12. Interference with advantageous relationships
    - Business relationships
    - Family relationships

It is important to have a good understanding of the legal definitions of the major torts. These definitions, along with examples and actual pharmacy practice cases, will provide the substance for upcoming chapters. This text will not discuss in detail every one of the topics of tort law, but will concentrate on the tort areas that are most relevant and common to the practice of pharmacy. These include negligence, products liability, misrepresentation, and, to a lesser degree, defamation and the intentional torts of false imprisonment and infliction of emotional distress.

Parties who have a tort claim brought against them, making them defendants in a legal action, have a right to raise defenses that may either mitigate or discharge the plaintiff's claim. The defendants

Table 1-1. Table of Tort Law Defenses

Tort	Defenses
Intentional torts (battery, assault, false imprisonment, etc.)	Consent Self defense, defense of others, or defense of property Necessity (private or public) Authority
Negligence	Contributory or comparative negligence Assumption of the risk
Strict liability	A showing of absence of fault
Products liability	Warranty breach claim Contributory or comparative negligence Assumption of the risk Disclaimer or failure to notify seller
Misrepresentation (fraud)	Truth or materiality of statement Proof of justifiable reliance
Misrepresentation (negligent misrepresentation)	Same defenses as for negligence
Defamation	Consent Truth of statement Person identified questionable Publication to a third person questionable Opinion
Nuisance	Not in violation of legislation or city ordinances
Invasion of privacy	Consent Authority
Interference with advantageous relationships	Justifiable purpose

may be limited in the scope of defenses they may bring, based upon the type of tort action. Table 1-1 lists the defenses that can be raised under a given tort action. These defenses will be elaborated upon in later chapters, using both examples and actual cases.

GENERAL REMEDIES TO TORT LAW CLAIMS

Plaintiffs who bring a tort action to court and receive a judgment in their favor will usually have entitlement to a court-determined remedy. The major category of remedies awarded to plaintiffs for damages they may have suffered is monetary compensation. A lesser category of tort claim awards is known as injunctive relief. Both of these remedy categories will be explained in detail in the later chapters of this book, and highlighted when discussing the individual tort topics. Table 1-2 provides an introduction to the types of monetary damage awards and the requirements for injunctive relief judgments.

Table 1-2. Table of Tort Remedies

Tort Remedy	Description
Monetary damages (ie, compensatory damages)	Compensatory damages compensate a plaintiff with a monetary reward for general and/or specific damages. General damages usually involve damages associated with pain and suffering. Specific damages usually involve losses that are not necessarily obvious and require an accurate accounting of loss (eg, lost wages and medical expenses).
Punitive damages	Are only awarded as punishment where there is intent to commit a tort or where the defendant acts willfully or with wanton disregard for others.
Nominal damages	A plaintiff is awarded an extremely small amount of money (eg, one dollar) as a result of the difficulty in setting a given amount of money to the tortious act and to show that the plaintiff has prevailed.
Injunctive relief	In cases where monetary damages are not adequate to repair the harm (eg, plaintiff wishes to get back a piece of personal property that is in the defendant's possession), a plaintiff may seek injunctive relief, such as an injunction, which is a court order requiring a person to do or cease doing a specific activity.

TORT LAW AND THE PRACTICE OF PHARMACY

The breadth of tort law categories, defenses, and remedies should demonstrate how vast the body of tort law is. This text will concentrate on those tort claims brought against pharmacists on a relatively consistent basis. These include the following:

- Negligence
- Products liability
- Invasion of privacy
- Misrepresentation
- Defamation
- False imprisonment
- Intentional infliction of emotional distress
- Interference with advantageous relationships

While many claims or lawsuits are settled before they go to court, there are a number of cases brought against pharmacists that are heard by both the trial and appellate courts each year. Some of the decisions in those cases yield favorable outcomes to the defendant pharmacist, and some do not. This text will examine cases that address different aspects of pharmacy-related tort claims to demonstrate how prior case law, standards of practice, and specific federal and state statutes and regulations help judges and juries reach their final verdicts. If you are or are soon to be a practicing pharmacist, reading and understanding these pharmacy-related tort cases will give you valuable insight on the way you practice within the pharmacy profession.

In reviewing an assigned case, the reader should extract from the case, in a concise manner, the following information:

- The cast of characters (who is the plaintiff, who is the defendant, and who are the witnesses?)
- A brief summation of the facts of the case
- The issue of the case
- The rule of law (what the case stands for and how it will serve as precedence for similar cases within that given jurisdiction)
- The court's analysis in how it arrived at its decision (often the analysis will be predicated on prior court decisions or statutory and regulatory laws within a given jurisdiction)
- The conclusion the court comes to in the case

Chapter 2 will provide an example of how to analyze a case and extract from it the important aspects described previously. This process is referred to as "briefing a case."

A large percentage of tort-related lawsuits brought against pharmacies and pharmacists occur as the result of some negligent act associated with practice. The majority of negligent actions are attributable to such matters as providing the patient with the wrong prescription drug, wrong strength, wrong directions, incomplete information during the consultation regarding appropriate drug warnings, or not using the patient's medication record or profile history properly to determine if there are problems associated with the taking of a prescribed drug.[4]

When analyzing a case that involves a possible or alleged negligent act on the part of a pharmacist, such a case may often focus on one of the four elements of negligence:

- Was there a *duty*?
- Was there a *breach of the duty*?
- Was the breach of the duty a *causation factor* in a resulting injury or harm?
- Was there *harm* or *injury* caused?

If any one element is missing from this list, even though the other three elements are present, the case may not proceed forward and the plaintiff will most likely lose. An example would be when a patient brings in a prescription to be filled by the pharmacist and the pharmacist fills the prescription with the wrong drug. If the patient takes one dose of the wrong drug but there is no resulting harm or injury to the patient in taking that one dose, any negligence case brought against the pharmacist would most likely not prevail. The analysis of the case scenario would go something like this:

- Was there a duty on the part of the pharmacist? Yes—when the pharmacist accepted the prescription to be filled, he or she assumed the duty or responsibility to fill it correctly.

- Was there a breach of the duty by the pharmacist? Yes—when the pharmacist filled the prescription with the wrong medication, he or she breached the duty or responsibility.
- Did the breach of duty by the pharmacist cause injury to the patient? Causation can be looked upon as the bridge between the breach and any injury caused. Because there was no resulting or provable injury to the patient, causation becomes a moot issue and the negligence claim by the patient would fail.

USING PAST CASE DECISIONS IN DECIDING PENDING CASES

When an attorney representing a plaintiff files a claim against a defendant, the attorney will commonly cite related past cases to show how the court ruled on a given matter and what analysis went into the past case decisions. Thus, precedence of past case decisions is a key factor in directing the thinking and logic of the court in reaching its decision on the case at bar.

While past cases can have a strong influence on the outcome of the case being decided, it is important to keep in mind that those past cases must have jurisdictional authority. Cases that are discussed in later chapters have originated in different state appellate courts or federal district or circuit courts. Thus, a case that has been decided in an appellate court in the state of Florida serves as a case having precedence in the state of Florida. That case technically does not serve as a precedent case for the state of California. However, California may have decided on a similar case whereby the rule of law for California follows the Florida rule of law. Such a case in California will serve as precedence for subsequent California court decision-making. Conversely, it is not uncommon for one state court's decision on a matter to be in direct opposition to another state court's decision on the same matter. Therefore, it is important to know a state or jurisdiction's ruling on a given or similar matter for the purpose of strengthening a client's legal arguments when the matter is brought before a court in that jurisdiction.

Circuit and district courts, which are part of the federal court system, have extended boundaries encompassing several states; the decisions from these courts serve as precedence for those boundaries of jurisdiction. The decisions made by the U.S. Supreme Court serve as precedence for all the states.

The principle in determining if the decision in a case has precedence in a given jurisdiction is associated with the term *stare decisis*, which requires that a court's decision-making follow the precedence of cases decided within that jurisdiction. Cases that have been decided outside the jurisdiction may still serve the court as a source of guidance, possibly to be adopted as that jurisdiction's decision on a yet-to-be-decided point.

While the cases presented in this text represent different jurisdictions, the reader will acquire a general sense of the direction of decision-making on the various tort law issues. Keep in mind that most jurisdictions have ascribed to the same outcomes presented in the cases that follow and have depended on other jurisdictions to formulate their decisions on pending matters not yet resolved by that jurisdiction.

UNDERSTANDING LEGAL TERMS

Many legal terms used in the pharmacy-related cases are understandably not common to the language of pharmacists. These terms will be explained in the core of the text where appropriate, and definitions of the terms can be found in the glossary following the last chapter. The cases, although abridged, have not been altered substantially in terms of the syntax and grammar used by the judge writing the court opinion. Therefore, it is essential that you understand the meaning of any "legalese" terms so that you do not miss some extremely important concept regarding either the procedural history of the case or the development of the court's opinion on a particular matter.

REFERENCES

1. Prosser WL, Wade JW, Schwartz VE. *Torts, Cases and Materials.* 7th ed. University Casebook Series. Mineola, NY: The Foundation Press; 1982.
2. *Lambert v. Bessey* (K.B. 1681) T., Raym. 421, 83 Eng. Rep. 220.
3. Keeton WP, Dobbs DB, Keeton RE, et al. *Prosser and Keeton on the Law of Torts.* 5th ed. St. Paul, MN: West Publishing Co.; 1984.
4. Baker KR. *The Pharmacist as Risk Manager* (from the Pharmacist's Journal 3rd ed.). Published by Pharmacists Mutual Insurance Co.; 1995.

QUESTIONS

1. Describe what you understand regarding the meaning of tort law, and provide some examples using actual facts based upon your own experiences that relate to tort law issues.
2. Before reading the chapters on negligence, try to explain what you think negligence means, and what you think are the elements of negligence that must be proven.
3. The torts of fraud and negligent misrepresentation might appear to you as being similar. Before reviewing the chapters on fraud and negligent misrepresentation, discuss what you understand to be the difference between these two torts.
4. Tort law cases are generally brought as civil cases in the courts. What is your understanding regarding the differences between a civil case and a criminal case? What remedies are sought in a civil case, and what remedies might be sought in a criminal case?
5. When a defendant must defend against a negligence suit brought by a plaintiff, provide your thoughts on what you think are the elements of the tort that need to be defended against. (Hint: Each tort has a set of elements that must be proven in order for the plaintiff to prevail. If any of those elements are missing, the plaintiff's case may not be sustainable.)

CHAPTER 2

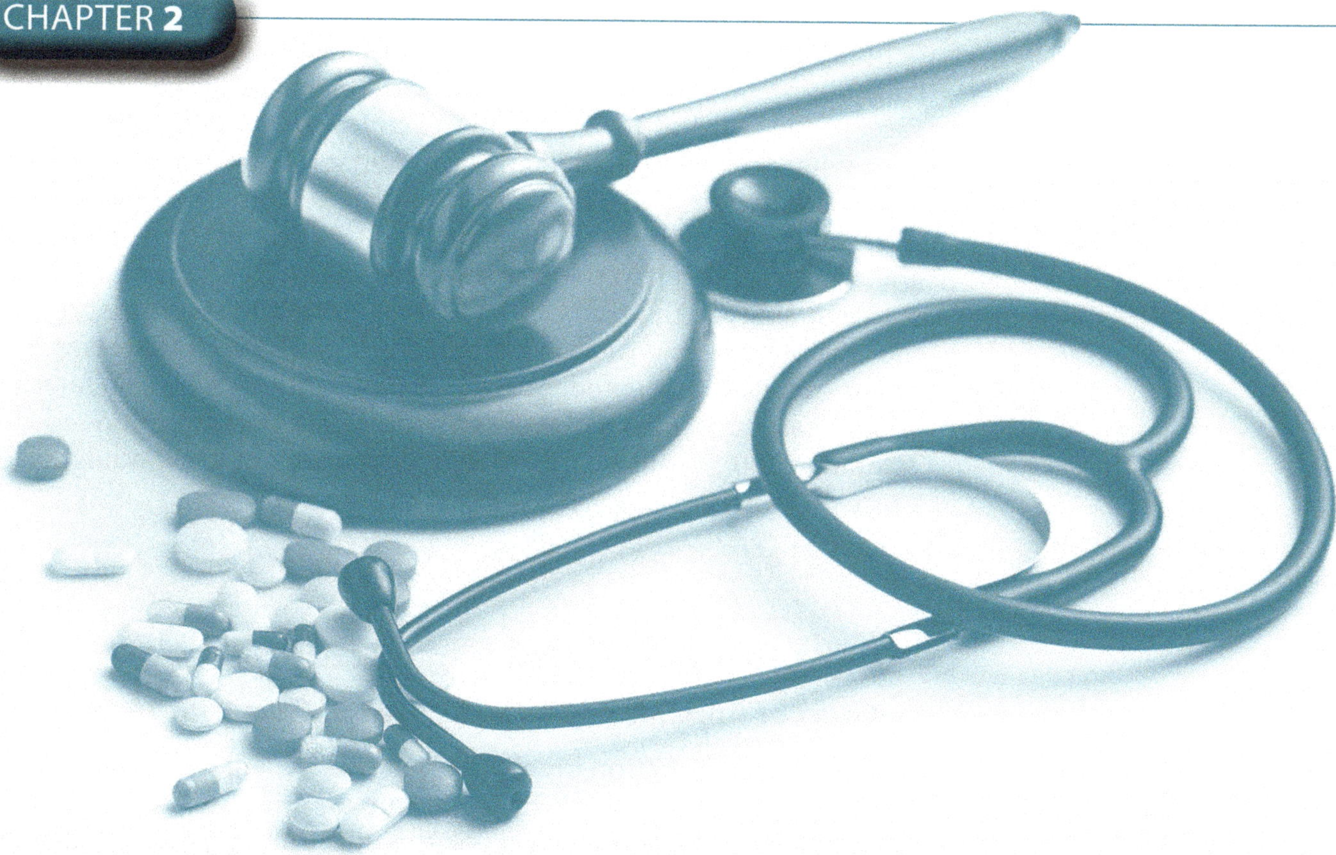

"Briefing" a Tort Law Case

Analyzing or "briefing" a case involves organizing the following key information about the case:

- The cast of characters (identifying the plaintiff, the defendant, and the witnesses)
- A brief summary of the facts of the case
- The issue of the case (the central question the court is deciding)
- The rule of law (what the case stands for and how it will serve as precedence for other cases of a similar nature within the given jurisdiction)
- The court's analysis (rationale of how the court arrived at its decision)
- The conclusion the court comes to in the case

Law school students use a tool known as the IRAC method to help them extract critical information from the written text of the court's decision in a case. The text of a given case can be many pages long. The purpose of the IRAC method, therefore, is to condense the case to preferably less than half a page, with simple wording that allows the student to have a full understanding of the case.

In the IRAC method, "I" stands for issue, "R" stands for rule, "A" stands for analysis, and "C" stands for conclusion. Breaking down a case within this framework of IRAC components will help to clarify both what the court decided and upon what facts it based its decision.

The following two cases are provided to demonstrate how the IRAC method operates. You might want to first read the two cases, and then come back to them to extract the IRAC elements. After you read and analyze the two cases yourself, compare your briefing with the author's briefing found immediately after each of the cases.

The first case presented, *Strunk v. Strunk,* although not a pharmacy-related case, provides a relatively simple fact pattern followed by a carefully thought-out analysis leading to a reasonable finding by the court.

STRUNK V. STRUNK

Court of Appeals of Kentucky, 445 S.W.2d 145, 1969

The specific question involved upon this appeal is: Does a court of equity have the power to permit a kidney to be removed from an incompetent ward of the state upon petition of his committee, who is also his mother, for the purpose of being transplanted into the body of his brother, who is dying of a fatal kidney disease? We are of the opinion it does.

The facts of the case are as follows: Arthur L. Strunk, 54 years of age, and Ava Strunk, 52 years of age, of Williamstown, Kentucky, are the parents of two sons. Tommy Strunk is 28 years of age, married, an employee of the Penn State Railroad, and a part-time student at the University of Cincinnati. Tommy is now suffering from chronic glomerulus nephritis, a fatal kidney disease. He is now being kept alive by frequent treatment on an artificial kidney, a procedure that cannot be continued much longer.

Jerry Strunk is 27 years of age, is incompetent, and, through proper legal proceedings, has been committed to the Frankfort State Hospital and School, which is a state institution maintained for the feeble-minded. He has an IQ of approximately 35, which corresponds with the mental age of approximately six years. He is further handicapped by a speech defect, which makes it difficult for him to communicate with persons who are not well acquainted with him. When it was determined that Tommy, in order to survive, would have to have a kidney, the doctors considered the possibility of using a kidney from a cadaver if and when one became available or one from a live donor if this could be made available. The entire family, his mother, father, and a number of collateral relatives were tested. Because of incompatibility of blood type or tissue, none were medically acceptable as live donors. As a last resort, Jerry was tested and found to be highly acceptable. This immediately presented the legal problem as to what, if anything, could be done by the family, especially the mother and the father to procure a transplant from Jerry to Tommy. The mother as a committee petitioned the county court for authority to proceed with the operation. The court found that the operation was necessary, that under the peculiar circumstances of this case it would not only be beneficial to Tommy but also be beneficial to Jerry because Jerry was greatly dependent upon Tommy, emotionally and psychologically, and that his well-being would be jeopardized more severely by the loss of his brother than by the removal of a kidney.

Appeal was taken to the Franklin Circuit Court, where the chancellor reviewed the record, examined the testimony of the witnesses, and adopted the findings of the county court.

A psychiatrist, in attendance to Jerry, who testified in the case, stated that in his opinion the death of Tommy under these circumstances would have "an extremely traumatic effect upon him" (Jerry).

The right to act for the incompetent in all cases has become recognized in this country as the doctrine of substituted judgment and is broad enough not only to cover property but also to cover all matters touching on the well-being of the ward. (The court referred to an English case in which the standard applied was whether the "lunatic would have approved if he had been capable of acting himself.")

We are of the opinion that a chancery court does have sufficient inherent power to authorize the operation. The circuit court having found that the operative procedures in this instance are to the best interest of Jerry Strunk and this finding having been based upon substantial evidence, we are of the opinion the judgment should be affirmed.

Dissenting Opinion

Apparently because of my indelible recollection of a government that, to the everlasting shame of its citizens, embarked on a program of genocide and experimentation with human bodies, I have been more troubled in reaching a decision in this case than in any other. My sympathies and emotions are torn between a compassion to aid an ailing young man and a duty to fully protect unfortunate members of society.

Briefing of the *Strunk* Case

Parties: Appellant: State on behalf of Jerry Strunk. Appellee: Parents of Jerry Strunk.

Facts: The appellees acting on behalf of their incompetent son Jerry Strunk, who is ward of the state, request that Jerry have a kidney surgically removed in order to be implanted into their other son, Tommy, who has chronic glomerulus nephritis and, without the replacement of a kidney from an appropriate donor, will have a limited period of survival.

Issue: Does a court of equity have the power to permit a kidney to be removed from an incompetent ward of the state upon petition of his parents for the purpose of being transplanted into the body of his brother, who is dying of a fatal kidney disease?

Rule: Under the doctrine of substituted judgment, those having the authority as guardian ad litem may decide for a ward of the state the fate of a surgical procedure such as a kidney transplant operation where there is a potential for that ward of the state to benefit another, as well as themselves.

Analysis: The right to act for an incompetent is allowed in this jurisdiction under the doctrine of substituted judgment. In this case such an operation is warranted since it would not only benefit Tommy but also benefit Jerry both emotionally and psychologically since in the balance Jerry's well-being would be jeopardized more severely by the loss of his brother than by the removal of a kidney.

Conclusion: The court has the power under the doctrine of substantial judgment to authorize a special operation involving a kidney removal and transplant that is arguably beneficial to both the donor and the recipient.

LASLEY V. SHRAKE'S COUNTRY CLUB PHARMACY

179 Ariz. 583; 880 P.2d 1129 (1994)

The plaintiffs appeal from the trial court's grant of a motion to dismiss in favor of Shrake's Country Club Pharmacy.

Facts: From 1960 to 1990, William K. Helms, MD (Helms) treated Mr. Lasley. Helms prescribed Doriden and codeine, which Lasley alleges are potent and addicting drugs. Lasley filled most of the prescriptions from Helms at Shrake's. For approximately 10 years, Shrake's mailed one or more of the allegedly addictive drugs to Lasley at his residence in another state.

Allegedly as a result of taking Doriden and codeine for an extended period of time and in combination, Lasley required hospitalization for Doriden detoxification and psychiatric treatment for addiction. He suffered from a major clinical depression and related disorders.

In March 1991, appellants filed their complaint against Helms and Shrake's. Appellants alleged that Shrake's had breached a duty to Lasley "to exercise that degree of care, skill, and learning expected of reasonable prudent pharmacies and pharmacists in the profession." Shrake's filed a motion to dismiss for failure to state a claim upon which relief could be granted. It argued that, as a matter of law, a pharmacist has neither a duty to warn of a prescribed drug's dangerous propensities nor a duty to control or keep track of a customer's reliance on drugs prescribed by a licensed treating physician.

In response, appellants argued that Shrake's owed a duty of reasonable care to Lasley and that whether it had breached the standard of care applicable to that duty was a question for the trier of fact. They presented to the trial court an affidavit from an expert and portions of the American Pharmaceutical Association Standards of Practice for the Profession of Pharmacy. Those documents indicated that the standard of care for a pharmacist includes obligations to advise a customer of the highly addictive nature of a prescribed drug and of the hazards of ingesting two or more drugs that adversely interact with one another. Appellants' evidence further stated that a pharmacist should advise the prescribing doctor if it appears that the patient is taking an addictive drug in quantities inconsistent with the manufacturer's recommended dosage guidelines.

The trial court granted the motion to dismiss. It found that Shrake's owed no duty to appellants to warn of addiction or to refuse prescriptions written by Helms. Following denial of appellants' motion for reconsideration, the trial court entered judgment dismissing the complaint against Shrake's with prejudice. Appellants timely appealed from the judgment.

Court's Analysis: A. Because this is a negligence action, we first determine whether Shrake's had "a duty to conform to a particular standard of conduct to protect [Lasley] against unreasonable risks of harm."[1] In other words, we must consider, as did the trial court, whether the relationship between Shrake's and Lasley required Shrake's to use care to avoid or prevent injury to Lasley.[2]

Shrake's contends that the trial court correctly ruled that Shrake's had no duty to warn Lasley or his physician of the potentially addictive nature of drugs legitimately prescribed for Lasley. We believe, however, that the trial court's ruling confuses the concept of duty with that of standard of care.

In *Markowitz*, the Arizona Supreme Court cautioned against confusing the existence of a duty with details of the standard of conduct.[3] Specific details of conduct do not determine whether a duty exists but instead bear on whether a defendant who owed a duty to the plaintiff breached the applicable standard of care.[4] In explaining the concept, the Coburn court quoted from Prosser and Keeton:

> It is better to reserve "duty" for the problem of the relation between individuals which imposes upon one a legal obligation for the benefit of the other, and to deal with particular conduct in terms of a legal standard of what is required to meet the obligation. In other words, "duty" is a question of whether the defendant is under any obligation for the benefit of the particular plaintiff; and in negligence cases, the duty [if it exists] is always the same—to conform to the legal standard of reasonable conduct in the light of the apparent risk. What the defendant must do, or must not do, is a question of the standard of conduct required to satisfy the duty.[5]

In its answer, Shrake's admitted that it owed a duty to Lasley to comply with the applicable standard of care. We agree. Thus, the answer to the threshold question in this appeal is that Shrake's did owe a duty of reasonable care to Lasley. The trial court therefore erred in finding, as a matter of law, that Shrake's owed no duty to Lasley.

B. Once the court determines that a duty exists, the next question is whether the defendant breached the standard of care established pursuant to the duty.[6] In most cases, whether the defendant's conduct met the standard of care is a question for the trier of fact.[7] In some instances, however, the court may decide as a matter of law that the defendant did not breach the applicable standard of conduct and thus was not negligent.[8] Thus, even though the trial court incorrectly granted summary judgment based on duty, if we can say as a matter of law that Shrake's did not breach its standard of care, we may affirm the trial court's judgment in favor of Shrake's.[9]

In an ordinary negligence action, the standard of care imposed is that of the conduct of a reasonably prudent person under the circumstances.[10] Health care providers and other professionals, however, are held to a higher standard of care than that of the ordinary prudent person when the alleged negligence involves the defendant's area of expertise. In these cases, the standard is based on "the usual conduct of other members of the defendant's profession in similar circumstances … [and] the plaintiff must present evidence of the accepted professional conduct" so that the jury can measure the defendant's conduct against the applicable standard. The plaintiff then must show that the defendant's conduct did not adhere to the standard. We impose this higher standard of care upon pharmacists because they are professionals in the health care area. Arizona courts have not yet considered whether the scope of a pharmacist's duty of reasonable care includes an obligation to warn customers of possible adverse effects of prescribed medications. Other jurisdictions, however, have resolved this question, and we look to their decisions for guidance.[11] Two distinct approaches have emerged for considering whether pharmacists have a duty to warn their customers.

As Shrake's asserts, the majority of jurisdictions that have considered the scope of a pharmacist's duty to warn customers have concluded, in various factual settings, that no such duty exists. Some courts, considering whether a pharmacist has a duty to warn the customer of possible adverse side effects of prescribed medications, have held that no such duty exists.[12] In these cases, the courts generally reason that imposing a duty to warn on the pharmacist would place the pharmacist between the physician, who knows the patient's physical condition, and the patient and that recognizing such a duty could lead to harmful interference in the patient-physician relationship.[13]

Other courts, considering the duty to warn in a factual situation similar to that before us, have concluded that pharmacists have no legal duty to warn the patient or physician when the physician prescribes excessive doses of a drug.[14] Those courts conclude that the physician, not the pharmacist, has the duty to prescribe drugs properly and to warn the patient of any dangers from taking the medication. Imposing a duty to warn on pharmacists would compel them to second guess every prescription physicians write if the pharmacists wished to escape liability.[15]

We reject the analysis relied upon in these decisions for the reasons stated in *Markowitz*. The decisions do precisely what the Markowitz court cautioned against; they use details of the standard of conduct to determine whether a duty exists.

Other jurisdictions, applying the same distinction between duty and standard of conduct as that explained in *Markowitz*, have concluded that whether a failure to warn violates the applicable standard of conduct in a particular situation generally presents a question of fact for the jury. In *Dooley v. Everett*, the plaintiff alleged that the pharmacy had a duty to warn a customer or the customer's physician or both of the potential adverse interaction between two drugs prescribed by the same physician on different days and filled by the same pharmacist on different days.[16] The pharmacy moved for summary judgment, arguing that as a matter of law the pharmacist owes no duty to his customer to warn of potential drug interactions. In opposition to the motion, the plaintiff filed an expert's affidavit that set forth various standards of care that the pharmacy allegedly had violated.

The *Dooley* court first noted the distinction between duty and standard of care and determined that the pharmacy owed its customer a duty to use due care under the attendant circumstances.[17] The court then considered whether the scope of the duty the pharmacist owed the customer included an obligation to warn. The court concluded that, because the plaintiffs had introduced expert testimony to dispute the pharmacy's argument that warning of potential drug interactions was not a part of its duty, the disputed issue of fact prevented the granting of summary judgment.[18]

Similarly, in *Hand v. Krakowski*, the court reversed summary judgment in favor of a pharmacy, finding that a jury question existed when the pharmacist knew that the customer was an alcoholic and knew or should have known that the prescribed drugs were contraindicated with the use of alcohol.[19] Under those circumstances, the court believed that the pharmacist may have had a duty to warn the customer of the danger involved and to inquire of the prescribing doctor whether the drugs should be discontinued.[20] In *Riff v. Morgan Pharmacy*, the court affirmed a jury verdict that found the pharmacy jointly liable for injuries sustained from a potentially toxic drug prescribed without a warning describing side effects that could result from exceeding the maximum safe dosage.[21] The court held that "the pharmacy had a legal duty to exercise due care and diligence in the performance of its professional duties."[22] The court concluded "the plaintiff had presented sufficient credible evidence to establish that the pharmacy breached its duty by failing to warn the patient or notify the physician of inadequacies on the face of the prescription that created a substantial risk of serious harm to the plaintiff."[23]

In response to Shrake's motion to dismiss, appellants presented an affidavit from an expert stating that the standard of care applicable to a pharmacist includes a responsibility to advise a customer of the addictive nature of a drug, to warn of the hazards of ingesting two or more drugs that adversely interact with one another, and to discuss with the physician the addictive nature of a prescribed drug and the dangers of long-term prescription of the drug. Appellants also presented excerpts from the American Pharmaceutical Association Standards of Practice for the Profession of Pharmacy that described similar standards. On this record, we cannot say as a matter of law that Shrake's did not breach the standard of care for the duty it owed to Lasley.

Conclusion: For the reasons explained previously, we reverse the trial court's grant of summary judgment in favor of Shrake's and remand to the trial court for further proceedings.

Briefing of the *Lasley* Case

This is an example of how the case may be synthesized down, using the IRAC method plus identification of the cast of characters and a brief statement of the facts:

Parties: Lasley is the plaintiff. Shrake's Pharmacy is the defendant.

Facts: Over a 10-year period, Lasley has been receiving prescriptions for Doriden and codeine written by Dr. Helms. These prescriptions have been filled at Shrake's Pharmacy. Lasley claims that as a result of taking these drugs over a long period of time, he required hospitalization for treatment of Doriden detoxification, addiction, and major depression. Lasley blames Shrake's Pharmacy personnel for not exercising its duty of due care by not advising Lasley of the highly addictive nature of the drugs prescribed and taking such drugs in quantities inconsistent with the manufacturer's recommended dosages.

Issue: Does a pharmacy have a duty to warn either the customer or the customer's physician that prolonged use of a prescription drug dispensed by the pharmacy or use of the drug in combination with another prescribed drug may lead to addiction or adverse side effects?

Rule: The pharmacy does have a duty to warn the patient about the possible dangers of the prolonged use of a drug alone or with other drugs causing addiction and other adverse effects.

Analysis: The defendant, Shrake's Pharmacy, had a duty to the plaintiff to exercise reasonable care to prevent harm. In addition, the concept of standard of care should not be confused with the concept of duty. According to *Coburn v. City of Tucson*, 691 P.2d 1078 (Ariz. 1984), "one's conduct should not determine whether a duty exists, but instead bear on whether a defendant who owed a duty to the plaintiff breached a reasonable standard of care owed to the plaintiff." The defendant did not meet the standard of care that was an obligation based upon the duty owed to the plaintiff. The standard of care required of the defendant was the type of conduct expected of a reasonably prudent person who had a duty of providing due care to the plaintiff. In fact, health care professionals such as pharmacists are held to a higher standard of care than that of the ordinary prudent person based upon the defendant's area of expertise and the importance of care provided when it involves a patient's health.

Conclusion: The trial court's decision was reversed, ruling that the defendant owed a duty of due care to the plaintiff. The case was remanded to the trial court for further proceedings.

REFERENCES

1. *Alhambra School Dist. v. Maricopa County Superior Court*, 165 Ariz. 36, 41, 796 P.2d 470. 473 (1990).
2. *Markowitz v. Arizona Parks Bd.*, 146 Ariz. 352, 356, 706 P.2d 364, 368 (1985); *Bellezzo v. State*, 174 Ariz. 548, 550, 851 P.2d 647, 849 (App. 1992).
3. 146 Ariz. at 355, 706 P.2d at 367; see also *Coburn v. City of Tucson*, 143 Ariz. 50, 51-52, 691 P.2d 1078, 1079-1080 (1984).
4. *Markowitz*, 146 Ariz. at 355, 706 P.2d at 367.
5. 143 Ariz. at 52, 691 P.2d at 1080 (quoting W. Page Keeton et al., *Prosser and Keeton on the Law of Torts* § 53, at 356 [5th ed. 1984]).
6. *Markowitz*, 146 Ariz. at 356, 706 P.2d at 366.
7. *Bellezzo*, 174 Ariz. at 551, 851 P.2d at 850.
8. *Id.* (citing *Markowitz*, 146 Ariz. at 357, 706 P.2d at 369).
9. See *Gary Outdoor Advertising Co. v. Sun Lodge, Inc.*, 133 Ariz. 240, 242, 650 P.2d 1222, 1224 (1982).
10. *Bell v. Maricopa Medical Ctr.*, 157 Ariz. 192, 194, 755 P.2d 1180, 1182 (App. 1988).
11. See *Bellezzo*, 174 Ariz. at 551-552, 851 P.2d at 850-851.
12. *Ramirez v. Richardson-Merrell, Inc.*, 628 F. Supp. 85 (E.D. Pa. 1986); *Leesley v. West*, 165 Ill. App. 3d 135, 522 N.E.2d 1246 (Ill. 1988); *Ingram v. Hook's Drugs, Inc.* 476 N.E.2d 881 (Ind. App.1985); *Nichols v. Central Merchandise, Inc.* 817 P.2d 1131 (Kan. App. 1991).
13. See *Ramirez*, 628 F. Supp. at 88; *Nichols, 817* P.2d at 1133.
14. *Jones v. Irvin*, 602 F. Supp. 399 (S.D. III. 1985; *Pysz* v. *Henry's Drug*, 457 So. 2d 561 (Fla. Dist. Ct. App. 1984; *Kampe v. Howard Stark Professional Pharmacy*, 841 S.W.2d 223 [Mo. App. 1992] Inc.).
15. *Jones*, 602 F. Supp. at 402; *Pysz*, 457 So. 2d at 562; *Fakhouri v. Taylor*, 622 N.E.2d 1204 (111.1993).
16. *Dooley v. Everett*, 805 S.W.2d 380 (Tenn. App. 1990).

17. 805 S.W.2d at 384.
18. *Id.* at 386.
19. *Hand v. Krakowski*, 89 A.D.2d 650, 453 N.Y.S.2d 121 (App. Div. 1982).
20. 453 NYS.2d at 123.
21. *Riff v. Morgan Pharmacy* 508 A.2d 1247 (Pa. Super. 1986), *appeal denied*, 524 A.2d 494 (Pa. 1987).
22. 508 A.2d at 1251-1252.
23. 508 A.2d at 1252.

QUESTIONS

1. What reasoning do you believe the trial court (the lower court) employed to come to the conclusion that no duty existed on the part of the pharmacy?
2. After reading this case, how would you explain to someone the difference between "duty" and "standard of practice"? What exactly is meant by "standard of practice"?
3. What happens when a case is "remanded"?
4. At the present time, are there state or federal statutes that you could argue would support the nature of the duty described in this case? (For example, how would OBRA 90 [Omnibus Budgetary Reconciliation Act of 1990] or state patient consultation laws apply?)
5. As a practicing pharmacist, would you have done anything differently from what Shrake's did?
6. Do you feel that the following parties should be fully or partially liable (comparable negligence) for the outcome that occurred? Give your reasons for your responses.
   a. The pharmacist(s) who filled or provided the medication to the plaintiff
   b. The pharmacy (Shrake's Pharmacy)
   c. The plaintiff's physician (William Helms, MD)
   d. The plaintiff (Mr. Lasley)

CHAPTER 3

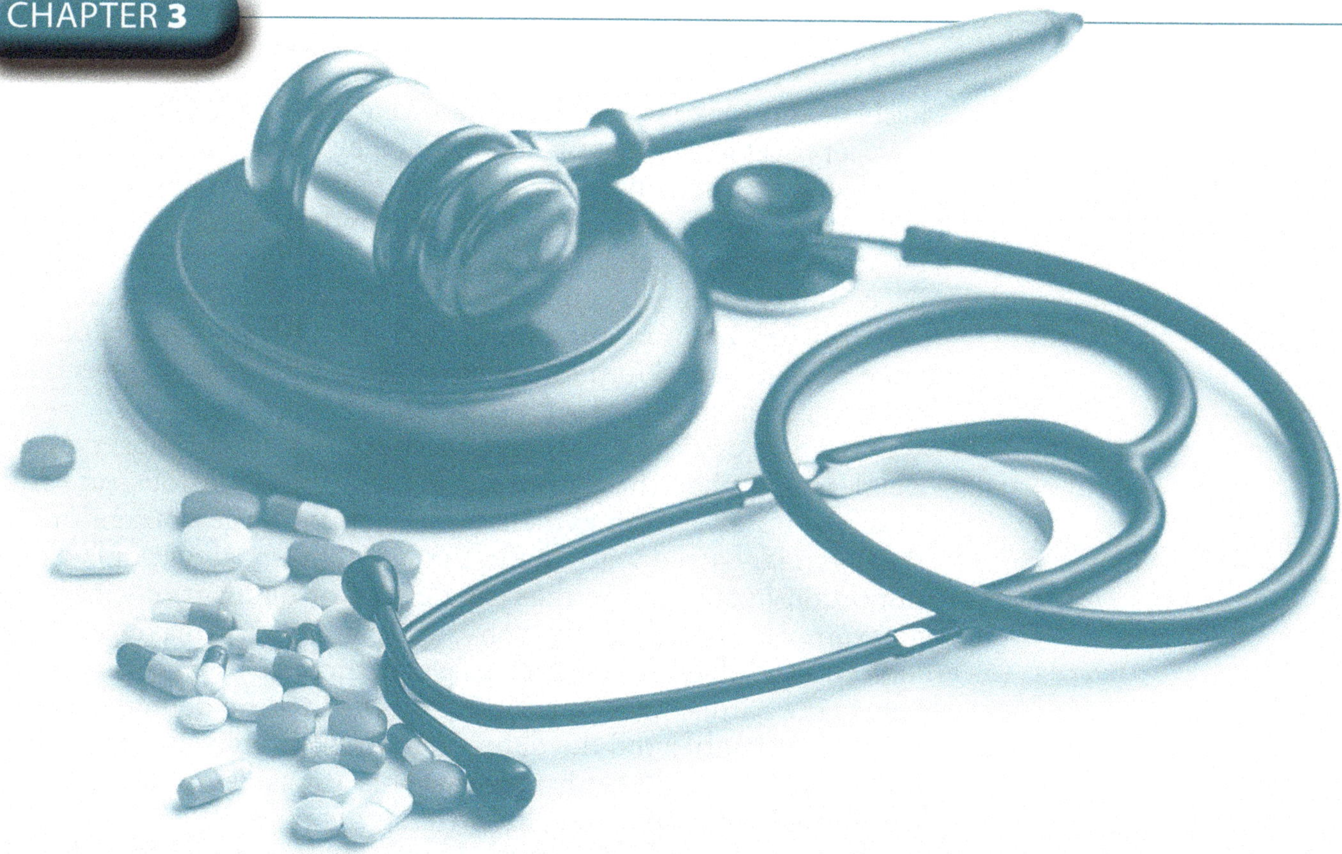

Intentional Torts Encountered in Pharmacy Practice

INTRODUCTION

In Chapter 1, the outline of intentional torts included battery, assault, false imprisonment, intentional infliction of emotional distress, trespass to land, trespass to chattels, and conversion. In order to give the reader a sense of how intentional torts occur in the area of pharmacy practice, cases where intentional tort issues have been decided upon will be the topics for discussion in this chapter. Therefore, not all of the intentional tort areas will be covered since case law pertaining to pharmacy practice is either insufficient (eg, conversion [taking something that belongs to another]) or, for all practical purposes, not applicable (eg, trespass to land or trespass to chattel [mainly involves animals]). Cases involving battery, assault, false imprisonment, and intentional infliction of emotional distress, however, do arise in the realm of pharmacy practice.

Before we discuss the three intentional torts noted previously, it is important to understand what is meant by the term "intent."

INTENT

Each of the four intentional torts discussed in the following must have a provable element of "intent." Unlike evidence, which is based on objective observance, intent is generally viewed from a subjective perspective. Subjectivity is a state of mind in which the defendant has exclusive knowledge in attaining a specific purpose with substantial certainty.[1] As an example, if the defendant wishes to hit someone with his fist, he must somehow think about it as a result of some issue that provoked him into accomplishing the specific objective of making physical contact with the plaintiff.

Objective evidence confirms in the mind of the observer that the defendant had the purpose of committing a tortious act.[2] If the observer notes certain evidence that supports the contention that the defendant acted with intent, that objective observation becomes important in supporting that the defendant had tortious intent. As an example, if the defendant physically hits the plaintiff, one might look to such objective evidence as: was there a verbal confrontation before the battery with supporting words that the defendant would strike the plaintiff; did the defendant raise his voice in anger; or did the defendant clench his fists or raise his arms in a threatening manner immediately preceding his striking the plaintiff?[3]

The cases presented in this chapter will focus on the objective evidence presented, as well as the result caused by the defendant's intentional action.

Battery and Assault

Battery and *assault* are two separate intentional torts, each having its own definition:

Battery: *The defendant's intentional infliction of a harmful or offensive contact on the plaintiff, lacking plaintiff's consent.*

Assault: *The defendant's intent to cause in the plaintiff a reasonable apprehension of an immediate contact or offensive contact.*

The following 1906 Minnesota case demonstrates two important issues: (1) whether a health care professional can be involved in the commission of a battery, and (2) whether consent to perform a given procedure was even necessary, or if the plaintiff gave implied consent authorizing a physical contact to occur.

ANNA MOHR V. CORNELIUS WILLIAMS

95 Minn. 261; 104 N.W.12 - Supreme Ct. Minnesota, 1905

Desired Remedy: Plaintiff Anna Mohr seeks relief from physician Cornelius Williams for battery after Williams performed surgery on an area of her body to which she did not consent.

Issue: Did Dr. Williams's surgery on a portion of Anna Mohr's body that was not consented to by plaintiff Mohr constitute battery?

Facts of Case: Plaintiff Mohr consulted defendant physician Dr. Williams concerning a difficulty with her right ear. The defendant examined the right ear and advised an operation to which the plaintiff consented. While under anesthesia, the defendant examined the left ear, and found it to be in a more serious state, and in greater need of an operation. Dr. Williams proceeded to operate on the plaintiff's left ear. The plaintiff had not previously experienced any difficulty with her left ear, and was not informed prior to the operation that any difficulty existed regarding her left ear. Mohr claimed after the operation that her hearing was greatly impaired in her left ear. The plaintiff brought suit claiming that the defendant had no authority to perform the operation on her left ear without the plaintiff's expressed or implied consent, and as a result of not having the consent of plaintiff, the defendant's action constituted a battery.

Case Analysis: In order for a battery to be established by the plaintiff, the plaintiff must prove that the defendant intentionally inflicted a harmful or offensive contact on the plaintiff, lacking the plaintiff's consent. Even though the defendant believed the plaintiff implicitly allowed him to perform the operation on the left ear by her consent to an operation on the right ear, the specific and expressed form of consent was to perform an operation on the plaintiff's right ear only. The argument by the defendant was that the discovery of the danger to the left ear was only found once the patient was anesthetized, and rather than wake the patient to give consent, the defendant believed he had authority to operate on the left ear based upon an emergency need to do so.

Case Holding: The appellate court confirmed the trial court's decision, finding for the plaintiff on the basis that the defendant did, in fact, commit battery on the plaintiff by intentionally inflicting a harmful contact with the plaintiff without her consent.

The *Happel* case in the following presents an unusual result charging a pharmacist and pharmacy with battery for the filling of a prescription with a drug where the patient is known to have an allergic predisposition to the dispensed drug.

HAPPEL V. WAL-MART

U.S. District Court 2007 Lexis 52288, Illinois 2007

Desired Remedy: Mrs. Happel seeks damages based upon her claim of battery (among other actionable claims) against Wal-Mart as a result of Wal-Mart filling and dispensing a Toradol prescription when the Wal-Mart employees were informed that Mrs. Happel is allergic to aspirin, acetaminophen, and ibuprofen as noted in the computerized records kept by Wal-Mart.

Issues: When Mrs. Happel took the Toradol medication dispensed by Wal-Mart, who had knowledge of a possible allergic disposition she may have to the drug, and after she experienced a series of drug-related reactions, can the dispensing of the Toradol and the harm that Mrs. Happel experienced as a result of taking the medication be sufficient to have her succeed on a battery claim against Wal-Mart?

Facts of Case: Mrs. Happel's physician prescribed Toradol for menstrual cramps. Mrs. Happel is allergic to aspirin, acetaminophen, and ibuprofen, and that information is noted in her computerized profile at Wal-Mart, where she routinely fills her prescriptions. The plaintiff's husband went to pick up Toradol Rx and he states that he informed one of the pharmacy personnel of his wife's allergies. Upon filling the prescription, the pharmacist filling the prescription appeared to overlook the possibility of cross-allergenicity upon dispensing the prescription and does not recall the specifics of what happened at the time of dispensing the medication to Mr. Happel. Mrs. Happel initially experiences difficulty in breathing and calls Wal-Mart and was told that she should not have any adverse reactions to the drug. She was later rushed to the ER in anaphylactic shock, and claims that besides almost dying, she still experiences incidences of asthma attacks as well as petit mal seizures, and that her multiple sclerosis has worsened. Among several causes of action that she brings against Wal-Mart is the claim of battery. Wal-Mart moves for summary judgment on this claim indicating there was no intentional offensive contact with the plaintiff by any member of the Wal-Mart staff.

Case Analysis: Regarding the claim of "battery" (there were also other claims stated such as "negligence"), the court noted that in order to prove "battery" the plaintiff must show that Wal-Mart intended to cause a harmful contact, that a harmful contact resulted, and that plaintiff did not consent to the contact. "The contact requirement may be met by showing that the defendant caused the plaintiff to come into contact with a foreign substance in a way that may reasonably be regarded as offensive." Further, "although Mrs. Happel actually ingested the Toradol knowing that she was taking the medicine, she had no idea that the defendant allegedly gave her a poison to her system. ... This act completely lacked consent. The known allergic action was certain to cause her harm." Thus, the medication should not have been filled." Prevailing on a "battery" count would entitle the plaintiff to punitive damages for the intentional act.

Case Holding: The appeals court affirmed the trial court's ruling that Wal-Mart's actions in this case satisfied the elements of a "battery" that would entitle Mrs. Happel to punitive damages in addition to compensatory damages.

FALSE IMPRISONMENT AND INTENTIONAL INFLICTION OF EMOTIONAL DISTRESS (IIED)

The intentional torts of *false imprisonment* and *infliction of emotional distress* are defined in the following manner:

False Imprisonment **definition:** The defendant intends to cause and actually causes the plaintiff to be confined or restrained to a bounded area, usually against the plaintiff's will.

Intentional Infliction of Emotional Distress (IIED) **definition:** The defendant demonstrates extreme and outrageous conduct with the intent to cause the plaintiff to suffer severe mental distress.

It is not uncommon that when a plaintiff brings an intentional tort action against a defendant, the plaintiff will identify several intentional torts in the complaint. As an example, if the plaintiff is subjected to false imprisonment, he or she will generally consider that action as extreme and outrageous conduct on the part of the defendant, and will, therefore, likely also bring a second cause of action for IIED in addition to the primary one of false imprisonment.

TAYLOR V. JOHNSON & WAL-MART

Court of Appeal of Louisiana, Third Circuit 796 So. 2d 11; 2001 La. App.

Desired Remedy: Defendants James Hill (pharmacist) and Wal-Mart appeal a trial court judgment in favor of plaintiff Ginger Taylor, who brought an action against the defendants for false imprisonment and intentional or negligent infliction of emotional distress.

Issues: Was plaintiff Ginger Taylor falsely imprisoned and arrested based upon the actions of Wal-Mart and its employees as the result of her being suspicious of illegally ordering a prescription for a controlled substance, Darvon Compound 65? Further, if Ms. Taylor was falsely imprisoned and arrested, should she also have entitlement to damages for either intentional or negligent infliction of emotional distress?

Facts of Case: Ginger Taylor, complaining of pain associated with an abscessed tooth, called Dr. B. C. Hollier, an oral surgeon, to obtain a prescription for pain medication. Dr. Hollier called Jim Hill, a pharmacist at Wal-Mart, and ordered a prescription for Darvon Compound 65, a Class IV narcotic. After Jim Hill took down the information and filled the prescription, he decided to verify the prescription with Dr. Hollier.

Jim Hill said he was suspicious because the phone connection was not clear when he spoke with Dr. Hollier. It did not sound as if Dr. Hollier had pronounced his own name correctly. He attempted to reach Dr. Hollier twice with no success. Finally, he spoke to Dr. Hollier's answering service and discovered Dr. Hollier was not on call that weekend. Mr. Hill spoke to Dr. Hollier's partner, Dr. Marks, who was on call and who told him it was unlikely Dr. Hollier called in the prescription. Dr. Marks explained to Mr. Hill their office had a policy that only the on-call dentist would phone in prescriptions. This increased Mr. Hill's suspicions. He ultimately decided to call Trooper Ledet of the Diversion Investigative Unit whose responsibilities included investigating prescription fraud.

When Ms. Taylor arrived at Wal-Mart to pick up her prescription, Ms. Janice Johnson Aymond, the pharmacy clerk, told her it would be a few more minutes and asked her to wait. Ms. Taylor waited a short time and checked again to see if the prescription was ready. Again she was told it would be a few minutes. While waiting, Ms. Taylor moved freely around the store. She did some shopping. At no time did Mr. Hill or any employee of Wal-Mart attempt to physically detain her. At no time was she told she could not leave the store.

Upon being contacted by Mr. Hill, Trooper Ledet immediately went to the Wal-Mart pharmacy. Upon arrival, Mr. Hill explained to Trooper Ledet why he was suspicious of Ms. Taylor. He identified her for the trooper. After identifying her, he continued with his duties at the pharmacy and had no further contact with Ms. Taylor.

Trooper Ledet conducted the investigation and made all the decisions from that point forward. He ultimately placed Ms. Taylor under arrest, handcuffed her, and took her outside.

Deputies from the Rapides Parish Sheriff's Office transported her to jail. She was booked. Later that evening, a Rapides Parish Sheriff's deputy contacted Dr. Hollier, who verified the prescription. Ms. Taylor was released.

Wal-Mart and James Hill appeal this judgment, arguing that the court erred in assessing any liability on their part. Plaintiffs answered the appeal, requesting that appellants be cast with the full amount of the judgment.

Case Analysis: The appellate court, in order to find that false imprisonment did in fact exist, the defendant would have needed the intent to cause the plaintiff to be confined or restrained to a bounded area usually against the plaintiff's will. The appellate court found the record void of any evidence that Mr. Hill or any other Wal-Mart employee detained Ms. Taylor, restricted her movement in the store, advised her she could not leave, or caused her to be arrested. Ms. Taylor did other shopping while she waited. She testified that at one point she had grown so tired of waiting she nearly left the store. When Trooper Ledet arrived, he conducted his own investigation and did not rely on Mr. Hill's suspicions in ultimately making the decision to arrest Ms. Hill. Thus, false imprisonment is not a valid theory of recovery in this case as it pertains to Mr. Hill and Wal-Mart.

It was the court's opinion that Mr. Hill's actions were logical. He acted logically by calling the authorities to report a call-in prescription that appeared suspicious. Having found Mr. Hill's actions logical, it follows that he acted reasonably. Having found reasonable action on the part of Mr. Hill and Wal-Mart, there cannot be a corresponding negligent or intentional infliction of emotional distress.

Case Holding: The appellate court viewed no applicable legal theory under which Ms. Taylor could recover damages from Wal-Mart or Mr. James Hill. However, Ms. Taylor may have an actionable case against the Rapides Parish Sheriff's Office.

JACK ECKERD CORPORATION V. DELORES SMITH

Court of Appeals of Florida, First District 558 So.2d 1060; 1990

Desired Remedy: Delores Smith seeks both compensatory and punitive damages for allegedly being accused of stealing a retail item from Jack Eckerd Pharmacy, for being falsely imprisoned, and for mental suffering occasioned by the defendant's wrongful interference with the plaintiff's peaceful security of person and reputation.

Issues: If a plaintiff, such as Delores Smith, mistakenly places a store's item in her purse (her prescription drugs) without paying, does the store's management have reasonable cause to falsely imprison the plaintiff and call law enforcement to further investigate whether criminal activity has occurred?

Facts of Case: Late one evening after work, Delores Smith went to Eckerd to pick up two prescriptions. She went to the pharmacy counter where she received her medicine from a clerk and signed a prescription logbook. Because of her husband's insurance, Smith was only required to pay $1.00 on each prescription. According to Smith, she offered to pay the pharmacy clerk, but was told that she needed to pay at the front of the store. She picked up a few more items and returned to the front counter. Smith testified that she laid all of her items, including the medicine in a prescription bag, on the counter. The cashier, Elizabeth Robinson, rang up the items and asked for $11.18. Smith gave Robinson $20.00 and received $8.82 in change. According to Smith, Robinson put the household items in a small bag and her prescription medicine in her purse. Smith attempted to leave the store and an alarm went off.

Smith returned to Robinson in an attempt to determine what had caused the alarm to go off. They determined that the household items were accounted for on Smith's receipt and were somewhat perplexed when the assistant manager, Alfred Lederer, joined them at the cashier's desk. At this point, Smith took the prescription bag from her purse, commenting that perhaps her medicine was the problem. According to Smith, she paid Robinson $2.00 for the medicine in Lederer's presence; but Lederer disputes this, testifying that without authority, Robinson permitted Smith to pay when Lederer had gone to the back of the store to talk to the pharmacy clerk. Smith claims that she inadvertently placed the prescription bag in her purse forgetting about it, but having every intention of paying.

When Lederer returned from the back of the store after talking to the pharmacy clerk, he asked Smith to accompany him to his office. He began filling out a report and shortly thereafter, Officer Green arrived. Smith became upset and started crying. Officer Green testified that he didn't remember her offering any explanation of the circumstances. Based on the facts that Officer Green learned from Lederer—that Ms. Smith had been told by the pharmacy clerk to return to the front of the store to pay for her medicine, and that her medicine was concealed in her bag and had not been paid for when she attempted to leave the store—Officer Green determined there was probable cause to arrest. He did not take Smith to the jail to book her, but instead gave her a notice to appear. Before Smith left, Lederer took her medicine as evidence and gave her $2.00 back.

When Smith's case regarding her criminal charge for theft came before the court, the prosecutor dismissed the case. Thereafter, Smith filed a complaint against Eckerd alleging false imprisonment. Smith testified at her civil hearing that after the alarm went off, she realized that Robinson had mistakenly overlooked her prescriptions.

The jury returned a verdict finding that Eckerd had maliciously prosecuted and falsely imprisoned Delores Smith. They awarded her $25,000.00 compensatory damages, and $100,000.00 punitive damages against Eckerd.

Case Analysis: The appellate court had issue with the punitive damages award based upon its belief that the defendant had no evil intent for how it pursued the plaintiff. However, based on the evidence presented, the appellate court concluded

> "that while the defendant has become liable to plaintiff to provide compensation to her for humiliation, indignity, and mental suffering occasioned by the defendant's wrongful interference with her peaceful security of person and reputation, the wrong done was the result of an honest, but mistaken suspicion on the part of the defendants. Had the defendant's servants stripped plaintiff of her clothing in an effort to find articles supposed have been stolen, or beat her in an effort to make her confess ..., the situation would have been different and a finding of malicious and wanton wrong doing might have been sustained. But in this case the force and detention employed was no greater than would have been the case had plaintiff's guilt of theft been established."

Smith states that Eckerd should have conducted a more thorough inspection before calling a law enforcement officer and that the failure to do so justifies the award of the punitive damages. It is the view of the appellate court that the brief investigation, which established that Smith was leaving a protected area with concealed merchandise, was an honest mistaken effort to comply with a Florida statute that gives a merchant immunity from prosecution for false imprisonment if he/she acts with probable cause and calls law enforcement immediately after taking a shoplifting suspect into custody.

Case Holding: The appellate court affirmed the lower court's decision in part, allowing compensatory damages to the extent of $25,000 to be awarded based upon the humiliation, indignity, and mental suffering the plaintiff endured by the defendant's wrongful interference with her peaceful security of person and reputation. However, the appellate court reversed the lower court's decision in allowing punitive damages in the amount of $100,000 to be awarded, reasoning that it could not find evidence of evil intent by the defendant in requesting that Ms. Smith remain and be subjected to a reasonable search based upon Florida's statute giving merchants immunity for conducting such reasonable searches to ensure items are not stolen from the store premises.

GORDON V. FROST & TREASURY DRUG

Court of Appeals of Georgia, 193 Ga. App. 517; 388 S.E.2d 362; 1989

Desired Remedy: Mrs. Gordon seeks damages for false imprisonment and intentional infliction of emotional distress (IIED) against pharmacist Frost and Treasury Drug for allegedly attempting to obtain a controlled substance over the telephone. Mrs. Gordon's husband also seeks damages based upon a loss of consortium claim as a result of his wife's alleged findings of illegally attempting to gain possession of controlled substances.

Issues: Does a pharmacist have a right to detain a customer if he or she believes, without doing a thorough or reasonable investigation, that the customer had a controlled substance phoned into the pharmacy illegally?

Facts of Case: On March 17, 1986, Mrs. Gordon awoke with a migraine headache. After unsuccessfully attempting to sleep it away, she decided to take some prescribed Fiorinal #3 with Codeine, which she was out of. Mrs. Gordon called Treasury Drug, where she had been a customer for over four years, to get the prescription for Fiorinal #3 with Codeine filled. Frost had known Mrs. Gordon for over two years and had filled such a Fiorinal prescription for her on several occasions.

Upon calling the pharmacy, Mrs. Gordon was told that her prescription could not be filled without the doctor's DEA number. Mrs. Gordon stated that she did not have the number, that it should be obtained from the doctor's office, and that she had given the doctor's telephone number to the woman with whom she had first spoken. Allegedly, a call did come from the doctor's office approving the prescription and providing the necessary information.

Believing that the caller requesting Fiorinal was a representative from Mrs. Gordon's physician's office, Frost called the doctor's office to inquire about the prescription but everyone at the office was out to lunch.

Approximately two hours later, Mrs. Gordon called the pharmacy, identified herself, and asked whether or not her prescription was ready. She was told that it would be ready in a couple minutes, by the time of her arrival. In the meantime, Frost spoke with the prescribing physician's office and learned that no one from the office had recently prescribed Fiorinal #3 with Codeine for Mrs. Gordon. Frost did not inquire further as to whether or not the doctor would have permitted the prescription, did not check the store computer to see the status of the Fiorinal prescription, and did not call Mrs. Gordon to attempt to clarify the situation. Mrs. Gordon's physician did not believe Mrs. Gordon abused the prescribed medications and probably would have refilled the Fiorinal prescription. Prior to this incident, Frost had stated to the intern pharmacist that Mrs. Gordon was a hypochondriac and took a lot of medication.

After learning that the initial call had not come from the doctor's office, Frost reached the conclusion that Mrs. Gordon was attempting to fraudulently acquire the prescription. Consequently, Frost called the DEA to report her suspicion. The DEA told Frost it would send someone to take care of the situation and instructed her to try to keep Mrs. Gordon at the store.

Mrs. Gordon arrived at the pharmacy, identified herself to the intern, and stated that she was there to pick up her prescription. She was told she would have to wait. She spoke briefly to Frost about some other medication that Frost had sold her the week before. Shortly thereafter, a police officer arrived and arrested Mrs. Gordon for violation of the Georgia Controlled Substances Act.

Mrs. Gordon was shocked, upset, and hysterical, and at first could not understand why she was being arrested. She asked to contact her husband and her physician. Another customer observed Mrs. Gordon's distress, her being yelled at by the police officer, and her pleas to contact her husband and doctor.

The pharmacists informed the officer that they would prosecute and Frost signed a "Citizen's Arrest Form." Mrs. Gordon was taken to jail and remained there for eight or nine hours. She was fingerprinted, photographed, and handcuffed. Following a preliminary hearing and pursuant to Frost's suggestion, a narcotics division detective subpoenaed a computer list of all prescriptions obtained by Mrs. Gordon from the drug store. Frost assisted the detective by going over the list and underlining the "hypnotics." After the evidence gathered was provided to the district attorney's office, the district attorney ultimately decided not to bring charges.

Case Analysis: The appeals court reviewed the tort of IIED and noted that in order to be a successful claim, "the defendant's actions had to be terrifying or insulting to the plaintiff as to naturally humiliate, embarrass, or frighten the plaintiff," and such actions will be considered outrageous and extreme. Nevertheless, there was reasonable suspicion on the part of pharmacist Frost in deciding to have the matter reported to the police.

Case Holding: While the trial court entered judgment in favor of Mrs. Gordon's claim for IIED and her husband's corresponding claim for loss of consortium, the appellate court reversed the trial court's decision based upon pharmacist Frost's responsibility to report what he thought was an illegal matter, even though he could have engaged in a more thorough investigation on his own.

COMMON DEFENSES APPLIED TO INTENTIONAL TORTS

Among the common defenses applied to intentional torts are (a) self-defense; (b) defense of others; (c) necessity; (d) authority; (e) consent; or (f) disproving any of the elements of the intentional tort rule. In consideration of pharmacy-related intentional tort cases, the major defenses that apply are usually in the category of the latter two defenses—consent and disproving any of the elements that make up the intentional tort rule.

Consent

In the *Mohr* case discussed earlier, the defendant raised the defense or privilege of consent. The plaintiff claimed that consent was only given for surgery on her right ear, and not on the left ear as well. The defendant argued that consent was implied, and that when the plaintiff subjected herself to surgery, any further problems identified would be treated on an emergency basis.

The opinion of the court in *Mohr* was that there was neither implied consent nor an emergency to perform the surgery on the plaintiff's left ear without first informing the plaintiff of the need and acquiring a clear consent from the plaintiff.

The categories of consent may be viewed in the following ways:

Express Consent: Occurs when the plaintiff clearly communicates his or her permission to perform a specific service, thus granting the defendant the right to act in performing that service.

Implied Consent: Occurs when the plaintiff's conduct, viewed by a reasonable person, would serve as evidence that the plaintiff permitted the defendant to act on the plaintiff's behalf.

Consent as a Matter of Law: Consent will exist as a matter of law if (1) under an emergency circumstance in order to prevent death or serious injury; (2) a reasonable person would be expected to consent under the circumstances; and (3) there is no reason to believe that the plaintiff would not consent.[3]

The other major defense to intentional torts involving pharmacy practice is to look at the specific tort's rule to attempt to prove that a particular element of that rule was missing or that the evidence did not support it. As examples, consider the following:

a. ***Battery:*** In order for a battery to exist, the plaintiff must show that the defendant had an intent to cause the battery, and/or that the degree of contact was either harmful or offensive.

b. ***False Imprisonment:*** In order to prove there was a false imprisonment, again the element of intent to restrict the movement of the plaintiff must be demonstrated, and there must be an actual showing of unreasonable confinement or restraint along with an unreasonable delay in the plaintiff's movement contrary to his or her will.

c. ***Intentional Infliction of Emotional Distress (IIED):*** There must be clear evidence of intent on the part of the defendant to cause an extreme and outrageous act that results in the plaintiff suffering severe emotional distress. Such conduct by the defendant would extend beyond the boundaries of that which is considered decent or tolerated by a civilized society. To illustrate this point of extreme and outrageous behavior, imagine a pharmacist telling a healthy patient—as a practical joke—that based upon the medication she is taking, he is amazed she is alive today.

REFERENCES

1. Dobbs, DB. *The Law of Torts, Hornbook Series*. St. Paul, MN: West Group Publishing; 2000:47-49.
2. *Ibid.* at 49.
3. Barpassers Series, Vol. L *Torts*. Seventh Ed. (1992).
4. Statutes from various states allowing for reasonable customer detention if shoplifting is suspected: Mass. Gen. L. Ann. 231 §§94B; Colo. Rev. Stats §18-4-407; Ariz. Rev. Stats §13-1805; Md. Cts. & Jud Pro. Code §5-402; 11 Del. Code Ann. §840; Iowa Code Ann. §808.12; and Fla. Stat Ann. §8812.015.
5. Dobbs, DB. *The Law of Torts, Hornbook Series*. St. Paul, MN: West Group Publishing; 2000, and *Wal-Mart Stores, Inc. v. Mitchell*, S. W.2d 616, 618 (Ky App. 1994).

QUESTIONS

1. What factors distinguish the intentional tort of battery from the intentional tort of assault?
2. If a battery is committed, does the party who is the subject of that battery need to be conscious or aware that this tort is occurring?
3. If an owner or manager of a pharmacy restricts a suspected shoplifter from leaving the pharmacy until searched, and finds nothing has been taken or stolen, will the individual who has been restricted from leaving the pharmacy have an undisputed case for being falsely imprisoned? Or does the shop owner/manager have some protections regarding this issue of customer detention if there is a reasonable belief that the customer may have shoplifted? (See Torts Restatement §120A.) Most states have created statutory laws that provide merchants with a privilege and protections if there is probable cause of shoplifting by a customer.[4] Case law also supports the reasonable detention of a suspected shoplifter "for a reasonable time to accomplish the investigation or perhaps to await the arrival of police officers."[5]
4. In the *Mohr* case, the defendant physician argued that consent to operate on the left ear was implied, and if not implied, constituted an emergency. Why were both these defenses, as noted by the court, weak? Could a defense of "necessity" have been raised in this case? And if so, would the case have been decided differently?
5. In the *Gordon* case, the trial court found in favor of the plaintiffs on their claim of intentional infliction of emotional distress (IIED) and loss of consortium.
   (a) Regarding the matter of intentional infliction of emotional distress, what made the defendant's actions to be considered "extreme" and "outrageous" to allow the court to rule in favor of the plaintiffs?
   (b) Mr. Taylor also prevailed in his claim of loss of consortium. What, in your opinion, must exist in order for a plaintiff like Mr. Taylor to succeed in his loss of consortium claim?
6. What are some take-away messages from these cases as you consider your future practice of pharmacy?
7. Do you have an opinion as to whether or not the decision of a battery was correct in the *Happel* case? If you are not convinced that a battery exists in this case, what arguments would you pose in opposition based upon the elements for a battery not being met?

CHAPTER **4**

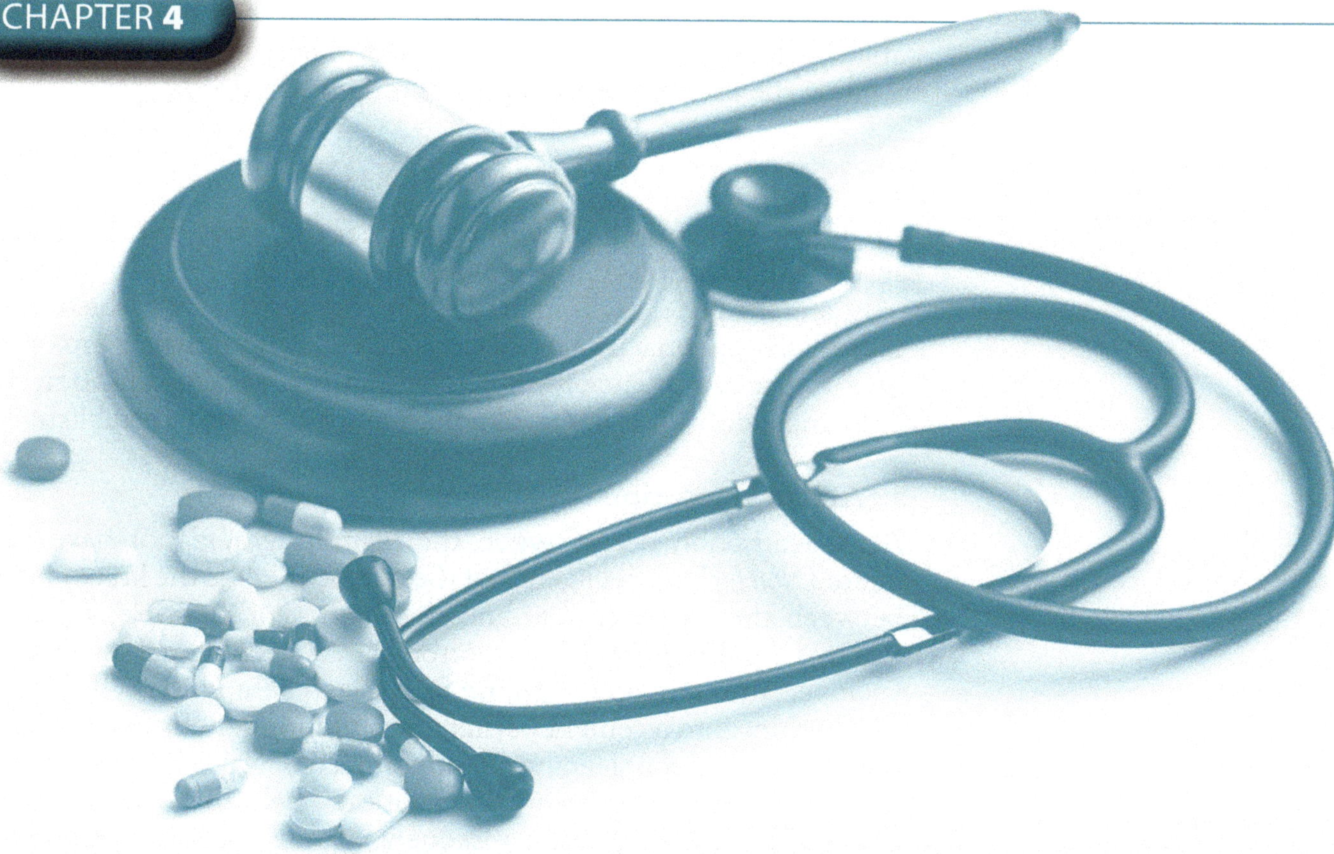

Background to Negligence in Pharmacy Practice: Elements of Negligence (Part I)

As noted in Chapter 1, there is a specific formula for providing evidence that *negligence* has occurred. Four elements must be proven to support a cause of action in *negligence*.

A DUTY MUST EXIST

The defendant assumed or owed some duty to the plaintiff. The defendant developed a relationship with the plaintiff whereby the defendant owed a duty of due care toward that plaintiff. As an example, when a pharmacist takes a prescription from a patient to be filled, once that prescription is taken from the patient, the pharmacist owes that patient a duty of due care in ensuring that the prescription will be filled correctly.

A BREACH OF DUTY OF DUE CARE

The defendant acted in a manner that breached the due care owed to the plaintiff. In the case of a pharmacist filling a prescription for a patient, after assuming the duty, the pharmacist may breach his duty by filling the prescription with the wrong medication.

CAUSATION OF HARM OR INJURY

The defendant's breach of duty was either the *actual* or the *proximate* cause of the plaintiff's injury. If a pharmacist filled a prescription incorrectly, and the patient was injured as the result of the error, the mistake made by the pharmacist may be considered as the actual or proximate cause of that injury. The proof of *actual* and/or *proximate* causation may be the most difficult element of a negligence analysis to establish.

a. Actual Causation

Actual causation occurs when the plaintiff would not have been injured *"but for"* the negligence of the defendant. It is the link or bridge between the *breach of duty* and the *injury*. For example, a patient receives a prescription filled in error with a sleeping pill instead of a laxative. After taking the pill, he falls asleep behind the wheel of his car, crashing into a cement barrier and suffering serious personal injuries. Based upon the sleeping pill's pharmacological effects, incorrectly filling the laxative prescription was more likely than not the actual cause of the accident and subsequent injuries. Such injuries would not have occurred *"but for"* the incorrect filling of the prescription.

Sometimes there may be several defendants who are viewed as being negligent by breaching their duty toward the plaintiff; however, it may be difficult to prove which one of them caused the harm or injury. The *"but for the negligence of the defendant"* analysis is mainly associated with one defendant that is closely linked to causing injury to the plaintiff. The *"substantial factor"* test or analysis is applied when there are two or more defendants, especially where negligence may be difficult or impossible to prove regarding the actions of any one of the defendants. When there is good reason to believe that several defendants, because of their close or similar relationships, are responsible for the defendant's injury, the *"substantial factor"* test is applied, implicating all the defendants as being responsible for the plaintiff's injury. The defendants can fight among themselves as to who may be solely or jointly culpable.

Examples of two such cases are found in the seminal case of *Summers v. Tice,* and the pharmaceutical company-related case of *Sindell v. Abbott Laboratories.*

In *Summers v. Tice,* two defendant hunters mistakenly shot their rifles at the same time at what they believed was a quail in the bushes, but turned out to be the plaintiff.[1] One of the fired shots hit the plaintiff. Because it was difficult to determine which one of bullets from the two guns fired by the defendants struck the plaintiff, the court ruled that both defendants were responsible since to have to prove whose rifle the bullet came from would be impractical and most likely impossible. The court's reasoning in *Summers* was founded upon the analysis that "*... both were negligent to plaintiff. They both brought about a situation where the negligence of one of them injured the plaintiff; hence it should rest with them each to absolve himself if he can.*"

In *Sindell v. Abbott Laboratories*, a plaintiff was injured indirectly by acquiring vaginal carcinoma as the result of her mother taking the drug diethylstilbestrol (DES) when she was pregnant with the plaintiff.[2] The drug was used to prevent miscarriage at the time. The difficulty in this case was attempting to identify which drug company was responsible for providing the plaintiff's mother with the drug—approximately 195 pharmaceutical companies manufactured the drug at the time, and no information was available through the pharmacy where the prescription was filled as to which manufacturer's DES was used. The theory that the court used in deciding this case involved a market share analysis:

> "... we hold it to be reasonable in the present context to measure the likelihood that any of the defendants supplied the product which allegedly injured plaintiff by the percentage which the DES sold by each of them for the purpose of preventing miscarriage bears to the entire production of the drug sold by all for that purpose." Plaintiff asserts that 6 or 7 companies "produced 90 percent of the DES marketed." As a result, the court concluded that "each defendant will be held liable for the proportion of the judgment represented by its share of that market unless it demonstrates that it could not have made the product which caused plaintiff's injuries. . . ."

b. Proximate Causation

Proximate causation is found when it is *foreseeable* that the defendant's breach of duty owed to the plaintiff would cause the injury incurred by the plaintiff. The link or bridge between the *breach of duty* and the *injury* caused is possibly more difficult to prove since it may be more remote.

As an example, a pharmacist prepares a young woman patient's prescription without a safety-proof vial. The patient takes the vial of medicine home and places it in a relatively safe place. Unfortunately, the patient's two-year-old son gets hold of the vial, consumes the contents, and becomes deathly ill. Aside from the fact that there is an existing law requiring a pharmacist to place certain medications in child-resistant safety containers, did the pharmacist, by issuing a non-child-resistant safety container to the patient, breach a duty of due care that was sufficient to be the proximate cause of the child's serious injury? In other words, is it reasonably *foreseeable* that a patient of the nature described earlier might have a family of young children and that by providing the medicine in a container that is not safety proof, one of those children could possibly gain access to and open such a container? Because of the depth of the matter of *proximate cause* involving a number of considerations and because of the variations that occur within the multitude of negligent cases, a further discussion has been reserved in the following pages of this chapter to hopefully provide a better understanding of this rather complex causation concept.

HARM OR INJURY

The last element that must be proven in a negligence case is resultant *harm* or *injury* caused to the plaintiff. If there is no harm or injury caused as a result of the *breach of duty*, a claim or cause of action in *negligence* will fail. Just because the patient received a prescription filled in error, as long as the patient did not take any of the medicine, a claim of negligence would fail since no injury could be accounted for as a result of the breach of duty.

MAJOR KEY PRINCIPLES ASSOCIATED WITH NEGLIGENCE

Within the sphere of *negligence*, there are an abundant number of terms, concepts, and divisions. Before proceeding to the negligence-based cases in the forthcoming chapters, it is important that the reader develop both an understanding and an appreciation for these negligence-related topics. To this end, we will continue our discussion with a more in-depth discussion of *proximate causation*.

PROXIMATE CAUSATION (REVISITED)

It is not the intent of the authors to dwell on this subject *ad nauseam*, but it is important that the student have a reasonable grasp of the *proximate cause* component to negligent actions. As somewhat alluded to before, a proximate cause analysis attempts to gauge how far you may be able to stretch liability for a given negligent action to the defendant, and to determine if there are definitive boundaries that the assessment of causation would be too difficult to attach once those boundaries have been exceeded.

William Prosser, in his torts casebook, analyzes the concept of proximate causation looking at *foreseeability* and *risk taking*.[3] Prosser uses the example of a car being driven at an excessive speed and the risk that the driver takes, viewing many of the conceivable things that can go wrong, thus creating a potential for causing foreseeable harm or a chain of undesirable events. Among those harms or undesirable events could be the following:

- Hitting another car and possibly injuring or killing the driver.
- The hit car going out of control and hitting a third and possibly a fourth car.
- Hitting another car and narrowly missing a pregnant woman who miscarriages as a result of becoming frightened.
- Striking a pedestrian who is left helpless in the street and run over by a second vehicle.

- After striking a pedestrian, someone else comes along to steal the stricken pedestrian's watch.
- The stricken pedestrian acquires pneumonia due to their weakened condition and dies.
- The stricken pedestrian, while on crutches, falls weeks later inducing new injuries.
- The stricken pedestrian, while hospitalized, receives negligent medical treatment causing his death.

Cases representing the previous scenarios have actually happened, and have held the initiating defendant (the one driving the car who set off the various events) responsible for not exercising reasonable due care and for being the proximate cause of the resulting injuries. Some of the previous examples may provide the reader with a sense that the resultant injuries are somewhat remote from the defendant's initial action. According to Prosser, the proximate cause rule attempts to protect a victim or plaintiff from the risk that the risk-taker or defendant takes that ultimately caused the plaintiff's injury. The previous examples attempt to display the limits or boundaries of "*foreseeability*" in that in some way the defendant set things in motion to put the plaintiff in such a position that additional bad things happened to him or her.

There is also an "*unforeseeable*" element associated with proximate cause. Assume that while you are rushing down a walkway, you negligently bump into someone relatively hard, knocking them to the ground. Unbeknownst to you, the individual is a hemophiliac who starts to bleed profusely and dies. The question then becomes, would you be liable for causing such a horrible and unforeseeable outcome? Most jurisdictions would apply the so-called *thin skull doctrine*, which stands for "taking your victim as you find him." In other words, while the result of your rushing down the walkway and possibly banging into another person was foreseeable, the seriousness of the damage caused could not have been reasonably foreseeable.

When an injury to a plaintiff is the result of possible acts of other defendants or forces, the concept of *indirect causation* may be present, giving rise to an *intervening force* analysis. For example, if the commercial building that the defendant owns experiences a cyclonic storm of extensive intensity whereby the roof caves in killing one of the employees within the building, assuming the roof is in good condition—a fact that will need to be proven to show that the defendant was not neglectful in caring for the maintenance of the roof—the cause of the plaintiff's death would appear to be attributable to the intervening force of the cyclonic storm and not attributable to the defendant's lack of responsibility in the upkeep of his roof. Often intervening forces are commonly associated with acts of god, animals, or persons other than the defendant or plaintiff. If the defendant's roof was in excellent shape, and a natural consequence of a powerful force such as a devastating cyclonic storm was the exclusive reason for the roof to cave in, then this intervening force would be classified as an *independent superseding intervening force*. Under such a circumstance, there would be no liability imputed on the defendant. However, if the defendant's roof was in disrepair and only a minor wind caused the roof to collapse, then the intervening force of the minor wind would, generally, not be considered an *independent superseding intervening force* sufficient to hold the defendant liable for the resulting death of the plaintiff. Another way this latter result would be expressed is by the terminology *"dependent intervening force."*

To further elucidate the concept of *dependent intervening force*, consider the following example: The plaintiff is injured in an auto accident caused by the defendant, and then rushed to a hospital to receive medical care that is negligently administered. The question becomes whether or not it was *foreseeable* that the plaintiff would receive negligent care. Most cases would find that the negligent act in the administration of medical care was not a superseding intervening force, and thus would be categorized as a dependent intervening force. Therefore, the resultant injuries caused to the plaintiff by the defendant were foreseeable and the proximate cause of the plaintiff's total injuries since the defendant placed the plaintiff in a position whereby such resultant injuries would not have occurred but for the negligence of the defendant.

RES IPSA LOQUITUR

Sometimes it may be impossible to know the identity of the defendant who caused the negligent act. Nonetheless, a negligent act did occur and the plaintiff was injured. The doctrine of *res ipsa loquitur* ("the thing speaks for itself") has been the governing principle in these types of cases. This doctrine attributes negligence to a party if all three of the following conditions are established:

- The event causing the plaintiff's injury would not have occurred unless someone such as the defendant was negligent.
- There is a more-than-likely possibility that the defendant caused the injury to the plaintiff since the event was caused by an instrumentality in the exclusive control of the defendant.
- The plaintiff did not contribute to the event that caused his or her injury.

Kambat v. St. Francis Hospital provides an example of a *res ipsa loquitur* issue.[4] In *Kambat*, during the performance of a surgical operation, an 18-by-18-in laparotomy pad was mistakenly left in the abdomen of the plaintiff who died some 30 days after the surgical procedure as a result of a systemic infection associated with complications from non-removal of the pad.

Plaintiff's counsel presented evidence that the type of surgery the plaintiff underwent mandated the use of these particular pads. Therefore, the one that was found in the plaintiff's abdomen must have been the result of its use by the defendant during the surgical procedure. Thus, the negligent event must have been caused by an agency or instrumentality within the exclusive control of the defendant. Further, it is reasonably clear that the pad left in the abdominal cavity of the plaintiff was not due to any voluntary action or contribution on the part of the plaintiff.

VICARIOUS LIABILITY (RESPONDEAT SUPERIOR)

When an employee of a corporation, for example, is involved in causing a negligent act, it is not uncommon that the corporation, as the employer, is sued in addition to the employee. This imputing of liability on the corporate structure for the acts of a single employee is generally founded upon two major principles: (1) The employee who caused the negligent act was acting within the scope of practice required by the corporation, and (2) the corporation or business entity will generally have more money, or so-called deeper pockets, than the single employee tortfeasor to appropriately compensate the plaintiff for the injury. As a general rule, a pharmacist employed by a chain pharmacy who commits a negligent act as an employee acting within the scope of his or her employment will cause the business entity that he or she works for to be held liable for the employee's actions. The term *respondeat superior* is aligned to vicarious liability in that it denotes a master-servant relationship.

One of the major issues in vicarious liability cases is determining whether or not the employee was acting within his or her scope of professional practice. Generally, this matter may be for the jury to decide, based upon the facts of each individual case. However, in pharmacy practice, since most negligent acts center around errors in preparing patient prescriptions, a definite scope of practice, imputing of liability to the employer tends to be more straightforward.

PREMISES LIABILITY

A collateral issue regarding any business entity is the possibility of a customer entering the business premises and getting injured because of some negligent condition associated with those premises. Examples of this occur when something spills onto the floor, causing a customer to slip and fall with resulting injury, or when something falls on a customer, causing injury. Depending upon the circumstances, premises liability cases are heavily dependent upon the facts of any given situation. *Rodgers v. Hook-SuperX Inc.* is an example of a potential premises liability issue.[5]

In *Rodgers*, a customer (plaintiff) leaving a pharmacy is attacked by two men who take the plaintiff's purse and knock her to the ground on the sidewalk and parking area immediately in front of the pharmacy. The plaintiff noted several matters that suggest the pharmacy was negligent regarding its duty to the plaintiff: (1) The pharmacy should have provided better protection for patrons who enter and exit the pharmacy (suggesting a guard); (2) there was a robbery that occurred two months before in this general area; and (3) the lighting just outside the pharmacy was inadequate. The court, in coming to its decision, looked at whether or not the attack on the plaintiff was reasonably foreseeable. The court concluded that an attack two months previously did not make an attack on the plaintiff reasonably foreseeable, and that the store lighting was sufficient and was not a factor in the attack on the plaintiff.

NEGLIGENCE PER SE

The application of "*negligence per se*" arises when a statute or regulation is violated. This rule of negligence holds "that a violation of a statute is negligence in itself if it causes harm of the kind the statute was intended to avoid and to a person within the class of persons the statute was intended to protect."[6] Perhaps the best example of the application of this rule regarding pharmacy practice is where there is a state statute or regulation requiring the pharmacist to verbally consult a patient on the common severe adverse reactions of a new drug the patient will be taking. The pharmacist neglects to consult with the patient on one of the severe adverse effects of a drug that could have been avoided had the pharmacist properly instructed the patient on how to use it in order to avoid the untoward effect. As a result, the patient suffers an injury that could have been avoided had the pharmacist properly consulted the patient. In this scenario the statute or regulation imposed a duty on the pharmacist to counsel patients within the class of persons who receive a prescription for the first time in order to prevent major problems that can be associated with taking that prescription. The fact that the pharmacist ignored following the requirements of the law will be viewed as *negligence per se*.

DEFENSES TO NEGLIGENT CLAIMS: WHERE AN ELEMENT OF THE NEGLIGENCE FORMULA CANNOT BE PROVEN

A major defense for a defendant faced with a negligence claim is to argue that one of the four elements—duty, breach of duty, causation, or injury—is lacking. Remember, all these elements must be present and provable in order for a plaintiff to succeed in a *negligence* claim. Also, just because an injury happens to the plaintiff, it does not necessarily mean that it is tied to a breach of duty.

Sometimes the more difficult element to prove in a negligence case is the element of *causation*. In Chapter 6, cases involving causation will be discussed to give the reader a better understanding of how the difficulty in proving this element can operate as a defense for the defendant. The issues of *duty, breach of duty*, and *injury* are fact driven, and the outcome of a particular case, while depending heavily on the facts, may in some ways differ from jurisdiction to jurisdiction.

CONTRIBUTORY OR COMPARATIVE NEGLIGENCE

The plaintiff may have, in some way, added to his or her resultant injury, thus allowing the defendant to argue that the plaintiff was either a *contributor* to his or her negligence or *comparatively* negligent. Depending upon the jurisdiction, a court will use the rule of either *contributory negligence* or *comparative negligence*.

In those jurisdictions that find that there is contributory negligence on the part of the plaintiff, the case will generally be dismissed against the plaintiff. Usually the degree or percentage of plaintiff contribution to the negligence is not considered. There are, however, some situations where even though the plaintiff may have contributed to his own negligence, the defendant may have had the opportunity to avoid injuring the plaintiff. This *doctrine of last clear chance* applies when the plaintiff's negligent action precedes the defendant's negligence whereby the defendant had the opportunity or time to avoid causing injury or further injury to the plaintiff.

An example of this would be if a pharmacist fills a refill prescription incorrectly. The patient notices that the refill drug does not look the same as previous prescriptions she has gotten over the last five years. The patient starts taking the first dose of this incorrect medication without inquiring if it is the correct medication. The pharmacist, shortly after the patient takes the first dose, realizes he dispensed the incorrect medication and decides not to call the patient to correct the mistake since the pharmacist believes this wrong drug will not hurt her. However, the patient gets very sick and must be hospitalized as a result of the adverse effects from this incorrectly dispensed prescription. One might argue that it would be reasonable for the patient to call the pharmacy to check on whether or not the drug dispensed was the same as she has always gotten. The fact that she did not raises a presumption that she may have contributed to the negligence. However, once the pharmacist found out that he dispensed the wrong drug, he in fact had a *last clear chance* to correct the error. He did not, and as a result, by not taking the *last clear chance*, his negligence will not be dismissed.

In the majority of jurisdictions, the rule of *comparative negligence* is the more common approach where the plaintiff shares in being partly negligent. In jurisdictions that apply the *comparative negligence* rule, the jury will be asked to apportion the percentage of negligence attributable to both parties. Thus, as an example, and based upon the facts of the case, the jury might find that the plaintiff was 20% responsible for her resultant injury, and the defendant contributed to the plaintiff's injury to the order of 80%. Therefore, if there was to be a total $100,000 award based upon the damages incurred, the plaintiff would only be entitled to $80,000 of the damage judgment. In a small number of jurisdictions that apply the *comparative negligence* rule, if it were found that the plaintiff contributed to 51% or more of his or her injuries, the plaintiff would lose his or her entitlement to any award that would otherwise be less than 49%.

ASSUMPTION OF RISK

Under the *assumption of risk* defense, the defendant would attempt to show that the plaintiff consented to undertake or assume the risk imposed by the defendant. The plaintiff, therefore, knowing such risk is involved, if injured, would be barred from recovery from the defendant. This particular defense or concept is really not commonly applied to pharmacy practice. Assumption of the risk does occur in pharmacy and medical cases where a patient may, for example, consent to the risk of taking an experimental drug to hopefully manage a rare form of cancer. However, in these types of cases, the patient is usually provided with an informed consent notice that must be signed, and that carefully states the known adverse effects and problems with the experimental or investigational drug, and the possibility of the patient experiencing those effects or problems.

The principle of *assumption of risk* has been absorbed into the doctrines of *contributory* or *comparative negligence* in many jurisdictions.[7]

REFERENCES

1. *Summers v. Tice*, 33 Cal.2d 80, 199 P.2d 1 (Calif. Sup. Ct. 1948).
2. *Sindell v. Abbott Laboratories*, 26 Ca1.3d 588, 163 Cal. Rptr. 132,607 P.2d 924 (Calif. Sup. Ct. 1980).
3. Prosser WL, et al. *Torts, Cases and Materials*. 7th ed. Mineola, NY: The Foundation Press; 1982:144, 364-370.
4. *Kambat v. St. Francis Hospital*, 89 N.Y.2d 489, 678 N.E.2d 456,655 N.Y.S.2d 844 (Court of Appeals of N.Y. 1997).
5. *Rodgers v. Hook-SuperX Inc.*, 562 N.E.2d 358 (Ill. App. Ct. 1990).
6. Dobbs DB. *The Law of Torts (Hornbook Series)*. St. Paul, MN: West Group Publishing; 2000:315.
7. *Id.* at 541-546.

QUESTIONS

1. An example was given in the text of the chapter whereby a pharmacist filled a prescription for a woman who had young children, and did not place the medications in a child-resistant container. As a result, one of the children easily opened the container, consumed the contents, and became deathly ill. What if the facts of this case were changed whereby the pharmacist filled the prescription with the wrong drug, placed the medication in a safety-proof container, and when the mother came home, she removed the safety cap and forgot to put it back, and as a result her young child consumed the contents and became deathly ill? Would the pharmacist be held negligent under these facts even though the mother was an intervening factor by forgetting to put the cap back on the medication?
2. In consideration of whether or not vicarious liability exists regarding the actions of a pharmacy's delivery person, what if that delivery person leaves a prescription in the wrong place at a person's

residence who is not home at the time of the delivery, and a small child from next door finds and consumes it, and is injured as a result? Is liability imputed back to the employer? What if the delivery person, using the employer's car to make deliveries, gets into an accident on the way back to the pharmacy? Or the delivery person, using his own car, gets into an accident on his way home after making deliveries for his employer pharmacy?

3. Explain the difference between a jurisdiction that employs a *contributory negligence* standard versus a jurisdiction that follows a *comparative negligence* standard. In the following example, what would be the outcome for both the plaintiff and the defendant if a *comparative negligence* standard is applied: Plaintiff is crossing the street when the light is red; defendant is speeding at 40 mph in a 20-mph zone and hits plaintiff, causing $1,000,000 in damages. If the jury finds the plaintiff 60% negligent and the defendant 40% negligent, what entitlement to the $1,000,000 jury judgment does the plaintiff have? What would be the outcome in a jurisdiction that applies the *contributory negligence* standard?

CHAPTER 5

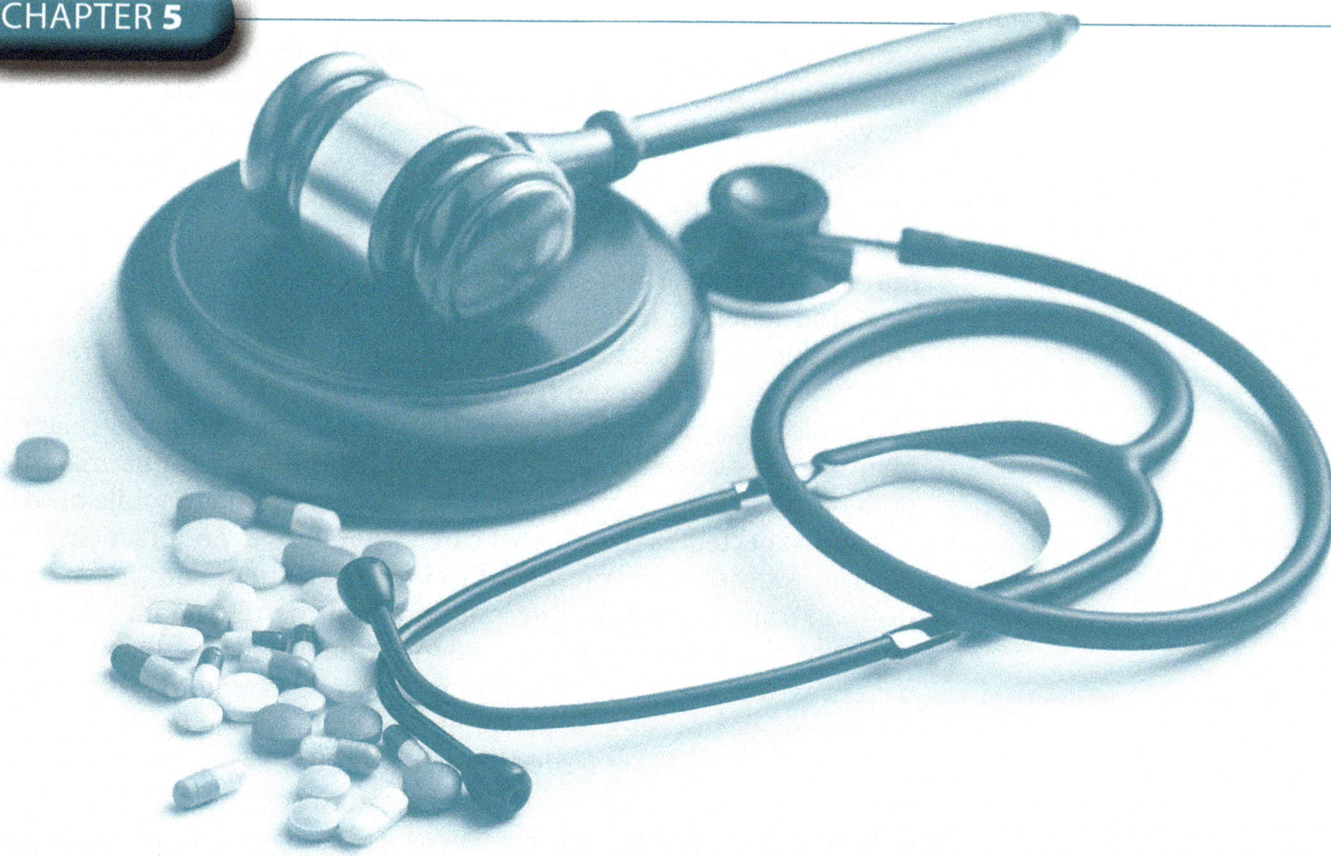

Negligence (Part II): Duty and Breach of Duty

THE MERGING OF STANDARD OF CARE AND DUTY

All of us have expectations as to how we should be treated in our interactions with others. We generally expect to be treated with respect, fairness, and concern for our needs. Overall such treatment should be standard and reasonable. It has been stated that, "the standard of care ... is the duty to exercise the care that would be exercised by a reasonable and prudent person under the same or similar circumstances to avoid or minimize risks of harm to others."[1] The court in *Gossett v. Jackson* stated the "*standard of care*" in the following terms, "... negligence is the failure to exercise that degree of care which an ordinarily prudent person would exercise under the same or similar circumstances to avoid injury to another."[2]

When the so-called prudent person is associated with a professional class, such as pharmacists, the standard of care expected of those professionals may evolve into duties owed to those seeking their services. There are, however, examples of contradictions whereby not providing a specific standard of care—even if such standard of care is not recognized as a duty—would still be considered a breach of duty under a negligence analysis.

To illustrate the entanglement courts sometimes face when determining whether or not a pharmacist practiced a certain standard of care, and whether that standard of care was a definable duty on the part of the pharmacist to service the needs of a patient, several issues are expanded upon in the following.

A major and established standard of care expected of all practicing pharmacists—which courts are not divided on—is that pharmacists fill each processed prescription correctly. This requirement, while both logical and expected, is the duty of care required of every practicing pharmacist. If a case were presented in which a patient sues for an injury from an improperly filled prescription, and the defendant pharmacist claims he owes no duty of due care to fill that prescription correctly, the patient would win the case barring no strong countering defense (eg, prescribing doctor wrote a prescription for the wrong drug).

The standard of care issues involving other pharmacy practice matters have not always been clear or uniform as to whether or not a duty of due care existed on the part of a pharmacist. The following are examples where the courts have been divided as to whether a standard of care translates into a required duty on the part of the pharmacist:

- The pharmacist's duty to warn patients about the adverse effects associated with their prescribed drugs
- The pharmacist's duty to monitor a patient's drug history
- The pharmacist's duty to control the patient's refills

The majority of states have adopted laws mandating the aforementioned standards of care be treated as duties required of the pharmacist in the performance of his or her job. If a pharmacist opts not to follow its state's laws regarding any imposed duty to warn, monitor, or properly refill prescriptions, this would generally be a clear breach of one's professional duty as a pharmacist. Remember, if a law has been created requiring a specific duty on the part of the pharmacist, any breach or nonfulfillment of that law creates *negligence per se*, thereby establishing the breach of duty component of the negligence formula.

The cases presented later in the chapter are examples of how the courts have analyzed the different standards of practice pertaining to drug warning, drug monitoring, and drug refilling absent clear statutory or regulatory guidance.

PHARMACIST'S DUTY TO WARN

Prior to the enactment of federal or state laws, a number of states found that a pharmacist had a duty to warn patients when a prescribed drug had a potential for being harmful when taken with other substances. In *Hand v. Krakowski*, the pharmacist knew that the patient was an alcoholic and knew that the prescription drug dispensed would interact with alcohol, causing serious harm. The *Hand* court found that the pharmacist not only had a duty to warn the patient about the potential serious interaction but had a duty to inform the prescriber as well.[3] In a similar case, *Perkins v. Windsor Hasp. Corp.*, the patient was also an alcoholic who claimed that she was not warned about the interaction of the prescribed drug with alcohol, and as a result, was injured from taking the combination.[4] The *Perkins* court held that the defendant pharmacy owed the plaintiff patient a duty to warn.

A smaller number of other states viewed the results of the pharmacist's duty to warn differently. In *Ingram v. Hook's Drugs, Inc.*, the court concluded that the pharmacist had no duty to warn a patient about the adverse effects of Valium.[5] The court's reasoning was based upon the pharmacist imposing on the patient-physician relationship, which could be disruptive to the patient's medication treatment. The court in *McKee v. American Home Products Corp.* maintained a similar position in a situation where the patient took a specific prescription drug over a 10-year period, resulting in adverse effects due to the extended period of time the medication was taken, and where the possibility of these adverse effects should have been brought to the attention of the patient.[6] Although the theme of interference with the physician-patient relationship was raised, the court did find that the pharmacist had a duty to alert the patient if a dispensing error occurred, the dose was lethal, the written instructions were inadequate, or there were contraindications or incompatibilities.

Keep in mind there are different characteristics associated with the pharmacist's role as a provider of information to the patient. The real issue is—what information does the pharmacist have a duty to convey to the patient? Based upon the principle that a professional such as a pharmacist is required to exercise that degree of care that a prudent pharmacist would exercise under similar circumstances based upon his or her skills, knowledge, and experience, the courts have routinely shown that pharmacists have more duties than simply the accurate filling of patients' prescriptions. The laws in many states are adopted from the federal OBRA 90 law that requires that the pharmacist counsel all Medicaid and Medicare prescription recipients on the use of their prescription drugs, how to properly store their drugs, and what the common severe adverse effects or serious interactions that might be experienced with prescription medications.

The following cases are examples of how the courts have decided on specific fact patterns dealing with whether or not there is a *duty to warn.*

CHINEY V. AMERICAN DRUG STORES, INC.

Missouri Ct. of Appeals 21 S.W.3d 14, 2000

Desired Remedy: The plaintiff seeks compensatory damages for a breach of a duty that caused her to become hospitalized when she went to the defendant pharmacy for the first time and asked that an albuterol inhaler be given to her without a prescription because she had it before at another pharmacy and there was an emergency need for it.

Issue: Is a pharmacist and pharmacy required, because of an established duty, to provide a patient with a prescription drug when that patient has never been to that pharmacy before, and demands the drug based on an emergency need?

Facts of Case: Ms. Chiney suffers from asthma, which she treats through the use of the prescription medication Proventil (albuterol). In her petition, she alleges: on October 1, 1994, she went to the Osco Drug Store in Kansas City, Missouri because she was suffering from an acute asthmatic attack and had run out of albuterol. She did not have a prescription. She therefore requested that pharmacist Stan Hodges either provide the inhaler to her or call the doctor or hospital to verify she was "entitled to" the albuterol. Mr. Hodges did not do as she requested, and she therefore had to travel by ambulance to Truman Medical Center for treatment. As a result, Ms. Chiney suffered damage to her breathing.

Defendants filed a motion for summary judgment on the grounds that Mr. Hodges had no legal duty to either fill Ms. Chiney's prescription or call the doctor or hospital when she had no current prescription. The trial court granted summary judgment on behalf of defendants on February 2, 1999, and it is from this judgment that Ms. Chiney now appeals.

Case Analysis: The appeals court, using other cases that set the precedence, found that "a mere request for assistance does not create a legal duty to help another. While recognizing a moral and humane duty to aid a person in distress or danger, in the absence of some special relation between the parties, the law generally imposes no legal duty to do so. However, if there was a special relationship between the two parties, then a duty on the part of Hodges to assist Chiney would probably exist." The relationship between Mr. Hodges and Ms. Chiney was one of a pharmacist to a potential customer. The pharmacy practice laws at the time in Missouri define the role of a pharmacist as a dispenser of drugs pursuant to a prescription order. "The definition does not describe or anticipate the practice of pharmacy to include calling a doctor to see if a potential customer, who does not have a written prescription, is entitled to a prescription medication when he or she requests that medication due to an immediate need."

Case Holding: The appeals court found in favor of the defendant.

COTTAM V. CVS PHARMACY

Supreme Ct. of Mass.; 436 Mass. 316; 764 N.E.2d 814; 2002

Desired Relief: Mr. Cottam seeks compensatory damages from defendant CVS Pharmacy for breaching its duty to inform Mr. Cottam that the trazodone prescription he received and took could cause priapism.

Issue: Does a pharmacy have a duty to warn its customers of the potential side effects of the prescription drugs it dispenses?

Facts of Case: The plaintiff, Robert L. Cottam, suffered permanent injury when he failed to seek timely medical attention for a side effect he experienced after taking the prescription drug trazodone for depression. He had obtained the drug at a CVS Pharmacy (CVS). Cottam alleges that CVS was negligent in failing to warn him of the side effect and its seriousness.

In May of 1994, CVS implemented a computer system designed to provide its customers with written information about the risks and side effects of prescription drugs. The computer produced this information in one of two ways: a short, condensed form (short form) or a longer and more inclusive form (long form). CVS's corporate policy required its pharmacists to distribute the long form when filling new prescriptions. The CVS policy also required its pharmacists to review the information on both the long and short forms with the customer. Cottam testified that the pharmacist gave him only the short-form warning, which provided:

> "**Possible Side Effects:** *Commonly: drowsiness. Very unlikely, but report: Dizziness, fainting, blood in urine, heart problems, breathing problems.*"

The plaintiff testified that the pharmacist discussed the medication with him, but that the sole warning she provided was that the drug may cause drowsiness. The defendant pharmacist testified that she had given Cottam the long-form warning, which included a warning about the risk of priapism, defined as an erection that is persistent, not produced by sexual stimulation and not relieved by orgasm. Specifically, the long form included the following: "SIDE EFFECTS: ... Notify your doctor if you develop ... painful erections ...." The manufacturer's package insert, which Cottam also did not receive, and which was not in CVS's corporate policy to distribute, read:

"**Warnings:** *Trazodone has been associated with the occurrence of priapism in approximately 1/3rd of the cases reported, surgical intervention was required and, in a portion of these cases, permanent impairment of erectile function or impotence resulted. Male patients with prolonged or inappropriate erections should immediately discontinue the drug and consult their physician."*

The pharmacist admitted that she did not orally advise Cottam about the risk of priapism. The plaintiff's physician testified that he had warned Cottam that priapism was a potential side effect before prescribing the medication.

Cottam took his first dose of trazodone at night before bed and awoke the next morning with an erection that persisted throughout the day. The erection became uncomfortable later that evening. Cottam did not contact his doctor, deciding instead to wait until the following day when he had a previously scheduled appointment with his primary care physician. He took his second dose of trazodone before bed that evening. On learning of Cottam's condition, the physician sent him immediately to a urologist. The urologist diagnosed Cottam's condition as priapism and immediately admitted him to the hospital to undergo emergency surgery. Because Cottam had waited approximately 30 h before seeking medical attention, the surgery left him permanently impotent. Ideally, Cottam should have sought medical attention within six hours. Cottam claimed that he would have sought medical attention earlier had he been informed that priapism is a potential and serious side effect of trazodone.

Case Analysis: To recover for negligence, a plaintiff must show "the existence of an act or omission in violation of a ... duty owed to the plaintiffs by the defendant." Subject to Massachusetts not having a law that requires a pharmacist to warn patients about adverse reactions that can occur with a given dispensed drug, this court looked to existing social values and customs, as well as to appropriate social policy. "A number of jurisdictions have addressed the issue, and the overwhelming majority hold that in general, a pharmacy has no duty to warn its customers of side effects. We similarly hold that, generally, a pharmacy has no duty to warn its customers of the side effects of prescription drugs." *(In California, this issue is addressed by regulation requiring that a pharmacist orally consult with a patient receiving a prescription for the first time and informing the patient of the "common severe adverse effects" associated with the drug prescribed [Title 16, CA Code of Regs. §1707.2].)*

Other jurisdictions have reached this result by extending to pharmacies the "learned intermediary doctrine ...." The doctrine provides that "a prescription drug manufacturer's duty to warn of dangers associated with its product runs only to the physician; it is the physician's duty to warn the ultimate consumer."

However, a pharmacy may voluntarily assume a duty that would not otherwise be imposed on it. Massachusetts recognizes that "a duty voluntarily assumed must be performed with due care." If a person voluntarily assumes a duty or undertakes to render services to another that should have been seen as necessary for his or her protection, that person may be liable for harm caused because of the negligent performance of his or her undertaking. Where a pharmacy provides a detailed list of warnings, or, by way of advertising, promises to provide customers with information, it may thereby undertake a duty to provide complete warnings and information. We thus conclude that ... CVS's argument that it did not assume a duty to warn of all side effects would be unavailing. Also, of pertinent concern is that Cottam's physician provided testimony that he did instruct Cottam about the possible problem with priapism.

Case Holding: Based upon the evidence and testimony of witnesses, the jury found CVS 51% negligent and Cottam 49% negligent, and awarded Cottam damages (after reduction for comparative negligence) in the amount of $357,000. The Supreme Court of Massachusetts affirmed the judgment.

DOOLEY V. REVCO DISCOUNT DRUG CENTERS

Tenn. Ct. of Appeals; 805 S.W.2d 380; 1990

Desired Remedy: The plaintiff appeals the trial court's rendering of summary judgment on behalf of defendant Revco Discount Drug Centers as a result of the Dooley child receiving erythromycin that the defendant pharmacy dispensed while the plaintiff was still taking theophylline dispensed earlier by the same pharmacy. The Dooley child suffered from cerebral seizures as a result of the toxic levels of theophylline in the blood. The pharmacist on duty did not know of the erythromycin–theophylline toxic interaction and, as a result, did not warn the patient of the interaction. The plaintiff's parents sued on a negligence theory that the pharmacist had a duty to warn of the drug interaction yet did not do so.

Issues: If a defendant pharmacist fails to warn a plaintiff patient of a serious drug interaction that causes the patient harm when the drugs are taken together, will that defendant pharmacist be held negligent for such a failure to warn the patient?

Facts of Case: Dr. Leon Everett began treating the minor plaintiff Brandon Dooley in June 1985 when Brandon was three years old. Brandon was hospitalized in June 1985 for pneumonia and, during this hospitalization, Dr. Everett prescribed an asthma medication known as theophylline. In January 1986, Dr. Everett diagnosed Brandon as suffering from asthma and again prescribed theophylline for Brandon.

On December 17, 1987, Dr. Everett prescribed erythromycin for Brandon at 400 mg four times per day for a period of 10 days. This prescription was filled by Revco on December 17, 1987. At the time erythromycin was prescribed for Brandon, he was still taking 200 mg of theophylline three times per day as per Dr. Everett's orders. On December 23, 1987, Brandon suffered cerebral seizures as the result of toxic levels of theophylline in his blood.

At the time erythromycin was prescribed by Dr. Everett and the prescription was dispensed by Revco, the package insert for erythromycin provided in pertinent part:

> Recent data from studies of Erythromycin reveal that its use in patients who are receiving high doses of Theophylline may be associated with an increase of serum Theophylline levels and potential Theophylline toxicity. In case of Theophylline toxicity and/or elevated serum Theophylline levels, the dose of Theophylline should be reduced while the patient is receiving concomitant Erythromycin therapy.

At the time Revco filled the erythromycin prescription, Revco did not warn or explain the potential for interaction to the plaintiffs. Also, Revco did not alert Dr. Everett of the potential interaction or possible effects of using erythromycin concurrently with theophylline.

The pharmacist on duty at the time Brandon's prescription was delivered did not know that erythromycin could interact with theophylline. He did not know that this combination of drugs posed a risk of serious injury to Brandon.

An expert witness on plaintiffs' behalf stated that "pharmacy is a profession that requires considerable knowledge about drugs and how they affect the human body"; that "pharmacists recognize that there exists a standard of care applicable to the practice of pharmacy in [Tennessee]"; that "there are certain duties and responsibilities generally accepted by the members of the pharmacy community"; that the "accepted standard of care of professional practice for the profession of pharmacy as they existed in Lawrenceburg, Tennessee, and similar communities in 1987" included that "pharmacies maintain a patient profile system"; and that "the patient profile should be reviewed by the pharmacist prior to filling a new prescription for several purposes" including a determination of whether the new drug prescribed for the patient and presented for filling to the pharmacist interacts with any other drug currently ordered for the patient.

The expert witness further testified that the standard of care also required the pharmacist alerted to the interaction to call the erythromycin prescriber, alert him or her to the potential interaction, and/or advise the patient or patient's representative of the potential interaction and encourage him or her to (1) have his or her serum theophylline levels monitored and/or (2) be alert for side effects of theophylline toxicity. It is difficult to articulate what the standard of care requires of a pharmacist without knowing the exact circumstances under which the prescription for Ery-Ped was presented but, regardless of the circumstances, the pharmacist is required to alert the patient or the patient's representative to the potential interaction.

The expert witness also testified that "there exists and did exist in 1983, 1984, 1985, 1986, and 1987, computer technology which was available to pharmacists to identify drug interactions in general and the erythromycin and theophylline interaction in particular."

Revco's motion for summary judgment was made on the sole basis that, as a matter of law, the pharmacist does not have a duty to warn his customer that there exists a potential drug interaction.

Case Analysis: Duty, in the context of a case where negligence is alleged, raises the question of whether the defendant is under any obligation required by law for the benefit of the particular plaintiff. Revco owes a duty to its customer to refrain from negligently doing or failing to do an act that would injure its customer. One who undertakes to render services in the practice of a profession or trade is required to exercise the skill and knowledge normally possessed by members of that profession or trade in good standing in similar communities.

"The practice of pharmacy" means "the practice of that profession concerned with the art and science of preparing, compounding, and dispensing of drugs and devices, whether dispensed on the prescription of a medical practitioner or legally dispensed or sold directly to the ultimate consumer, and includes the proper and safe storage and distribution of drugs, the maintenance of proper records, therefore, and the responsibility of relating information as required concerning such drugs and medicines and their therapeutic values and uses in the treatment and prevention of disease."

Case Holding: The appeals court reversed the trial court's granting of summary judgment in favor of Revco and remands for a trial on the merits, the collection of costs, which are assessed to Revco.[7]

PHARMACIST'S DUTY TO MONITOR

Prior to OBRA 90 and the institution of state legislation and regulations to hold the pharmacist to a duty of due care in the monitoring of patients' prescription drugs, the courts were slow to impose this duty on the pharmacist. Some courts, however, had limited duty-to-monitor provisions. *Gassen v. East Jefferson General Hospital* required that the pharmacist contact the prescriber only to inform him or her if there was a questionable error or mistake in a patient's prescription.[8] Other courts simply dismissed the pharmacist's role or duty in monitoring prescriptions. These courts made point of the fact that all monitoring of medications the patient is taking is the physician's responsibility exclusively. Some courts have even gone as far as to state that the pharmacist has no duty to even warn the customer or notify the prescriber that a drug is being prescribed in dangerous amounts, or that the patient is being overmedicated, or that serious drug interactions could occur; such monitoring and discussion of problems was strictly within the jurisdiction of the prescriber, and not the pharmacist.[9]

Since monitoring has become increasingly associated with the duty to warn, the majority of states are now recognizing the importance of pharmacists and pharmacies maintaining patient medication profile records to ensure that patients and their physicians are alerted to potential drug interactions, cross-allergenicity, duplication, drug misuse, and drug abuse problems. The following case provides an example of a pharmacy that marketed itself as maintaining patient medication profiles on its patients in order to prevent harmful drug interactions, yet failed to live up to its advertised drug monitoring standard of care.

BAKER V. ARBOR DRUGS, INC.

Court of Appeals of Michigan, 544 N.W.2d 727; 1996

Desired Remedy: The plaintiff's estate claims that Arbor Drugs acted negligently when the defendant pharmacist did not check a "drug–drug" interaction computer program in the pharmacy when it dispensed Travist-D (a decongestant) to plaintiff, who was also taking Parnate (MOA [monoamine oxidase inhibitors] inhibitor), causing the plaintiff to suffer a severe stroke. The plaintiff later committed suicide due to his stroke condition.

Issues: Is the defendant pharmacist negligent in a state that, at the time, did not require by law that pharmacists review patients' drug–drug interactions, despite the pharmacy advertising that its drug–drug interaction computer program reviews all potential drug–drug interactions, and that for the patient, "You can't do any better than what Arbor Drug offers¿"

Facts of Case: This case concerns the scope of a pharmacy's duty to a customer. The decedent, Robert F. Baker, and the plaintiff were married. Dr. Arthur Hewitt had prescribed the drug Parnate for the decedent's depression after an attempted suicide in October 1989. Parnate is grouped in a class of drugs known as monoamine oxidase inhibitors and can cause severe complications if taken with certain foods or other medications. The decedent was well aware of the dangers of adverse reactions with Parnate and strictly followed instructions given by his physician and the drug's manufacturer.

On February 26, 1992, the decedent developed a cold, and went to see Dr. Henry Tomashevski at the Park Medical Center. A notation in Dr. Tomashevski's medical records indicated that the decedent was taking Parnate. Additionally, the plaintiff testified at her deposition that the decedent told her that he had twice informed Dr. Tomashevski during the examination that he was taking Parnate. Dr. Tomashevski prescribed two medications for the decedent: Ceftin (an antibiotic) and Tavist-D (a decongestant).

The decedent went to the Arbor Drugs store where he normally went to have his prescription for Parnate filled. The decedent had had his prescription for Parnate filled at Arbor Drugs 11 days earlier. Penelope Serafim was the pharmacist who filled the prescriptions for Ceftin and Tavist-D. Serafim testified at her deposition that she was not aware that the decedent was taking Parnate when she filled his prescriptions for Ceftin and Tavist-D. According to Serafim, because of Arbor Drugs' computer system known as "Arbortech Plus," a drug interaction was detected between Tavist-D and Parnate, which had been filled earlier. Serafim testified that she did not personally see the interaction indicated on the computer, probably because a technician overrode it. Serafim, however, was sure that the computer detected the interaction because the letter "I" appeared next to the price on the prescription label. Serafim further testified that she was personally aware that Parnate and Tavist-D should not be taken at the same time. Had she known that the decedent was taking Parnate, Serafim would not have filled the prescription for Tavist-D.

The decedent purchased his cold medications and consumed the prescribed doses at home. Later that evening, he complained to his wife that he was not feeling well. They referred to the patient information literature provided with Parnate, and believed that he was suffering from a hypertensive attack. The plaintiff took the decedent to the hospital, where he was diagnosed as having suffered a stroke. The stroke was a result of ingesting both Parnate and Tavist-D. On July 16, 1992, the decedent committed suicide. He left a note claiming that, among other things, the stroke was too much for him.

Case Analysis: In determining whether a duty exists, courts look to different variables, including foreseeability of the harm, existence of a relationship between the parties involved, degree of certainty of injury, closeness of connection between the conduct and injury, moral blame attached to the conduct, policy of preventing future harm, and the burdens and consequences of imposing a duty and the resulting liability for breach.

Case Holding: In Michigan, at the time of this case, the pharmacist owed no duty to a customer to monitor his or her drug usage or to advise the patient about drug–drug interactions, regardless of how severe. It is, however, the plaintiff's contention that the defendant voluntarily assumed a duty in this case because of the implementation and use of its computer system known as Arbortech Plus. The plaintiff has presented evidence that the defendant implemented, used, and advertised through the media that it used, the Arbortech Plus computer system to monitor its customers medication profiles for adverse drug interactions. The defendant has advertised that its Arbortech Plus computer system was designed in part to detect harmful drug interactions. Therefore, the defendant voluntarily assumed a duty of care when it implemented the Arbortech Plus system and then advertised that this system would detect harmful drug interactions for its customers.

> "How can you avoid harmful drug interactions? Simple. Get your prescription filled at Arbor Drugs where Arbortech Plus provides your Arbor pharmacist with your complete medication history, so we're aware of any possible medication interactions. Arbortech Plus. You can't get any better …."

Accordingly, the appeals court held that the defendant voluntarily assumed a duty to utilize the Arbortech Plus computer technology with due care and found that the trial court erred in concluding that the defendant owed no duty to the plaintiff's decedent in this case and erred in granting summary disposition in the defendant's favor on this basis.

RAPID REFILLING OF PRESCRIPTIONS

Again, some states, prior to state statutes and regulations requiring a duty, were reluctant to impose a duty to prevent pharmacists refilling prescriptions at a frequency inconsistent with a prescriber's refill schedule directions. In *Laribee v. Super X Drug Corp.*, the defendant pharmacist refilled prescriptions for the plaintiff patient at shorter intervals than was authorized. As a result, the plaintiff died of an excessive use of the drug. The court positioned on the side of the defendant, claiming that the "danger of disobeying the prescription directions was as obvious to the customer as it was to the pharmacist, and that the customer's disobedience to her doctor's orders was not due to (1) the pharmacist's failure to warn her of the dangers associated with not following the method for taking the medication and (2) selling of refills in advance of the time allotted."[10]

Other courts recognized the seriousness of this matter of not holding the pharmacist accountable when systems were in place to allow the pharmacist to intervene and control the rate at which patients would acquire their refills. *Cafarelle v. CVS, Inc.* is such a case whereby a child's death could have possibly been averted had the pharmacist acted in a responsible manner.[11] The *Cafarelle* case is an excellent example of how the tools and knowledge of the pharmacist were misused. The *Cafarelle* case is presented in the following for this reason.

In *McLaughlin v. Hook's SuperX, Inc.*, also presented later, the court used a three-prong analysis to determine whether or not a pharmacist has an expanded duty beyond that of correctly filling prescriptions.[12] Like *Cafarelle*, the pharmacy in *McLaughlin* refilled prescriptions for the plaintiff patient at a two and a half times faster rate than was authorized by the prescriber. The *McLaughlin* court ruled that the pharmacy, based upon satisfying the three-prong test, did owe a duty of care not to refill the plaintiff patient's prescriptions at the frequent rate that it did.

Given the fact that pharmacies now have computerized programming to track refill information pertaining to a patient's prescription drug use, there should be no reason why the medication usage intervals as authorized by the prescriber should not be carefully adhered to.[13]

MCLAUGHLIN V. HOOK'S SUPERX, INC.

Supreme Court of Indiana, 642 N.E.2d. 514; 1994

Desired Remedy: Plaintiff McLaughlin seeks recovery against Hook's on the theory that it breached its duty of care by failing to stop filling the controlled substance prescription because the defendant pharmacists knew or should have known that McLaughlin was consuming the drugs so frequently that it posed a threat to his health.

Issues: Where a pharmacy customer is having a prescription for a controlled substance refilled at an unreasonably faster rate than the rate prescribed, does the pharmacist have a duty to cease refilling the drug at the unreasonable rate even though the physician may approve refills at intervals not in conformance with the manner the drug was prescribed?

Facts of Case: Patrick McLaughlin injured his back while working as a lumberjack in the state of Washington. In the course of treatment for that injury, he became addicted to propoxyphene. He was treated for the addiction in 1982, 1983, and 1987, but he did not stop using the drug. In 1988, because he was still experiencing pain from the injury, he began treatment with Dr. Bernard Edwards. Over a period of months in 1988, McLaughlin obtained prescriptions for drugs containing propoxyphene from Dr. Edwards. Most of these prescriptions were filled at a Hook's drugstore in South Bend by pharmacists Kathy O'Dell and Craig Merrick. The prescriptions were dispensed on the basis of written prescriptions from Dr. Edwards brought to Hook's by McLaughlin, on the basis of telephone calls to the store from the doctor's office, or as refills.

McLaughlin consumed these drugs at a rate much faster than prescribed. Hooks' records show that dozens of prescriptions for Darvocet or Darvon were filled for McLaughlin between May 1987 and December 1988. For example, during one 60-day period in 1988, McLaughlin received 24-four separate refills of propoxyphene compounds, totaling 1072 tablets. If consumed according to the prescription, the number of tablets would have lasted a period of 138 days; McLaughlin consumed the tablets in 62 days, almost two and one half times faster than the prescription ordered. In one month alone, propoxyphene prescriptions were filled 12 times, which means that McLaughlin or his wife appeared in the Hook's store once every two or three days.

In late 1988, after Dr. Edwards apparently became aware that McLaughlin was consuming propoxyphene drugs at a rate much faster than prescribed, he refused to furnish any more prescriptions. Shortly thereafter, McLaughlin's wife found her husband holding a shotgun to his head at a time of depression. He did not pull the trigger. Following treatment for drug addiction in early 1989, McLaughlin stopped taking all prescription pain medication.

Case Analysis: The appeals court analyzed the facts of the case looking at the following principles:

- Was there a ***Relationship***? It has long been established that the existence of a duty upon one party to act in a certain way toward another arises out of the relationship between them. It is a matter of common expectation, as well as statute, that pharmacists possess expertise regarding the dispensing of prescription drugs. It is also a matter of common understanding that customers rely upon pharmacists for that expertise. Upon this basis, we conclude that the relationship between pharmacist and customer is sufficiently close to justify imposing a duty.
- Was there a ***Foreseeability*** of harm or injury being caused? The court notes that it is well established that a duty is imposed only where a reasonably foreseeable victim is injured by reasonably foreseeable harm. It is not disputed here that one who consumes sufficient quantities of addictive substances may become addicted to them, and that such an addiction carries with it certain reasonably foreseeable consequences.
- Does ***Public Policy*** on the matter exist?

> "What the public policy of a state, is must be determined from a consideration of its constitution, its statutes, the practice of its officers in the course of administration, and the decisions of its court of last resort .... We perceive three policy considerations at stake here: preventing intentional and unintentional drug abuse, not jeopardizing the physician/patient relationship, and avoiding unnecessary health care costs."

State law provides that a pharmacist shall exercise his or her professional judgment in the best interest of the patient's health when engaging in the practice of pharmacy. Also, under Indiana State law, "a pharmacist has a duty to honor all prescriptions from a practitioner or from a physician .... Before honoring a prescription, the pharmacist shall take reasonable steps to determine whether the prescription has been issued in compliance with the laws of the state where it originated. The pharmacist is immune from criminal prosecution or civil liability if he or she, in good faith, refuses to honor a prescription because, in his professional judgment, the honoring of the prescription would (1) be contrary to law; (2) be against the best interest of the patient; (3) aid or abet an addiction or habit; or (4) be contrary to the health and safety of the patient."

Case Holding: The Indiana Supreme Court affirms the trial court's finding that a duty did exist on the part of the defendant pharmacy and the pharmacist, and denies Hook's motion for summary judgment.

CAFARELLE V. CVS, INC.

Superior Court of Mass., 1996 LEXIS 421

Desired Remedy: Plaintiff parents seek compensatory damages in the death of their daughter due to the negligent acts of the defendant pharmacy.

Issues: Is a pharmacist negligent by refilling a drug for a patient sooner than the refill schedule allows, thereby causing the patient to overuse the refilled drug, ultimately leading to her death?

Facts of Case: On July 3, 1991, Jennifer died from acute respiratory failure associated with a severe asthma condition from which she suffered since infancy. At the time of her death, Jennifer was 13 years old .... The clinical diagnosis at the time of her death was asthma with acute exacerbation and severe acute respiratory distress.

In the year before her death, Dr. Lawrence and his associates treated Jennifer approximately once per month. During that period, Dr. Lawrence prescribed a Proventil inhaler to Jennifer to be used on an "as needed" basis. At the time of her death, Jennifer was also taking Theodur tablets, Intal/Alupent (administered through an electrical nebulizer), Alupent tablets, and Azmacort. Proventil and Azmacort are beta-agonists and are used to treat the symptoms of asthma by opening up the lung passages; they do not affect the inflammation in the lungs.

The Proventil inhaler prescribed by Dr. Lawrence contained 200 metered doses. At eight puffs per day, the inhaler would last about one month. Dr. Lawrence testified at his deposition that when he first issued the inhaler to Jennifer, he instructed her on the proper breathing technique and he advised her not to use the inhaler more than two puffs up to four times a day, at a maximum. Dr. Lawrence stated that he discussed with Jennifer and her mother the consequences of exceeding the recommended maximum dosage. Dr. Lawrence also stated that he told them that overuse of the inhaler could result in possible accelerated heart rate or cardiac arrhythmia and the masking of worsening symptoms of asthma. In the seven-month period before Jennifer's death, Dr. Lawrence and his associates issued her a number of prescriptions for Proventil inhalers, all of which were filled at the defendant pharmacy.

During the relevant time period, CVS had an in-store computer used by the pharmacists when filling and refilling customer prescriptions. This computer system allowed the pharmacist to access a customer's prescription profile showing the customer's entire prescription history at that store. When a prescription was initially filled, the pharmacist would type into the computer the number of days the prescription should last based on the quantity and dosage prescribed by the physician. If a customer requested a refill too soon, the computer alerted the pharmacist with a warning prompt. The purpose of the warning prompt was for insurance payment purposes and also to alert the pharmacist that the customer may be overusing the medication. The pharmacist must manually override the warning prompt if he makes the decision to dispense the prescription in spite of the warning. According to plaintiffs' expert, Dr. Thomas M. Golbert ("Dr. Golbert"), CVS pharmacists filled Jennifer's prescriptions for Proventil inhalers approximately three times more frequently than is standard practice or recommended use of these medications.

A CVS pharmacist, James Grohman ("Grohman") testified that a pharmacist has a duty to alert the doctor when the pharmacy computer alert warns that the customer may be overusing the prescribed medication and that the pharmacist also has a duty to warn the patient that she may be overusing the medication. CVS has produced no documentation that any of its pharmacists ever warned the prescribing physician that Jennifer was overusing any of her medications. However, Grohman stated in his deposition that he called Dr. Lawrence's office and told the secretary that he had concerns about Jennifer's overuse of the

Proventil inhalers. Grohman also stated that he told Mrs. Cafarelle that Jennifer was overusing the inhalers. Conversely, Jennifer's parents contend in their answers to interrogatories that CVS did not inform them of the dangers associated with overusing the asthma medication. Whether Mr. Grohman provided these warnings is a disputed factual issue that cannot be resolved on summary judgment.

Sometime in April 1991, Grohman entered a new prescription for Jennifer's inhaler into the pharmacy computer as a 15-day supply, as opposed to the previous 25-day supply. However, Jennifer was given the usual 17-g inhaler canister, which should have lasted her for at least 25 days if used as recommended. CVS treated another prescription on May 13, 1991 as a 15-day supply. Grohman stated that he informed Dr. Lawrence's office that this change was needed to provide the medication to Jennifer at a faster rate and to ensure that the insurance company would pay for the medication. Grohman testified that he received approval of this change from a staff member at Dr. Lawrence's office. However, the prescriptions that CVS has presented allegedly authorizing these changes do not indicate a reduction in the amount of medicine Jennifer received or a change in the rate at which the inhaler was supposed to be used. Again, these are simply disputed factual issues.

Case Analysis: The CVS computer system alerted the CVS pharmacists that Jennifer was getting the inhalers at improper intervals. The pharmacists were aware of the length of time the inhalers should have lasted if used properly. The risk of her overuse of the medication was not only foreseeable, but it was foreseen by the CVS pharmacists. These pharmacists should also have known of the dangers associated with the overuse of the inhalers.

A pharmacist is usually in the best position to know when a patient is refilling prescriptions at too fast a rate, and to alert the patient and the physician of the situation. In this way, pharmacists and physicians can work together to provide the best care available to all patients. The CVS Pharmacist Responsibilities & Professional Practices states that "each prescription must be analyzed individually to determine its merit and medical necessity" and that a pharmacist must use her sound professional judgment in determining whether to refuse to fill a prescription.

Case Holding: The court held that CVS had a duty to exercise that degree of care that an ordinarily prudent pharmacist would have exercised under the same or similar circumstances, and that a jury may determine upon the evidence that CVS breached its duty of care by failing adequately to warn the plaintiffs or Jennifer's doctors that she was overusing the prescribed medication.

REFERENCES

1. *Mansfield v. Circle K Corp*. 877 P. 2d 1120 (Okla. 1994).
2. *Gossett v. Jackson*, 249 Va. 549, 457 S.E.2d 97 (Va.1995).

3. *Hand v. Krakowski*, 453 N.Y.S.2d 121 (N.Y. 1982).
4. *Perkins v. Windsor Hosp. Corp.*, 455 A.2d 810 (Vt. 1982).
5. *Ingram v. Hook's Drugs, Inc.*, 476 N.E.2d 881 (Ind. Ct. App. 1985).
6. *McKee v. American Home Products Corp.*, 113 Wash.2d 701, 782 P. 2d 1045 (1989).
7. *Gassen v. East Jefferson General Hospital*, 628 So.2d 256 (La. Ct. App. 1993).
8. *Kampe v. Howard Stark Professional Pharmacy, Inc.*, 841 S.W.2d 223 (Mo. Ct. App. 1992).
9. *Walker v. Jack Eckerd Corp.*, 209 Ga. 517, 434 S.E. 2d 63 (Ga. 1993).
10. *Laribee v. SuperX Drug Corp.*, 1987 Ohio App. Lexis 7861.
11. *Cafarelle v. CVS, Inc.*, 805 S.W.2d 380 (Tenn. App. 1990).
12. *McLaughlin v. Hook's SuperX, Inc.*, 642 N.E.2d 514 (Ind. 1994).
13. *Speer v. United States*, 512 F. Supp. 670 (N.D. Tex. 1981).

QUESTIONS

1. In the *Chiney* case, if the patient had an expired prescription on file with the pharmacy for her asthma medication, would the pharmacist have a duty to provide appropriate assistance?
2. Given that no prescription was on file for Chiney, and the pharmacist had no duty to provide assistance or services, what options would the pharmacist have if he were feeling charitable and decided to help *Chiney*?
3. In the *Cottam* case, was it fair for Cottam to sue CVS when he had received the needed warnings about his medication from his physician?
4. If Cottam had phoned the pharmacist as soon as he realized he was having a reaction to the medication, would the pharmacist have a duty to provide advice?
5. What does the judgment in *Cottam* tell us about the level of Cottam's comparative negligence?
6. In *Dooley v. Revco*, there appears to be some technology (computer programs) available to assist the pharmacist in detecting drug interactions. Do you think the argument that a pharmacist must warn a patient of potential drug–drug interactions is any stronger today given our advanced technology?
7. Do you think the *Revco* pharmacist had a duty to warn the parents of patient Dooley given that Dooley's physician didn't know there could be a drug–drug interaction?
8. What lessons can be learned from *Baker v. Arbor Drugs*?
9. In the *Hook's* case, do you agree there are instances when a pharmacist should fill a prescription faster than intended by the prescriber?
10. What are the signs or symptoms of a patient addicted to opioid medication?
11. In the *Cafarelle* case, was the computer system helpful to the pharmacist in making decisions about early refills?
12. How much blame should be placed on CVS rather than on the prescribers who were generating the prescriptions?

CHAPTER 6

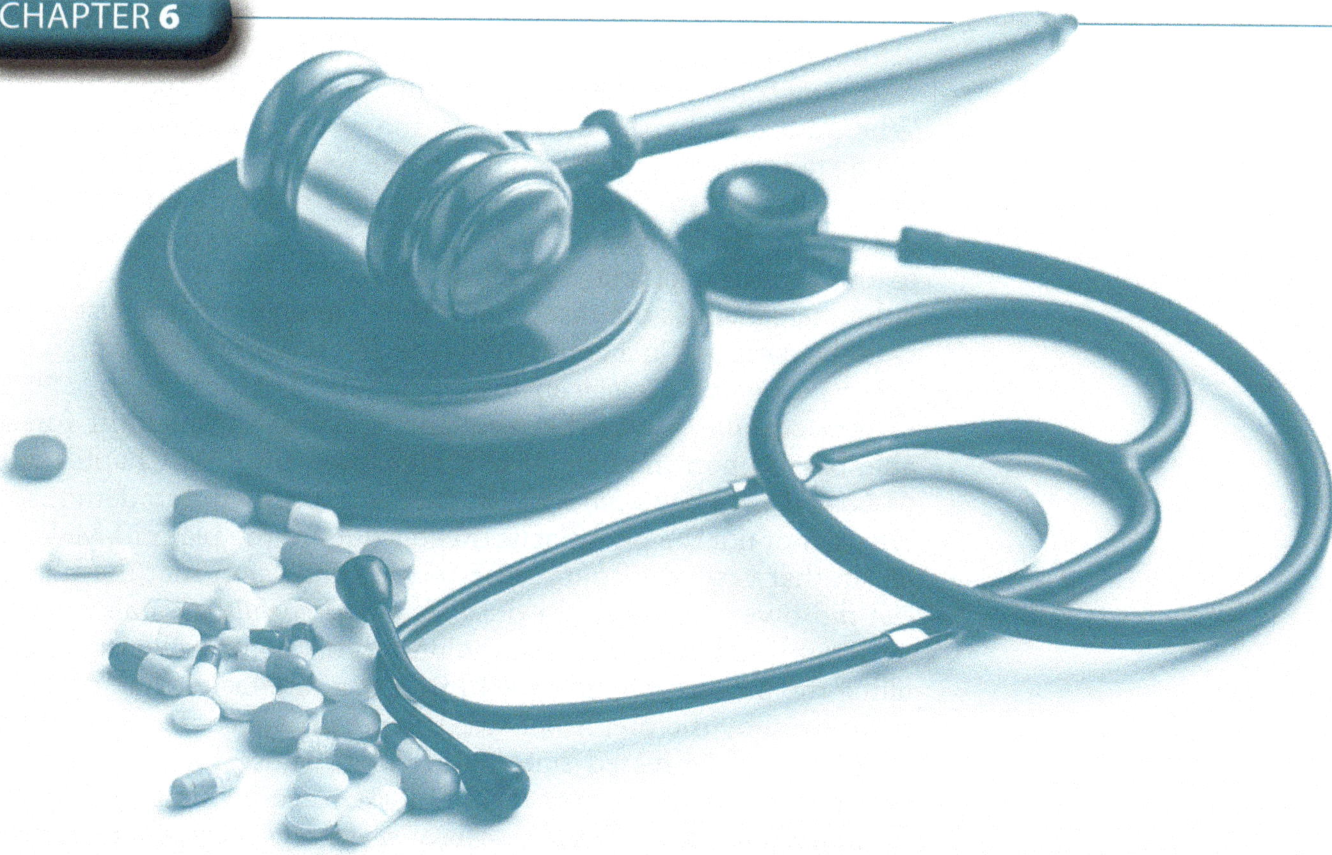

Negligence (Part II): Causation and Injury

As noted in Chapter 3, *causation* is basically the bridge between breach of duty and the resultant related injury. The causation component of negligence is not always straightforward and, thus, must take into account all the surrounding facts to determine if the resultant injury was foreseeable and linked to the breach of duty.

In this chapter, several pharmacy-related cases are presented that attempt to carefully analyze whether or not the causation link between the breach of duty and the resultant injury are clearly connected. Remember, some causation issues are objectively quite clear, such as in the case where a pharmacist incorrectly fills a prescription for a patient and one of the major side effects is drowsiness—an effect he would not experience if his prescription were filled with the correct drug. After taking the drug, the patient falls asleep while driving, gets into a serious accident, and is badly injured as a result.

From the simple facts in this hypothetical case, it appears more than likely that the furnishing of the wrong drug with the clear side effect of drowsiness was responsible for resultant injury. Certainly other facts may come into play: Did he drink alcohol after taking the drug? When did he take the drug? How many times before the accident did he take this wrong drug whereby he would have experienced the drowsiness effect? Was there some other independent intervening effect? Was there another driver involved who may have contributed to the serious accident? Many of these other facts or factors may either help dismiss the case against the defendant pharmacist or mitigate the damages in a comparative negligence arrangement.

In a *proximate causation* analysis, generally one looks to the element of foreseeability—was the resultant injury to the plaintiff foreseeable based upon the defendant's breach of duty? In Chapter 5, the *McLaughlin v. Hook's SuperX, Inc.* case was presented to demonstrate whether or not the pharmacist owed a duty to the plaintiff McLaughlin. In that case, the court came to the conclusion that the pharmacist did owe McLaughlin a duty. The *McLaughlin* case also goes on to determine whether or not the breach of the pharmacist's duty of filling the propoxyphene prescription at a rate faster than what was authorized by the prescriber was the proximate cause of placing the plaintiff in a depressed state sufficient to cause him to attempt to commit suicide. Review the facts of that case in Chapter 5 in order to understand the proximate causation analysis the court discusses later.

MCLAUGHLIN V. HOOK'S SUPERX, INC.

Supreme Court of Indiana 642 N.E.2d 514; 1994 Ind.

Review Facts Presented in Chapter 5

Court's Analysis on Causation Issue: The court addresses the foreseeability by making the statement, "It is not disputed here that one who consumes sufficient quantities of addictive substances may become addicted to them, and that such an addiction carries with it certain reasonably foreseeable consequences."

First, Hook's urges us to find the pharmacy and pharmacist not liable as a matter of law because McLaughlin's suicide attempt and his own wrongful conduct in consuming substances he knew were addictive constituted independent intervening causes sufficient to cut off any liability of Hook's. McLaughlin responds that the doctrine of intervening cause does not apply because McLaughlin's actions were foreseeable.

The authorities are clear that where the negligent actor's act or omission has the effect of setting in motion the chain of events leading to the injury, the key to holding that act or omission as the proximate cause of the injury is that the ultimate injury must be one that was foreseen or reasonably should have been foreseen, as the natural and probable consequence of the act or omission. Our case law recognizes this important limitation in determining whether the actor's act or omission is the proximate cause of the injury.

An intervening negligent act breaks the chain of causation only if the harm resulting from the intervening act could not have been reasonably foreseen by the original negligent actor.[1] An intervening cause is not a concurrent and contributing cause like the acts of joint tortfeasors, but instead is treated as a superseding cause that results in the original negligence being considered a remote cause and not a proximate cause.[2]

> "Accordingly, if harm is a natural, probable, and foreseeable consequence of the first negligent act or omission, the original wrongdoer may be held liable even though other independent agencies intervene between his negligence and the ultimate result. Generally, where harmful consequences are brought about by intervening and independent forces, the operation of which might have been reasonably foreseen, then the chain of causation extending from the original wrongful act to the injury is not broken by the intervening and independent forces, and the original wrongful act will be treated as a proximate cause; but, if the new independent intervening force was not reasonably foreseeable at the time of the actor's wrongful conduct, the consequences, ordinarily, are not caused by the original wrongful act ."

As was recently acknowledged by this court, Indiana decisions hold that suicide constitutes an intervening cause, as a matter of law, if committed by one who is sane enough to realize the effect of his actions.[3] Suicide by a sane person is sufficient to break the causal connection between the original negligence and the suicide.[4] In the *Riesbeck* case, a druggist negligently sold poison to the underage son of the decedent, who used the poison to kill himself. The court held that the pharmacist could not be held liable for that negligence because the decedent's suicide constituted an intervening cause:

> A voluntary, willful act of suicide of an injured person, who knows the purpose and physical effect of his act, is generally held to be such a new and independent agency as does not come within and complete a line of causation from the injury to the death so as to render the one responsible for the injury civilly liable for the death.[5]

That is, suicide constitutes an intervening cause only if it is the "voluntary" and "willful" act of the victim. Suicide induced by mental illness so severe that one cannot direct one's conduct does not constitute an intervening cause. We cannot say as a matter of law that the trial court erred in refusing to grant summary judgment for Hook's on this issue because the trial court may well have concluded that a genuine issue of material fact remained as to whether McLaughlin's suicide attempt was voluntary or whether it was involuntarily induced by a reaction to his drug addiction.

Holding: The Indiana Supreme Court denied Hook's motion for summary judgment and remands the case back to the trial court.

JANUARY V. BILLY JACK PEACE

Court of Appeals, Texas, 12th Dist. 738 S.W.2d355; 1987

Relief Sought: Plaintiffs, on behalf of the decedent, bring a negligence suit against the defendant pharmacist and pharmacy for selling strychnine to the decedent's husband, who used it to kill his wife. The husband claimed to the defendant pharmacist he was going to use it to kill wolves stalking his cows. The defendant pharmacist sold strychnine to him with the understanding it was for killing the wolves.

Issues: Should it have been foreseeable to the defendant pharmacist that the sale of the strychnine to the decedent's husband was for the purpose of killing his wife?

Facts and Procedural History: On November 5, 1982, Billy Jack Peace, a licensed pharmacist and owner of Peace Drug Store, received a telephone call from Murry Hugh January. January, a regular customer of Peace, requested some strychnine for the avowed purpose of killing wolves. January told Peace that he had been having problems with wolves attacking his cattle while they were calving. Peace advised January that he didn't have the poison in stock. Peace, according to his testimony, concluded that January wanted the strychnine "immediately" to prevent further loss of livestock. He stated,

> "At no time during my conversations with Murry Hugh January or anyone else, did I ever have any idea that Murry January was going to in some way use the strychnine

> purchased as outlined above to harm, injure, or kill his wife. There were no circumstances, inferences, statements or any other actions by any party that would have in any way led me to believe Murry Hugh January would use the strychnine for that reason. No statement, act or conduct in any way suggested that the strychnine would be used for any other purpose than to kill the wolves that were attacking Mr. January's cattle as he had reported to me in the telephone conversation."

The strychnine was given by Mr. January to his wife Deloris Faye January "… from which poison, after a period of intense and conscious physical pain and mental suffering, she died on November 13, 1982."

Reasoning: Foreseeability is satisfied by showing that the actor, as a person of ordinary intelligence, should have anticipated the danger to others by his negligent act. Foreseeability does not require that the actor anticipate just how the injury will grow out of the particularly dangerous situation. An act wanting in ordinary care, which actively aids in producing an injury as a direct and existing cause, need not be the sole cause; but it must be a concurring cause, and as such might reasonably have been contemplated as contributing to the result under the attending circumstances. It matters not what the actor believed would happen, but whether he ought to have reasonably foreseen that the event in question, or some similar event, would occur.

The evidence strongly supports that Peace had no knowledge of any facts, even remotely, suggesting that January, at the time he purchased the poison, had any motive to injure or murder his wife or any other person. Peace's affidavit testimony states, in effect, that he had no knowledge of any facts calculated to induce a belief that January had intentions to administer the poison to his wife or any other person. In fact, January informed him that wolves were killing his cows or newborn calves and he wanted the strychnine to poison the wolves before more cattle were lost.

Holding: The court granted the motion for summary judgment on behalf of the defendant and affirmed the lower court's decision.

BATTLE OF THE EXPERTS IN PROVING/DISPROVING CAUSATION

Generally attorneys on both sides of lawsuits involving malpractice will secure the experience, knowledge, and skills of expert witnesses to help explain why either the case should be dismissed against the defendant, or the preponderance of the evidence shows that the plaintiff's case against the defendant is sufficient to swing the judgment in favor of the plaintiff. Expert witnesses, while they play an important role in arguing why a duty or a standard of practice existed or did not exist, play an equally important role in being able to support or block the "causation" element at issue in a negligence case. The following case demonstrates how the so-called *battle of the experts* becomes an important element when a judge or jury must come to an opinion on a case. Judges and juries generally depend heavily on the opinions rendered by experts.

WAL-MART STORES, INC. V. KILGORE

Ct. of Appeals of Arkansas, Div. 2, 2004 Lexis 160

Relief Sought: Plaintiff John Kilgore seeks damages under a negligence theory that he received another Kilgore's medications that he took and caused him to suffer from post-traumatic stress disorder (PTSD).

Issues: If a plaintiff takes the incorrect drugs given to him by mistake by a defendant pharmacy, and apparently does not suffer from any of the direct pharmacological effects or side effects from those administered drugs, will the plaintiff be successful in bringing a causation claim of PTSD?

Facts and Procedural History: Plaintiff John Kilgore presented a prescription for cephalexin and Claritin-D 24 h to the defendant pharmacy on November 19, 1998. Instead of receiving his prescriptions, he mistakenly was given a bag containing medications meant for another customer who also had the last name "Kilgore." The medicine he received was triamterene w/ hydrochlorothiazide and Synthroid. John Kilgore took each of the medications for approximately two days, allegedly ingesting six triamterene hydrochlorothiazide capsules and two Synthroid tablets. Plaintiff filed a negligence suit against the defendant pharmacy on November 20, 2000, alleging that the medication error resulted in PTSD. After a four-day trial, the jury returned a verdict in favor of the plaintiff in the amount of $840,000. The defendant pharmacy appeals the case.

Reasoning: On appeal the plaintiff (appellee) called on two witnesses to testify that the ingestion of the medication mistakenly dispensed by pharmacy was the proximate cause of Mr. Kilgore's PTSD. The defendant pharmacy claims that neither of the medical experts testified with the requisite degree of medical certainty regarding proximate cause, and that without it, the jury was forced to speculate regarding the proximate cause of Mr. Kilgore's injury. Accordingly, the defendant pharmacy claims that the underlying jury verdict is not supported by substantial evidence.

Dr. Scott Stinnett, the plaintiff's witness and Mr. Kilgore's physician, offered his opinion at trial regarding the direct cause of Mr. Kilgore's PTSD:

> *Question – "Do you have an opinion as to the cause of his post-traumatic stress disorder?"*
> *Answer – "His symptoms, again, post the incident with the medication. He had not had symptoms prior to that."*

The defendant claims this testimony was not sufficiently specific. Additionally, plaintiffs called clinical psychotherapist Rodney Goodsell on the issue of proximate cause, and the following testimony occurred:

> *Question – "Do you have an opinion as to what caused the PTSD?"*
> *Answer – "I believe that it was from an overactive thyroid."*
>
> *Question – "As a result of the medication error?"*
> *Answer – "Yes, sir."*

The appellate court held that this is a simple negligence claim, and that as such, "expert testimony is required only when the asserted negligence does not lie within the jury's comprehension as a matter of common knowledge, when the applicable standard of care is not a matter of common knowledge, and when the jury must have the assistance of experts to decide the issue of negligence." According to the appellate court, Mr. Kilgore ingested the wrong medicine, provided to him by the defendant pharmacy and pharmacist. Later, Mr. Kilgore learned that he had taken the wrong medicine and that it could have seriously injured or killed him. Plaintiffs correctly assert that the jury could reasonably conclude that this information was the trauma that led to his PTSD and that there was substantial evidence to support that conclusion.

Holding: Based upon the appellate court's standard of review, it held that there was substantial evidence as to the elements of the negligence claim, and affirmed the trial court's decision in whole.

Post-Traumatic Stress Disorder (PTSD) Definition:

"A complex disorder in which the affected person's memory, emotional responses, intellectual processes, and nervous system have all been disrupted by one or more traumatic experiences. It is sometimes summarized as 'a normal reaction to abnormal events'. The DSM-IV-TR (the professional's diagnostic manual) classifies PTSD as an anxiety disorder."

JEANS V. CARAWAY PHARMACY

Ct. of Appeal of Louisiana, 649 So.2d 1141, 3rd Circuit 1995

Relief Sought: Plaintiff Jeans sues defendant Caraway Pharmacy in a negligence action for compounding an over-the-counter (OTC) product containing phenylpropanolamine that the plaintiff took and claims caused him to suffer a hypertensive crisis episode.

Issues: Was the plaintiff's ingestion of the phenylpropanolamine-compounded product prepared by the defendant pharmacy the cause-in-fact of his episode of hypertensive crisis?

Facts and Procedural History: Dalton Jeans, 49 years, took a dose of a homemade remedy containing phenylpropanolamine on the morning of November 14, 1990. That night he suffered a hypertensive (high blood pressure) crisis, with his blood pressure at one point reaching 270/150. He lived, but suffered brain damage. Based on his treating physician's opinion that the hypertensive crisis was caused by the medication, Jeans, joined by his wife and his son, sued the pharmacist, J. Garrett Caraway, who had prescribed and given him the medication. At the trial, a number of experts gave their opinions.

Causation is the only issue on appeal .... Causation is the only issue concerning which there are two permissible views of the evidence. The issue on appeal is whether the jury was clearly wrong in finding that the administration of phenylpropanolamine by the pharmacist, Caraway, was a cause-in-fact of Jeans' hypertensive crisis.

In tort cases and other civil actions, the plaintiff, in general, has the burden of proving every essential element of his case. In a malpractice claim the plaintiff must demonstrate by a preponderance of the evidence a causal nexus between the defendant's fault and the injury alleged.

Jeans had sinus problems. He had been treated by Dr. Richard Henry Kent, an allergy specialist, for years. One day in September 1990, some friends told Jeans about some medicine available at Caraway Pharmacy. Caraway, a pharmacist for over 30 years, had established a practice of concocting his own medications with mixtures of what he believed to be OTC drugs. There were several of these which he mixed up and gave names like Snoddgrass, Super Snoddgrass, Super de Snuff, Nu-Triphenyl TD, Redeye, Little Red, Goose Grease, and Bee Bottom Balm.

Caraway remembered when Jeans first came to see him in the fall of 1990. They talked a pretty good time, discussing what Jeans wanted and what he thought he needed. Jeans told him he had headaches and sinus problems. He questioned Mr. Jeans "about his health and things like that, which was normal procedure." "Then," he said, "I gave him some medication, one of my formulas that I routinely put together; and I told him how to take it and what to expect." They never talked about blood pressure. Dalton later called the pharmacy to complain that the Snoddgrass was not working. He was given Super Snoddgrass. This, too, failed to work so he was given Super De Snuff. He was finally given Nu-Triphenyl TD.

On the morning of November 14 at 8:00 AM, Dalton took his daily dose of the Nu-Triphenyl TD. This remedy, like the Snoddgrass concoctions in the Super de Snuff, contained phenylpropanolamine. Late that afternoon is when he suffered the hypertensive crisis.

The Caraway remedy that he named Nu-Triphenyl TD contained a ""Three Amines" sustained release tablet and one ibuprofen capsule. The "Three Amines" tablet consisted of 50 mg phenylpropanolamine, 25 mg pheniramine, and 25 mg pyrilamine.

In 1990 when Jeans bought these products from Caraway, the law required that the ingredients of the product be listed on the bottle and that all the manufacturer's labeling be included with the product. It is not denied that Caraway dispensed a prescription drug without a prescription, although not intentionally. He also did not deny that the bottles were improperly labeled; he admitted he was not aware of the changes in the law. The dispute in this case, however, is not about fault. The dispute is about cause. If the phenylpropanolamine found in the Nu-Triphenyl TD was not proved to have caused the hypertensive crisis suffered by Jeans, then Caraway's actions were not a cause-in-fact of his injuries.

Expert testimony by both sides was introduced on the issue of phenylpropanolamine's relation to the hypertensive crisis. It is distinctly within the province of the trial fact finder to assess the credibility of expert witnesses and the weight to be assigned to their testimony.

Dr. Kent, the allergy specialist, testified. During his treatment of Jeans over the years, he took his blood pressure routinely. On discovering on November 8, 1990, a blood pressure of 170/108, he told Jeans he ought to see another doctor about his blood pressure. He testified at the trial that he was unaware that Jeans was taking medication on the side, and he would not have prescribed phenylpropanolamine to a patient with blood pressure of 170/108.

Dr. R.D. Paraguya was the internist who treated Jeans when he arrived at Lake Charles Memorial Hospital on November 14. He diagnosed Jeans with hypertension secondary to medication because he had been told that Jeans was taking a decongestant. Dr. Paraguya stated that 50 mg of phenylpropanolamine was an OTC strength dosage, and that he would not expect a hypertensive crisis from that dosage. He was told at the hospital that the medication Jeans had been taking was strong. His discharge diagnosis was that the hypertensive crisis was probably caused by medication. The jury could have reasonably interpreted Dr. Paraguya's opinion as based on the belief that Jeans was taking phenylpropanolamine in stronger than therapeutic doses.

Dr. Neal Benowitz of San Francisco, an expert in clinical pharmacology, medical toxicology, and internal medicine with an emphasis on hypertension, testified for the plaintiffs. He explained that phenylpropanolamine constricts the blood vessels in the nose, and this is why it is used in medication for colds and hay fever. It can also constrict other blood vessels in the body. Dr. Benowitz was of the opinion that this constriction causes high blood pressure. He opined that taking the Nu-Triphenyl TD, which contained phenylpropanolamine, caused the hypertensive crisis in Jeans. Dr. Benowitz' explanation that this was an adverse drug reaction was based on three considerations. One was the nature of the reaction: he believed, though he had no scientific proof, that some very sensitive individuals could have elevated blood pressure even with standard doses of phenylpropanolamine. The second consideration was the time course of the reaction: the causal relationship in this case was supported by his study of Jeans' medical records and his findings that Jeans had normal or only mildly elevated blood pressure until about a week before the crisis, and then within a year after the crisis, his blood pressure was almost normal again without his having to take medication for lowering blood pressure. The third consideration supporting his opinion was that he could find nothing else in the medical records to explain the crisis.

Dr. Raymond Harbison, a pharmacologist and toxicologist, testified for the defendant. He was not himself a medical doctor but he was a professor in a medical school. He explained the effect that phenylpropanolamine would have in causing a hypertensive crisis. If too much phenylpropanolamine is ingested, it can cause significant constriction of the blood vessels throughout the body, and that constriction can result in an elevation of blood pressure. However, he was of the opinion that a therapeutic dose of a sustained release formulation of phenylpropanolamine would elevate the blood pressure only slightly, to an extent clinically insignificant. He stated that there must be an overdose of phenylpropanolamine to cause a significant increase in blood pressure like that seen in Jeans. Dr. Harbison was of the opinion that 50 mg of phenylpropanolamine found in the "Three Amines" tablet taken by Jeans in the morning would not cause a hypertensive crisis in the evening. It would all be out of his system by that time. He was aware that Jeans had been seeing Dr. Richard Kent for his allergy problems and, on a visit on November 8, six days before the hypertensive crisis, his blood pressure was 170/108. Although Dr. Harbison admitted that it was not wise to continue taking phenylpropanolamine when Jeans' blood pressure was 170/108 on November 8, he saw no evidence to suggest that 50 mg of phenylpropanolamine was high enough to have kicked this elevated blood pressure into a hypertensive crisis. Dr. Harbison also believed it was significant that Jeans had been exposed to phenylpropanolamine for a period of time before the hypertensive crisis on November 14, 1990, and he did not experience a hypertensive crisis during that period of exposure. Observing that Jeans had elevated blood pressures after the hypertensive crisis when he was not taking phenylpropanolamine, he gave this as another reason why this could not have been the cause of his high blood pressure.

Dr. Mark Strauss, a general internist, testified for the defendant. Fifty percent of his patients suffered from high blood pressure. He could not recall seeing a case where a therapeutic dose of phenylpropanolamine caused a hypertensive crisis. His opinion was that therapeutic doses of phenylpropanolamine would not cause a hypertensive crisis, nor would repeated doses. Taking more than the recommended dose could do it. Although phenylpropanolamine combined with antihistamines might increase the blood pressure, he was of the opinion that it did not cause Jeans' hypertensive crisis. He explained that there were other possible diagnoses of Jeans' elevated blood pressure, such as renal artery stenosis or seizure activity mimicking a hypertensive crisis.

Reasoning: The expert testimony, summed up, shows that phenylpropanolamine can cause an elevation in blood pressure. The facts reveal that Jeans took phenylpropanolamine over a period of time, administered to him by the defendant Caraway. The evidence fails, however, to prove that the phenylpropanolamine was the most probable cause of his blood pressure crisis on November 14, 1990. There is no evidence that he took doses in excess of therapeutic quantities, and many experts testified that it would take overdoses of phenylpropanolamine to cause a hypertensive crisis. Dr. Benowitz, the expert who believed therapeutic doses over a prolonged period could cause such a crisis, could offer no scientific proof for that hypothesis. Considering this testimony, we cannot say that the jury was clearly wrong in its determination that Caraway's actions were not a cause of Jeans' hypertensive crisis and resulting injuries. Although there was evidence that phenylpropanolamine can cause elevated blood pressure, there was testimony by several witnesses that 50 mg of phenylpropanolamine found in the "Three Amines" tablet taken by Jeans would not cause the significant increase in blood pressure he experienced on November 14.

Holding: The appeals court upheld the trial court verdict in favor of the defendant.

OSTROW V. NEW LONDON PHARMACY

Supreme Court of New York, 278 A.D.2d 718, 2000

Relief Sought: The plaintiff seeks damages in her negligence claim that receiving the wrong drug caused her ulcerative colitis to become worse.

Issues: If the plaintiff received the sulfa drug sulfadiazine instead of the prescribed drug sulfasalazine, would that be cause-in-fact to make her colitis condition worse?

Facts and Procedural History: The plaintiff mistakenly received the drug sulfadiazine instead of sulfasalazine for the treatment of her ulcerative colitis. The plaintiff was also using steroids in the management of the colitis condition. While the plaintiff claimed that her colitis condition worsened from being given the wrong drug, defense expert witnesses testified that the steroids were the cause for any exacerbation. The trial jury, after testimony by all parties, found that although the pharmacy had negligently dispensed the wrong drug, such negligence had not proximately caused the injuries of which the plaintiff complained.

Reasoning: There was sufficient evidence presented that the plaintiff failed to sustain her burden of proving that the worsening of her condition was not simply the natural progression of her admittedly preexisting disease, and the use of adjunct steroid therapy.

Holding: The appeals court confirmed the trial court's decision in favor of the defendant pharmacy, indicating that the worsening of her colitis condition was not caused by the administration of a similar sulfa medication.

SUPERSEDING EVENTS THAT BREAK THE CHAIN OF CAUSATION

As discussed in Chapter 4, superseding intervening events may cut the causation link between the defendant's duty and the resulting injury. These independent intervening forces may occur in different ways even though the pharmacist may be culpable to the patient in some way. Despite the fact that a prescription is filled incorrectly, mislabeled, or given out at a frequency greater than what was authorized by the prescriber, an independent intervening factor may disengage the pharmacist from being held negligent. The *Bikowicz* case presented in the following demonstrates how the plaintiff may be the intervening force, cutting off the liability claimed against the defendant.

BIKOWICZ V. STERLING DRUG

Supreme Court of New York, Appellate Div. 161 A.D.2d 982, 1990

Relief Sought: Plaintiff Marilyn Bikowicz commenced this negligence action against Sterling Drug seeking recovery for damages incurred as a result of her addiction to Talwin.

Issues: Did the defendant pharmacy owe a duty to warn the plaintiff of the possible dangers, such as addiction and physical damage to the leg and thigh area, from the continuous use of Talwin injections?

Facts and Procedural History: Dr. Rinse began administering Talwin to the plaintiff in 1968 as treatment for her migraine headaches. Originally, the injections were administered at Rinse's office or at a hospital. When the plaintiff told Rinse in February 1973 of an upcoming lengthy trip to Florida, Rinse wrote a prescription for Talwin, Dramamine, and disposable syringes. She also instructed the plaintiff's husband on how to administer the injections. Allegedly this prescription was not refillable yet the plaintiff, from 1973 through 1981, obtained many refills from Nedco Pharmacy through its respective owners, even though Rinse stopped treating the plaintiff in 1975. Defendant Sterling Drug was a second pharmacy the plaintiff went to in the 1970s.

By 1980, the plaintiff was allegedly injecting one shot per hour. When she was admitted to the hospital in July 1980 for an unrelated problem, she apparently realized that she was addicted to Talwin and her neurologist discussed the problem with Cunningham, a psychiatrist. As part of an overall treatment plan, Cunningham prescribed decreasing doses of Talwin over the period of the plaintiff's hospitalization. Upon her discharge from the hospital, however, the plaintiff told Cunningham of another impending trip, and Cunningham gave her a prescription for injectable Talwin that would reportedly last until the plaintiff's trip ended. This prescription was also allegedly non-refillable as originally written. Nonetheless, the plaintiff managed to obtain repeated refills from this prescription and the original 1973 prescription until she was admitted to a detoxification unit in 1981. As a result of repeated injections of Talwin in the leg and thigh area over the years, the plaintiff suffered serious and permanent damage to those areas.

... At trial, the jury concluded that any breach by defendants of their duty to warn of the risks associated with Talwin was not the proximate cause of the plaintiff's injuries.

Reasoning: In order to establish a *prima facie* case, a plaintiff must generally show that the "defendant's negligence was a substantial cause of the events which produced the injury."[6] Nonetheless, any break in the nexus between the defendant's negligence and the plaintiff's injury caused by the act of a third party or the plaintiff herself may affect the liability of the defendant.[7] Whether the defendant's liability is affected depends, in turn, on "whether the intervening act is a normal or foreseeable consequence of the situation created by the defendant's negligence."[8] If the intervening act is a natural, normal, and foreseeable consequence of the situation created by the defendant, the defendant will continue to be liable.[9] On the other hand, "an intervening act will be deemed a superseding cause and will serve to relieve defendant of liability when the act is of such an extraordinary nature or so attenuates defendant's negligence from the ultimate injury that responsibility for the injury may not be reasonably attributed to the defendant."[10] Accordingly, an intervening act that is "not foreseeable in the normal course of events or independent of or far removed from the defendant's conduct may well be a superseding act that breaks the causal nexus."[11]

Holding: The appeals court concurred with the trial court decision in favor of the defendant pharmacy.

REFERENCES

1. *Walker v. Rinck* (1992), Ind., 604 N.E.2d 591, 596.
2. *Havert v. Caldwell* (1983), Ind., 452 N.E.2d at 158 (citing 21 I.L.E. 330-333: Negligence § 67 (1959)).
3. *Kimberlin v. Delong* (1994), Ind., 637 N.E.2d 121 (the rule applies only where the original tortfeasor was negligent; the rule does not apply where the original tortfeasor acted intentionally).
4. Riesbeck Drug Co. v. Wray (1942), 111 Ind. App. 467, 39 N.E.2d 776.
5. *Ibid.* at 111 Ind. App. at 476, 39 N.E.2d at 780.
6. *Derdiarian v. Felix Contr. Corp.*, 51 N.Y.2d 308, 315; see *Kush v. City of Buffalo*, 59 N.Y.2d 26, 32-33; *Mack v. Altmans Stage Light. Co.*, 98 AD2d 468, 470.
7. *Kush v. City of Buffalo*, supra, at 33; see *Muhaymin v. Negron*, 86 AD2d 836, 838.
8. *Derdiarian v. Felix Contr. Corp.*, supra, at 315.
9. *Lynch v. Bay Ridge Obstetrical & Gynecological Assocs.*, 72 N.Y.2d 632, 636-637; *Kush v. City of Buffalo*, supra, at 33.
10. *Kush v. City of Buffalo*, supra, at 33.
11. *Lynch v. Bay Ridge Obstetrical & Gynecological Assocs.*, supra, at 636, quoting *Derdiarian v. Felix Contr. Corp.*, supra, at 315.

QUESTIONS

1. In the case of *January v. Billy Jack Peace*, should the pharmacist have been assigned some level of responsibility for providing the poison that was used in killing January's wife?
2. On which element of negligence do most cases hinge and for which expert witnesses are used?
3. In *Jeans v. Caraway Pharmacy*, which side had the stronger expert testimony? Why?
4. What type of expert testimony could have been used for either side to make their cases stronger?
5. In *Wal-Mart Stores, Inc. v. Kilgore*, what weaknesses appear on the part of the defendant Wal-Mart, possibly causing the pharmacy to lose?

6. In *Wal-Mart Stores, Inc. v. Kilgore*, what factors allowed the plaintiff Kilgore to be awarded $840,000? Would you have decided differently, and what arguments would you have made as the defendant's attorney?
7. In *Bikowicz v. Sterling Drug*, what was the intervening factor?
8. Was it fair that Sterling Drug faced no liability for the injury suffered by the plaintiff?
9. Other than civil proceedings, what other legal action could Sterling Drug and their pharmacists face for repeatedly refilling an expired prescription?

CHAPTER 7

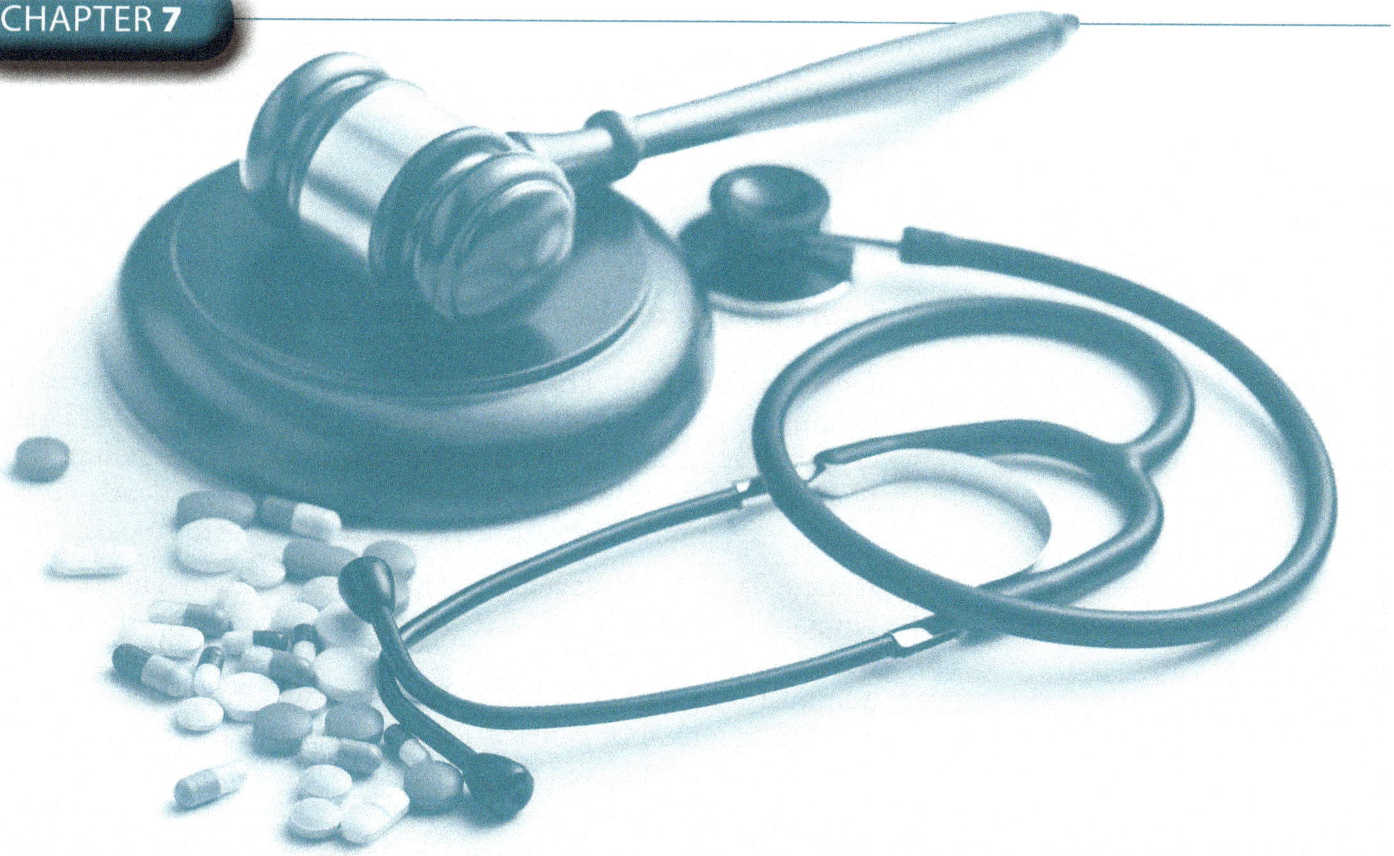

Negligence (Part III): Defenses

As discussed in Chapter 4, there are primarily four major defenses to negligence claims that a defendant may employ: (1) One or more elements of the negligence formula are missing; (2) contributory or comparative negligence exists; (3) assumption of the risk by the plaintiff; and (4) the statute of limitations. The following cases are used to illustrate each of these defenses.

WHERE ONE OR MORE ELEMENTS OF THE NEGLIGENCE FORMULA ARE MISSING

Often attorneys representing the defendant will attempt to dismiss negligence claims by demonstrating that one or more of the key components of the negligence formula are missing. Thus, if the defendant's attorney can show that there was no duty on the part of the pharmacist required, that the pharmacist did not breach his or her duty, or that the injury that occurred was not actually or proximately caused by the pharmacist's actions, then the defendant may have a good chance in having the case dismissed. The following case illustrates how the court concluded that there was no duty, thus no breach of duty, on the part of the defendant pharmacist.

HOOPER V. PERRY DRUG STORES

Court of Appeals Michigan, 1996

Desired Remedy: The defendant pharmacy seeks summary judgment in a case where a plaintiff was prescribed Seldane, erythromycin, and other medication filled by the defendant pharmacy that ultimately caused the plaintiff's death from myocardial infarction, secondary to coronary thrombosis.

Issues: Is a letter issued by the Department of Health and Human Services (DHHS) five weeks after the plaintiff's death that was due to the combination of Seldane and erythromycin administration stating that the use of the two drugs concurrently has the potential of causing life-threatening arrhythmias, and that the use of the two drugs together is contraindicated, sufficient to make the dispensing pharmacy liable to the plaintiff?

Facts of Case: Hooper's physician, Dr. Prabhaker, gave him prescriptions for Seldane and erythromycin. Hooper presented the prescriptions to a pharmacist at one of the defendant's stores. The pharmacist filled the prescriptions as written and dispensed the prescribed medications to Hooper, who thereafter ingested them. On July 7, 1992, Hooper died of a myocardial infarction, secondary to coronary thrombosis.

Seldane is "terfenadine." Erthromycin is a "macrolide" antibiotic. Almost two years before the death of the plaintiff's decedent in this case, an August 6, 1990 letter entitled "IMPORTANT DRUG WARNING " was issued by Marion Merrill Dow, Inc., the manufacturer of Seldane, to physicians and pharmacies, including Dr. Prabhaker and the defendant's store. This letter provided in relevant part as follows:

> ***General Precautions***
>
> Terfenadine undergoes extensive metabolism in the liver. Patients with impaired hepatic function (alcoholic cirrhosis, hepatitis) who are on ketoconazole or troleandomycin therapy or having conditions leading to QT prolongation (e.g., hypokalemia, congenital QT syndrome) may experience QT prolongation and/or ventricular tachycardia at the recommended dose. The effect of terfenadine in patients who are receiving agents which alter the QT interval is not known. These events have also occurred in patients on

macrolide antibiotics, including erythromycin, but causality is unclear. The events may be related to altered metabolism of the drug, to electrolyte imbalance, or both.

Drug Interactions

Preliminary evidence exists that concurrent ketoconazole or macrolide administration significantly alters the metabolism of terfenadine. Concurrent use of Seldane with ketoconazole or troleandomycin is not recommended. Concurrent use of other macrolides should be approached with caution.

On July 7, 1992, approximately five weeks after plaintiff's decedent had filled his prescription at the defendant's store, a DHHS news release stated that Marion Merrill Dow, Inc., had issued, pursuant to a request by the Food and Drug Administration, warnings to physicians and pharmacists that patients using Seldane may be in danger of developing life-threatening cardiac arrhythmias, and that the concurrent use of Seldane and erythromycin was contraindicated and must be avoided.

In September 1993, the plaintiff's representative filed a claim that the defendant's acts of dispensing Seldane and erythromycin for concurrent use were negligent acts that proximately caused the decedent's death.

The defendant moved for summary disposition … claiming that dismissal of plaintiffs claim was in order because it had no actionable duty to the plaintiff's decedent except to correctly fill his valid prescription. In response, the plaintiff claimed the defendant's duty to the plaintiff's decedent arose by virtue of the August 6, 1990 letter and that the defendant had breached its duty by failing to contact Dr. Prabhaker before dispensing Seldane and erythromycin to the plaintiff's decedent for concurrent use.

The trial court denied the defendant's motion, noting that the issue before it was whether the defendant had a duty to warn the physician, or anyone else, if the prescription was accurately filled. The court reasoned that although duty was an issue for the court to decide, a relationship existed that required the defendant to operate with ordinary care, and that whether it did so was for the jury to decide.

Case Analysis: A pharmacist owes a customer a duty to properly fill lawful prescriptions and may be held liable in tort for any breach of that duty.[1] Generally, however, a pharmacist will not be held liable for correctly filling a prescription issued by a licensed physician.[2] Thus, this court has held that a pharmacist owes no legal duty to warn a customer of the possible side effects of a prescribed medication where the prescription is proper on its face and neither the physician nor the manufacturer has required that any warning be given to the patient by the pharmacist.[3] This court has also held that a pharmacist owes no legal duty to monitor and intervene with a customer's reliance on drugs prescribed by a licensed physician.[4] The rationale for these rules is, in part, that "pharmacists should not be placed in the position of having to second-guess every prescription in an attempt to avoid tort liability."[5] In addition, this court has held that a pharmacist owes no legal duty either to discover a customer's addicted status or, failing such knowledge, to refuse to sell a nonprescription product to him or her."[6]

In this case, the August 6, 1990 letter did not state that Seldane and erythromycin were incompatible or that their concurrent use was contraindicated. Rather, the letter contemplated their concurrent use, albeit with "caution," thereby leaving the ultimate determination concerning their concurrent use with the physician. Rather, the first determination that Seldane and erythromycin were incompatible or their concurrent use contraindicated was the July 7, 1992 DHHS news release. Thus, assuming without deciding that a pharmacy has a duty not to fill two incompatible prescriptions,[7] we conclude that no such duty arose in this case where Seldane and erythromycin were not incompatible or their concurrent use was not contraindicated at the time the plaintiff's decedent fill his prescription at the defendant's store. Rather, we believe this case falls within the rule that "a pharmacist has no duty to warn the patient of *possible* side effects of a prescribed medication where the prescription is proper on its face and neither the physician nor the manufacturer has required any warning be given to the patient by the pharmacist."[8] To hold otherwise would require pharmacists to second-guess every prescription ordered by a doctor.[9]

Case Holding: The trial court's decision is reversed, and the defendant's motion for summary judgment granted.

CONTRIBUTORY AND COMPARATIVE NEGLIGENCE

Generally, those states that employ a contributory negligence defense may have a hard and set rule that bars the plaintiff from recovery if the plaintiff, in some way, contributed to his or her own negligence. Nevertheless, in a number of states that observe the contributory negligence defense, the use of the "last clear chance" doctrine may turn in the plaintiff's favor because the defendant may have been able to do something at the last second or minute to avert the negligent act. An example of this doctrine could be illustrated in the following manner:

> If a plaintiff got drunk and fell on a railroad track and lay there unconscious, and the engineer of a train coming down the track should discover the condition of the plaintiff as he approaches providing sufficient time to avoid running him down, the plaintiff's negligence on being on the track becomes irrelevant and he would be allowed to recover against the railroad if hit by the oncoming train. Even if the train had good brakes, the plaintiff could still recover on the basis of the engineer having sufficient time to discover the plaintiff's plight which would allow him through reasonable care to avoid hitting the plaintiff.[10]

Another variation of the "last clear chance" doctrine is the "discovered peril" doctrine used in other jurisdictions that employ the contributory negligence defense.[11] The "discovered peril" doctrine only applies if the defendant discovered the plaintiff's helpless condition and was negligent thereafter in failing to avoid injury.[12] The difference between this rule and the last-clear-chance rule is that the latter rule can be raised not only when the defendant actually discovered the danger but also when he should have discovered the danger.[13]

In the majority of jurisdictions that use the comparative negligence defense rule, a finding of negligence on the part of the plaintiff will reduce by some percentage the award that the plaintiff would have otherwise gotten. As an example, if it is found that a plaintiff contributed to 30% of the negligence, and the defendant was 70% negligent, then the plaintiff would only be entitled to 70% of the damages award.

In states where comparative negligence defenses apply, the courts may refer to the plaintiff as being contributorily negligent even though the standard used is comparative negligence.

The following case provides insight on how the court assesses damages when both sides bear responsibility for the resultant negligent act.

ORZEL V. SCOTT DRUG CO.

Supreme Ct. of Michigan, 537 N.W.2d 208, 1995

Relief Sought: Plaintiff John Orzel and his relatives commenced this negligence action against Scott Drug and other involved pharmacies seeking recovery for damages incurred as a result of his addiction, hallucinations, and paranoid schizophrenia resulting from the use of Talwin.

Issues: Is the continuous filling of prescriptions of Talwin at inappropriate intervals and without proper monitoring of the plaintiffs use of the drug that caused the plaintiffs addiction and mental changes sufficient to hold the defendant pharmacy negligent?

Facts of Case: In their complaint, the plaintiffs asserted that the defendant's negligence caused John Orzel to suffer the following damages:

> John J. Orzel became physically and psychologically addicted to Desoxyn, which resulted in auditory and visual hallucinations and mental illness including but not limited to paranoid schizophrenia. As a result of mental derangement and illness, the plaintiff has sustained pain, suffering, and disability including loss of earning capacity and has required medical aid and attention and hospital care and treatment.

The plaintiffs had claimed that the defendant pharmacy had breached common-law and statutory duties owed to John Orzel when it filled Desoxyn prescriptions for him without asking for identification or allowing an adequate interval between prescriptions (one-month refill periods were exceeded), and where the prescriptions read for purposes of "weight control" when they allegedly should have said "obesity." State law required that "for obesity" must be stated on a prescription as one of the allowed terms in order for the prescription to be legally dispensed.[14]

John Orzel testified that over time he knew that his purchase and use of Desoxyn was illegal. He also indicated that he was addicted to Desoxyn by July 1981. The plaintiffs additionally contend that by July 1981, John Orzel was no longer taking Desoxyn voluntarily, and that he was suffering from amphetamine psychosis to the point of being rendered legally insane so that he could not conform his conduct to the requirements of law.

In August 1981, John Orzel started going to the Figure Eight Weight Loss Clinic one to three times a week. There he would misrepresent to the physicians that he desired to lose weight, and the physicians would write him Desoxyn prescriptions for "weight control." It is uncontested that he never wanted or needed to lose weight, and that the only reason he went to the clinic was to obtain Desoxyn.

The defendant filled Desoxyn prescriptions for John Orzel, allegedly beginning in August 1981, and ending in January 1982. According to the evidence presented at trial, the defendant filled a total of between six and nine Desoxyn prescriptions for him, and each prescription was for a medically acceptable one month's supply of 30 tablets. Consequently, in total, John Orzel obtained between 180 and 270 Desoxyn tablets from the defendant. Each prescription that John Orzel presented to the defendant had been signed by a licensed physician.

From 1983 through 1986, he continued his drug use, purchasing and using mostly cocaine and Tylenol No. 4.

Dr. Finklestein, a psychiatrist and psychoanalyst who examined John Orzel in 1983, testified that he suffers from amphetamine psychosis. Dr. Finklestein attributed this psychosis to the heavy dosages of Desoxyn that John Orzel took in 1981, and opined that any subsequent drug use rendered him merely harder to treat.

Dr. Griffith, a psychiatrist who examined John Orzel in August 1986, testified that he suffers from paranoid schizophrenia induced by his Desoxyn consumption. Dr. Griffith explained that, although John Orzel was genetically predisposed to schizophrenia, the large doses of Desoxyn caused the onset of his schizophrenia.

> ... [T]he trial judge instructed the jury to apply comparative negligence principles to determine the extent of each party's responsibility for the damages, if any. The jury found the defendant negligent, and assessed plaintiffs' damages at $3.8 million. The jury also found John Orzel to be fifty percent comparatively negligent, and the verdict was reduced to $1.9 million.
>
> The defendant moved for judgment notwithstanding the verdict, and the trial judge granted the motion on the basis that John Orzel's illegal acts barred the plaintiffs' claim.

Case Analysis: When a plaintiff's action is based on his own illegal conduct, and the defendant has participated equally in the illegal activity, a common-law maxim, known as the "doctrine of *in pari delicto*," generally applies to bar the plaintiff's claim:

> [A]s between parties *in pari delicto*, that is equally in the wrong, the law will not lend itself to afford relief to one as against the other, but will leave them as it finds them. [1A CJS, Actions, § 29, p. 386. See also 1 Am. Jur. 2d, Actions, § 45, p. 752.]

The rationale that Michigan courts have used to support the wrongful-conduct rule are rooted in the public policy that courts should not lend their aid to a plaintiff who founded his or her cause of action on his or her own illegal conduct. If courts chose to regularly give their aid under such circumstances, several unacceptable consequences would result. First, by making relief potentially available for wrongdoers, courts in effect would condone and encourage illegal conduct. Second, some wrongdoers would be able to receive a profit or compensation as a result of their illegal acts. Third, and related to the two previously mentioned results, the public would view the legal system as a mockery of justice. Fourth, and finally, wrongdoers would be able to shift much of the responsibility for their illegal acts to other parties.

The mere fact that a plaintiff engaged in illegal conduct at the time of his or her injury does not mean that his or her claim is automatically barred under the wrongful-conduct rule. To implicate the wrongful-conduct rule, the plaintiff's conduct must be prohibited or almost entirely prohibited under a penal or criminal statute.

John Orzel's illegal conduct is of the type that warrants application of the wrongful-conduct rule. By his own admissions, as well as that of his counsel, he repeatedly violated several provisions of the controlled substances act when he obtained, possessed, and used Desoxyn without a valid prescription. The significant degree of harm and punishment associated with such violations, as well as the number of times that he committed them, makes his conduct distinguishable from a violation of a safety statute.

In view of all the facts in this case, we do not find it necessary to decide whether John Orzel was actually legally insane so that he could not be held criminally responsible for his actions. Proceeding on the assumption that John Orzel did at some point become legally insane, and that such insanity would excuse the illegal acts he committed while insane, we are still able to conclude that his illegal acts, committed while he was sane, proximately caused his damages. A review of the facts in this case makes clear that the illegal conduct that John Orzel engaged in while he was sane served as "a" proximate cause of his asserted injuries.

It is uncontested that John Orzel was sane when he first began to illegally purchase and use Desoxyn in November 1980. It was while he was sane that he decided to escalate his purchase and use of Desoxyn. The escalation continued quickly over the next several months, to the point that he became addicted to Desoxyn, and suffered hallucinations, amphetamine psychosis, and eventually legal insanity.

It is undisputed that both John Orzel and the defendant engaged in wrongful conduct. John Orzel's conduct was wrongful because he repeatedly made misrepresentations to doctors in order to obtain prescriptions for Desoxyn, he repeatedly presented prescriptions to be filled when they were written on the basis of such misrepresentations, he repeatedly presented prescriptions to be filled when they were written for persons with names other than his own, and he repeatedly purchased and used Desoxyn that he obtained pursuant to the false prescriptions. The defendant filled many Desoxyn prescriptions for John Orzel, and, when it did, its conduct was seriously blameworthy. The defendant filled Desoxyn prescriptions for John Orzel without first confirming his identity, it filled the prescriptions too frequently, and it filled them for arguably illegitimate purposes.

In comparing John Orzel's wrongful conduct with the defendant's wrongful conduct, we conclude that the two wrongdoers are equally at fault. Both parties played pivotal roles in making the illegal acts possible, and we cannot say that one party is more guilty than the other.

Case Holding: The appeals court held that plaintiffs' claim is barred since it is based, at least in part, on John Orzel's illegal conduct, and the trial court's decision to grant the defendant judgment notwithstanding the verdict is affirmed.

ASSUMPTION OF RISK

"Assumption of risk is not a defense much favored by the courts; and it has been cordially disliked by the friends of the plaintiff, because of its long history of defeating recovery in cases of genuine hardship—particularly in those of injuries to employees before the workmen's compensation acts."[15] For the most part, assumption of risk has merged into the defenses of comparative and contributory negligence. While the following case does not contain elements associated with pharmacy practice, it clearly discusses how assumption of risk has faded away as an affirmative defense and yielded to a contributory or comparative negligence defense.

BLACKBURN V. DAVID DORTA

Supreme Court of Florida, 348 So. 2d 287; 1977 Fla.

Discussion: Since the *Hoffman v. Jones* decision, contributory negligence no longer serves as a complete bar to plaintiff's recovery, but is to be considered in apportioning damages according to the principles of comparative negligence.[16] How then does the common-law doctrine of assumption of risk operate after the *Hoffman* case? If assumption of risk is equivalent to contributory negligence, then *Hoffman* mandates that it can no longer operate as a complete bar to recovery. However, if it has a distinct purpose apart from contributory negligence, its continued existence remains unaffected by *Hoffman*.

It is to be noted that assumption of risk is not a favored defense. There is a puissant drift toward abrogating the defense. The argument is that assumption of risk serves no purpose that is not subsumed by either the doctrine of contributory negligence or the common-law concept of duty. It is said that this redundancy results in confusion and, in some cases, denies recovery unjustly. The leading case in Florida dealing with the distinction between the doctrines recognizes that "at times the line of demarcation between contributory negligence and assumption of risk is exceedingly difficult to define."[17] The issue is most salient in states that have enacted comparative negligence legislation. Those statutes provide that the common-law defense of contributory negligence no longer necessarily acts as a complete bar to recovery. The effect of these statutes upon the doctrine of assumption of risk has proved to be controversial. Joining the intensifying assault upon the doctrine, a number of comparative negligence jurisdictions have abrogated assumption of risk (Alaska, Connecticut, New Hampshire, New Jersey, New Mexico, North Dakota, Utah, and Wisconsin). Those jurisdictions hold that assumption of risk is interchangeable with contributory negligence and should be treated equivalently. "Today we are invited to join this trend of dissatisfaction with the doctrine. For the reasons herein expressed, we accept the invitation."

The following states have indicated that although express assumption of risk is a viable defense, implied assumption of risk is equivalent to and should be treated like contributory negligence: Kansas, Maine, Minnesota, Oregon, Texas, Washington, and Wyoming. California and Hawaii have both indicated that assumption of risk may not be a defense when it overlaps with contributory negligence.[18]

... To sprinkle the term assumption of risk into the equation can only lead to confusion of a jury. An example of this concept is presented in the operation of a passenger train. It can be said that a passenger assumes the risk of lurches and jerks, which are ordinary and usual to the proper operation of the train, but that he does not assume the risk of extraordinary or unusual lurches and jerks resulting from substandard operation of the train. The same issue can be characterized in terms of the standard of care of the railroad. Thus, it can be said that the railroad owes a duty to operate train with the degree of care of an ordinary prudent person under similar circumstances, which includes some lurching and jerking while a train is in motion or commencing to move under ideal circumstances. So long as the lurching or jerking is not extraordinary due to substandard conduct of the railroad, there is no breach of duty and, hence, no negligence on the part of the railroad. The latter characterization of the issue clearly seems preferable and is consistent with the manner in which the jury is instructed under our standard jury instructions.

Application of pure or strict assumption of risk is exemplified by the hypothetical situation in which a landlord has negligently permitted his tenant's premises to become highly flammable and a fire ensues. The tenant returns from work to find the premises a blazing inferno with his infant child trapped within. He rushes in to retrieve the child and is injured in so doing. Under the pure doctrine of assumption of risk, the tenant is barred from recovery because it can be said he voluntarily exposed himself to a known risk. Under this view of assumption of risk, the tenant is precluded from recovery notwithstanding the fact that his conduct could be said to be entirely reasonable under the circumstances.[19]

There remains, then, for analysis only the principle of implied-qualified assumption of risk, and it can be demonstrated in the hypothetical recited earlier with the minor alteration that the tenant rushes into the blazing premises to retrieve his favorite fedora (a hat). Such conduct on the tenant's part clearly would be unreasonable. Consequently, his conduct can just as readily be characterized as contributory negligence. It is the failure to exercise the care of a reasonably prudent man under similar circumstances. It is this last category of assumption of risk that has caused persistent confusion in the law of torts because of the lack of analytic difference between it and contributory negligence. If the only significant form of assumption of risk (implied-qualified) is so readily characterized, conceptualized, and verbalized as contributory negligence, can there be any sound rationale for retaining it as a separate affirmative defense to negligent conduct that bars recovery altogether? In the absence of any historical imperative, the answer must be no.

Case Holding: The court held that the affirmative defense of implied assumption of risk is merged into the defense of contributory negligence and the principles of comparative negligence enunciated in *Hoffman v. Jones* shall apply in all cases where such defense is asserted.

EXCEEDING THE STATUTE OF LIMITATIONS

The statute of limitations sets the prescribed period of time in which a plaintiff may file his or her claim against the defendant. Each state has its own period of time allowed for the plaintiff to act on his or her claim. Generally, it is usually within a period of two to three years commencing when the negligent act has been discovered. After the statutory period has been reached, the plaintiff is barred from bringing a claim before the court.

FISHER V. WALGREENS

Court of Appeal of Louisiana, 746 So.2d 161, 1999

Desired Remedy: Plaintiff Fisher sues Walgreens by filing a negligence claim for the defendant pharmacy inappropriately filling a hand cream that caused the plaintiff to suffer from itching, swelling, and infection.

Issues: If a plaintiff does not file his or her negligence claim within the statute of limitation period allowed, is the plaintiff barred from any recovery?

Facts of Case: On January 12, 1998, the plaintiff, Aletha Fisher, filed suit against Walgreens Louisiana Corporation, Inc., (Walgreens), alleging that she sustained damages as a result of the defendant's employee negligently filling her prescription on January 9, 1997. She further alleged that she did not realize that the hand cream prescription had been improperly filled until January 11, 1997. Walgreens answered with a general denial, and then filed an exception of prescription, arguing the plaintiff's action had prescribed.

Pursuant to Article 3492 of the Louisiana Civil Code, a negligence action must be filed within one year "from the day injury or damage is sustained." (*This time period for the statute of limitations may vary in other jurisdictions.*)

The plaintiff argues that although the cream was prescribed, purchased, and used on January 9, 1997, she did not discover she was given the incorrect cream until January 11, 1997. She further argues that since January 11, 1998 was a Sunday, her suit was timely filed on January 12, 1998.

The long-standing rule of law is "an injured party need not have actual knowledge of his condition for purposes of starting the statute of limitations, as long as there is 'constructive notice,' that is information sufficient to incite curiosity, excite attention, or put a reasonable person on guard to call for inquiry."[20]

In her deposition, the plaintiff testified that she had used Topicort cream for a couple of years. It was prescribed by her physician to treat the dry skin on her hands caused by diabetes mellitus. She explained that she received a new prescription for Topicort on January 9, 1997, and went to Walgreens to have the prescription filled. The plaintiff further testified that in the past the Topicort cream she was given was in a blue-and-white tube. When she opened the bag to look at the cream on January 9, 1997, she immediately noticed this tube was red and white. She testified that she questioned Walgreens personnel as to the different color of the tube and further testified:

> … She told me it was the same cream, and I knew it wasn't because you could feel – When you put it on, it was like more of a greasier one than the first cream I had. (From Deposition of Althea Fisher)

During her deposition, the plaintiff was questioned as to the first time she noticed a problem with the cream, and she answered:

> That night [January 9, 1997] when I applied it, I told my son, I said—I screamed, "I don't feel good." I said, "It makes my hand feel like it is itching." Like red spots started breaking out on it. I said, "I don't know if it's the same cream or not." And I said, "I should get up and go and check this cream out." So I waited until the next morning and my hand was swollen up and it was red and infected. That's when I went to the doctor.

Later during the deposition, the following exchange took place:

> Before you went to the doctor, did it occur to you that maybe there was something wrong with the cream that you had put on your hand?
>
> It had to be, because like I say, I had used Topicort cream before and it had never done that.

The trial court found for the defendant based upon the dates noted, determining that the plaintiff did not act within the statute of limitations period.

Case Analysis: Applying the case law to this testimony, we find that the plaintiff had knowledge that she may have been given the incorrect cream on January 9, 1997. She also had knowledge that she sustained damage from the use of the cream.

Case Holding: Accordingly, the judgment of the trial court is affirmed.

KODERICK V. SNYDER BROTHERS DRUG, INC.

Court of Appeals of Minnesota, 413 N.W.2d 856; 1987 Minn. App.

Desired Remedy: The plaintiff claims that the pharmacy sold injectable Talwin, as a prescription, over an eight-year period knowing that it would result in injuries or problems for the plaintiff.

Issue: Is a claim brought by a plaintiff against a pharmacy eight years after an alleged harm or injury has been identified beyond the statute of limitations period? Also, would the claim involve the pharmacy under a theory of *respondeat superior* even though the prescriptions for Talwin were filled by a pharmacist employed by the pharmacy?

Facts of Case: In 1975, Joyce Koderick consulted Dr. Janna Peake for jaw pain. Dr. Peake prescribed an injectable pain killer called Talwin. Koderick filled her prescription at Snyder Brothers Drug. For the next eight years, Peake continued to prescribe Talwin, and Koderick filled the prescriptions at Snyder.

In December 1983, Roderick was hospitalized for ulcerated sores on her legs. Dr. Peake discontinued the Talwin and began prescribing Elavil (a mood-altering drug) and Dolophine (another pain killer). The last prescription for Talwin was filled in November of 1983. Koderick claims that Snyder continued to fill her prescriptions for other pain-killing drugs between November of 1983 and October of 1984.

In June 1986, Koderick served Snyder Brothers Drug with a summons and complaint alleging she suffered personal injuries as a result of Snyder's negligent sale of Talwin. (It was not determined in the case what the specific injuries were. The purpose of presenting the case is to concentrate on whether or not the statute of limitations was exceeded.)

Case Analysis: Questions of interest regarding the complaint filed were as follows:

1. What statute of limitations applies to the corporate defendant in a negligent sale of prescription drugs?
2. When does the cause of action accrue for negligent sale of a narcotic drug?

On appeal from summary judgment, the court determined whether any genuine issues of material fact existed and whether the law was properly applied.

Koderick argues that she is not suing the individual pharmacists but is suing Snyder Brothers Drug, Inc., a Minnesota corporation for negligence not only in the actual dispensing of the drug but in the maintenance of conditions under which the pharmacists worked, the record-keeping procedures of the business, and the lack of guidance and control exercised by Snyder. Koderick claims these are acts of negligence independent of any acts of the pharmacists and, therefore, the claim is controlled by the six-year general statute of limitation for injuries to the person.[21]

Snyder characterizes any potential liability as arising under a theory of *respondeat superior*. The court agrees. The complaint itself does not allege any independent negligence. Koderick's complaint states that Snyder "failed to use reasonable care in selling the narcotic Talwin to plaintiffs and sold the narcotic Talwin to plaintiffs negligently, unlawfully, and wantonly." The complaint alleges a negligent sale of Talwin through Snyder's employee pharmacists. These descriptions of negligence obviously relate to the duty to manage, control, and supervise, which is the basis of the doctrine of *respondeat superior*. Thus, Snyder stands in the shoes of its agent and a statute that bars a claim against the employee also will bar a claim against the employer.[22]

When a motion for summary judgment is made and supported as provided in Rule 56, an adverse party may not rest upon the mere averments or denials of his pleading but must present specific facts showing that there is a genuine issue for trial.[23] There are no facts introduced to support alleged independent acts of negligence. "As a general rule, the cause of action accrues when the accident occurs."[24]

There are instances in which strict application of that rule would create injustices, such as when no specific date of injury exists but the injury occurs over a period of time.[25] In such cases, the action accrues when "the plaintiff discovers, or in the exercise of reasonable diligence should have discovered, his illness."[26] Koderick argues that the continuous sale of Talwin over a period of eight years caused her injuries, so the "discovery of the injury" rule applies.

The trial court found that Koderick knew, or should have known, of her claimed injuries no later than December 1983 when she was hospitalized and the evidence supports this finding. Koderick, in fact, retained legal counsel and started discovery for suit against Dr. Peake at least by the spring of 1985, some six or seven months prior to the expiration of the two-year statute of limitation.

There is a second exception to the "time of accident" rule for applying statutes of limitation that has applied to physicians. This exception is known as the "termination of treatment" rule.[27] This exception exists because medical treatment frequently does not consist of a single act.[28] The courts also recognized that the relationship of trust between a patient and a physician during treatment may make it difficult for the patient to discover malpractice until the treatment relationship ends.[29]

Koderick argues that the "termination of treatment" rule also should apply to pharmacists. According to Koderick, after Dr. Peake discontinued the Talwin in December of 1983, the physician substituted Elavil and Dolophine for the treatment of Koderick's jaw pain. Koderick continued to fill these prescriptions at Snyder until October of 1984.

The "termination of treatment" rule cannot be applied. Pharmacists do not treat patients; they fill prescriptions for sale to the customer.[30] A pharmacist may have no idea as to what the customer is being treated for, or when the course of treatment ends.

In addition, the complaint specifically alleges that Talwin was the drug that caused the injuries. The course of treatment with Talwin ended when the last prescription was filled in November of 1983.

No matter which rule, discovery of injury, or termination of treatment is applied, Koderick's action was filed about six months after the two-year statute of limitation ran.

REFERENCES

1. *Adkins v. Mong*, 168 Mich. App. 726, 729; 425 N.W.2d 151 (1988).
2. *Id.*
3. *Stebbins v. Concord Wrigley Drugs, Inc.*, 164 Mich. App. 204, 218; 416 N.W.2d 381 (1987).
4. *Adkins*, supra at 732.
5. *Adkins*, supra at 730; *Stebbins*, supra at 216-217.
6. *Kintigh v. Abbot Pharmacy*, 200 Mich. App. 92, 94; 503 N.W.2d 657 (1993).
7. *Baker*, supra.
8. *Stebbins*, supra at 218 (emphasis supplied).
9. *Id.* at 216-217.
10. Prosser WL, Wade JW, Schwartz VE. *Torts Cases and Materials.* 7th ed. University Casebook Series. Mineola, NY: The Foundation Press; 1982:498-503.
11. Prosser WL, Keeton WP. *Prosser and Keeton on Torts.* 5th ed. St. Paul, MN: West Publishing Co.; 1984:465; *Esrey v. Southern Pacific Co.*, 1894, 103 Cal. 541, 37 P. 500; *Tempfer v. Joplin & Pittsburg Railway Co.*, 1913, 89 Kan. 374, 131 P. 592; *Labarge v. Pere Marquette Railroad Co.*, 1903, 134 Mich. 139, 95 N.W. 1073.
12. *Ibid.* at page 465.

13. *Ibid.* at pages 465-467.
14. *Orzel v. Scott Drug Co.*, 449 Mich. 550 (1995), pg. 553.
15. Prosser WL, Wade JW, Schwartz VE. *Torts Cases and Materials.* 7th ed. University Casebook Series. Mineola, NY: The Foundation Press; 1982:534-539.
16. *Hoffman v. Jones,* 280 So.2d 431 (Fla. 1973).
17. *Byers v. Gunn*, 81 So.2d 723, 727 (Fla. 1955).
18. *Li v. Yellow Cab Co.*, 13 Cal. 3d 804, 532 P.2d 1226, 119 Cal. Rptr. 858 (1975), and *Bulatao v. Kauai Motors, Ltd.*, 49 Haw. 1, 406 P. 2d 887 (1965).
19. *Morrison & Conklin Construction Co. v. Cooper,* 256 S.W.2d 505 (Ky. 1953); Restatement (Second) of Torts, § 496C, Comments d-g (1965).
20. *Boyd v. B.B.C. Brown Boveri, Inc.*, 26,889 (La.App. 2nd Cir.5/10/95), 656 So.2d 683, 688, writ not considered, 95-2387 (La.12/8/95), 664 So.2d 417.
21. Minn. Stat. § 541.05, subd. 1(5) (1982).
22. *Kambas v. St. Joseph's Mercy Hospital*, 33 Mich. App. 127, 128, 189 N.W.2d 879, 881 (1971), rev'd on other grounds, 389 Mich. 249, 205 N.W.2d 431 (1973).
23. Minn. R. Civ. P. 56.05.
24. *Dalton v. Dow Chemical Co.*, 280 Minn. 147, 151, 158 N.W.2d 580, 583 (1968).
25. *Id.*
26. *Id.*
27. *Schmit v. Esser*, 183 Minn. 354, 358, 236 N.W. 622, 624-25 (1931).
28. *Swang v. Hauser*, 288 Minn. 306, 309, 180 N.W.2d187, 189 (1970).
29. *Id.* at 309, 180 N.W.2d at 189-90.
30. Minn. Stat. § 151 (1982).

QUESTIONS

1. In *Hooper v. Perry Drug Stores*, what would have happened if the DHHS letter arrived before the prescription was dispensed?
2. If you knew that these drugs were contraindicated but the prescriber insisted you dispense them, would you comply?
3. In *Orzel v. Scott Drug Co.*, did the jury find correctly that the parties were equally to blame?
4. Should the defendant pharmacy face some kind of consequences for its actions? What type of consequences might it have faced after the civil case ended?
5. In *Fisher v. Walgreens*, does it make sense to use a statute of limitations? Is it fair to the plaintiff? How should a statute of limitations be determined?
6. In *Koderick v. Snyder Brothers Drug*, should the defendant face some kind of punishment for continually filling Koderick's prescriptions for pain medication?
7. If you were the plaintiff, how satisfied would you be with the performance of your legal representation?

CHAPTER 8

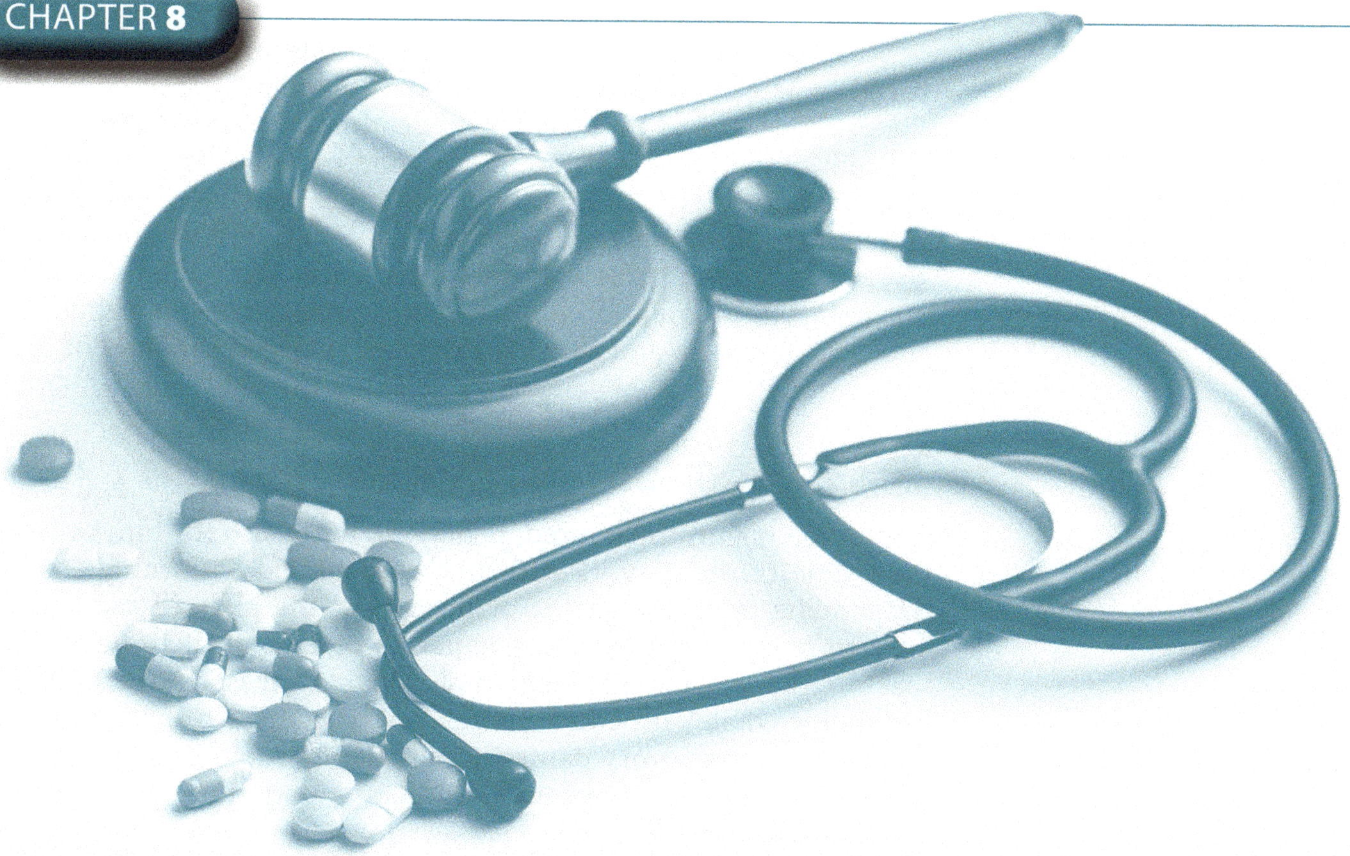

Negligence (Part IV): Remedies

Remedies or damages as the result of negligence, and other tort actions as well, are primarily identified as *compensatory damages. Punitive* and *nominal damages* may also be awarded depending on issues of intent and recklessness, and to prove a point. In addition, a spouse may have an opportunity to bring a claim for *loss of consortium* due to the nature of injury sustained by the plaintiff that may create a loss of the relationship between a husband and a wife.

COMPENSATORY DAMAGES

Compensatory damages attempt to make the plaintiff whole. They take into account the personal injury the plaintiff suffered along with the possible future loss that may be experienced. The plaintiff may be entitled to three categories of recovery under this damage category: (1) lost earnings and earning capacity, (2) medical and other expenses, and (3) pain and suffering experienced along with loss of enjoyment.

Wrongful deaths resulting from tort actions, and survivor benefits for the most part, are dealt with under both federal and state statutes. States, in regard to their wrongful death statutes, will differ in the amount of damages that may be awarded to survivors or beneficiaries for various claims. State survival statutes usually follow the common-law principles allowing the survivor, on behalf of the deceased, to seek to recover "whatever the deceased would have been able to sue for at the moment of death—for example, for his pain and suffering, loss of wages, and medical expenses between the time of injury and death."[1]

LOST EARNINGS AND EARNING CAPACITY

When the plaintiff is injured, it may be necessary for him or her to take time off from work and thus be deprived of earning a salary. Depending upon the extent of the injury, the plaintiff may not be able to return to work for some period of time, or may have to cut back on hours of work indefinitely. This decrease in the ability to work, for whatever period of time, is considered in the formula for granting compensatory damages to make up the difference of what the plaintiff would have earned during the period of his or her incapacity caused by the injury.

MEDICAL AND OTHER EXPENSES

The plaintiff may not only claim medical expenses that have already been paid, but may also set forth an estimate of what the medical expenses in the future will be as the result of the injury induced by the negligent act. This area of recovery involves such expenses as the costs of medical office visits, drugs, laboratory tests, physical therapy, medical devices, etc. as long as they are related to the injury induced by the negligent act.

PAIN AND SUFFERING AND LOSS OF ENJOYMENT

Plaintiffs who are injured as the result of a tortious encounter will generally experience pain and suffering. As a result, the courts will usually grant financial consideration for past, present, and future pain and suffering. The suffering takes into account both physical and mental suffering. The awards for pain and suffering claims are often difficult to quantify. While an injury may produce pain, sometimes with enduring consequences (eg, a back injury), there may be situations where the enduring pain and suffering may be the result of emotional trauma that may come with the loss of an arm or leg, or where the person is totally incapacitated (eg, body paralysis). Such emotional reactions to a trauma proximately caused by the tortious act fall within the definition of pain and suffering.[2]

If one is deprived of a life activity as a result of the tortious act, the plaintiff may seek remedy for such deprivation. If one loses his or her hearing and cannot enjoy listening to music, or has been incapacitated as the result of paralysis and cannot play a favorite sport, the plaintiff can claim loss of enjoyment under this remedy category.

LOSS OF CONSORTIUM AND NEGLIGENT INFLICTION OF EMOTIONAL DISTRESS

Often when a member of a family is injured, it may impact other members of the family, causing those members to lose some pleasure or companionship. Most commonly, a claim of *loss of consortium* occurs when one spouse may be deprived of the sexual relationship that existed before the tortious injury occurred. As a result, the spouse may join a complaint for a tortious injury sustained by the other spouse, raising his or her claim of loss of consortium.

A claim somewhat associated with loss of consortium, although separate, is the claim of *negligent infliction of emotional distress*. Here, the family member who witnesses the tortious act inflicted upon another member of the family may suffer extreme emotional distress sufficient to cause them to seek medical care. The consequences of emotional distress suffered by a family member may also be claimed as a separate cause of action by that family member. Keep in mind that the plaintiff herself may also bring an action involving negligent infliction of emotional distress.

The following three cases provide insight on how various damages are assessed and the financial awards rendered. Pay particular attention to the compensatory damages awarded in *Pressler v. Irvine Drugs,* the pecuniary and loss-of-consortium damages awarded in *Malone & Hyde, Inc. v. Hobrecht, et al.,* the reasons for awarding punitive damages in *McClure v. Walgreen*, and the reasons for denial of punitive and negligent-infliction-of-emotional-distress damages in *Baas v. Hoye Super Rexall Drug.*

PRESSLER V. IRVINE DRUGS

Court of Appeal of Calif. Fourth Appellate Dist. 169 Cal. App.3d 1244; 215 Cal. Rptr. 807; 1985 Cal. App.

Desired Remedy: The plaintiff claims he received the wrong form of insulin injection from the defendant pharmacy and is therefore entitled to compensatory damages based upon negligence on the part of the pharmacy and the pharmacists.

Issue: On a finding of negligence in this case, how would the court come to a decision in assessing the compensatory damages against the defendant?

Facts of Case: In September 1979, Michael Pressler, a diabetic who had required daily injections of insulin for approximately 20 years (since the age of 13), requested his usual semilente insulin at Danber Drugs. Pressler, was evidently given lente insulin by the pharmacist. Without noticing he was given lente rather than semilente (or being aware at the time of any distinction), he injected the drug for several days. As a result, the plaintiff experienced intermittent episodes of disorientation.

On September 30 when Pressler awoke, he felt unwell and continued to want to sleep. He did not awaken until 3:00 AM on October 1, having missed his scheduled employment as an accordion player the previous evening. On October 1, he called his girlfriend and told her he had discovered he had been using lente rather than semilente insulin. The evidence is unclear as to whether he did or did not discontinue using the lente insulin.

Pressler spent the following evening at his girlfriend's apartment. She was awakened at 2:00 AM by his heavy breathing and noticed he was losing body fluids and had become rigid. She called the paramedics who injected him with glucose and transported him to the hospital for further treatment.

Despite a return to his correct insulin, he continued to suffer hypoglycemic attacks. On two occasions, his condition warranted treatment by paramedics, while other instances required only the ingestion of orange juice or food. His parents, brother, and girlfriend reported noticeable changes in his physical abilities, mental attitude, ability to play the accordion, memory, and awareness of his own diabetic condition. In March 1981 Pressler, an expert skier, while executing an intermediate run in Sun Valley, crashed into a tree and suffered severe injuries. He has no recollection of the incident or its cause. However, eyewitnesses testified he suddenly went out of control, lost a ski, and, taking no evasive action whatever, shot over the edge of the run.

Pressler filed a complaint for malpractice and negligence on the part of Danber Pharmacy, Robert Robinson, the owner, and one of the pharmacists.

Case Analysis: The elements of negligence appear to be satisfied. The pharmacist and pharmacy owed Pressler a duty to provide him with the correct insulin product. The pharmacist and pharmacy breached that duty by providing him with the incorrect insulin that was the proximate cause of the harm that occurred to Pressler. Therefore, Pressler should be entitled to compensatory damages.

Case Holding: The trial court found no negligence on the part of Pressler or pharmacist Robinson (Robinson was absolved because there was no evidence he was the particular pharmacist on duty) but assigned liability to the pharmacy in the amount of $425,000. The jury broke down the lump sum award as follows:

- Medical -------------------------------------- $25,000
- Loss of earnings ---------------------------- $75,000
- Pain and Suffering damages --------------- $325,000

After the jury was dismissed, the court on its own motion reduced the general damages for pain and suffering by $75,000 pursuant to Sec. 3333.2 of the California Civil Code (allows for $250,000 as a maximum damage).

MALONE & HYDE, INC. V. HOBRECHT, ET AL.

Court of Appeals of Texas, Fourth Dist. 685 S.W.2d 739; 1985 Tex. App.

Desired Remedy: The pharmacy, Malone & Hyde, Inc., appeals the decision in this case brought by the decedent's (Roland Hobrecht) family whereby the court awarded damages for pecuniary loss and loss of consortium.

Issue: Did the trial court appropriately award pecuniary and loss-of-consortium damages as a result of the Malone & Hyde pharmacy's negligent act?

Facts of Case: Roland Hobrecht was a 66-year-old advertising executive. At the time of his death, he had been married to his wife, Antonia, for 39 years. The Hobrechts had three children.

In August of 1980, while on vacation, Mr. Hobrecht had to be hospitalized for an infection. After his condition stabilized, he and his wife went to his treating physician for his long-term problem with diabetes. Because of his diabetic condition being aggravated, he was hospitalized and released with a prescription for injectable insulin (Mr. Hobrecht had been on an oral hypoglycemic agent previously). His doctor wrote a prescription for NPH insulin, insulin syringes with 5/8 × 26 gauge needles. The doctor called the order into the defendant pharmacy where the Hobrechts routinely filled prescriptions. The pharmacist on duty, however, filled the prescription with a non-insulin syringe. The syringes provided to Mr. Hobrecht were 25 gauge, 5/8-inch syringes with a total capacity of 3 cc and did not have the "units" marked on the barrel for the routine provision of the proper dosing of the insulin (which has a maximum volume of 1 cc = 100 units).

Mr. Hobrecht's prescription directions required him to inject himself with 25 units of NPH insulin each day. As a result of using the wrong syringe, the plaintiff injected himself with approximately six times his prescribed dosage of insulin on two consecutive days (representing 150 units of insulin each time). The plaintiff was taken to the hospital where he died 30 days later.

Case Analysis: The trial jury, finding negligence on the part of the pharmacy, awarded the plaintiff's family $250,000 to Mrs. Hobrecht for pecuniary loss, $25,000 for loss of consortium before the death of her husband, and $250,000 for loss of consortium, which Mrs. Hobrecht would sustain after the death of her husband.

Also, included in the jury verdict was the following: an award of $50,000 to John Hobrecht, the adult son of the decedent as pecuniary loss; an award of $30,000 to Richard Hobrecht, another adult son of the decedent, as pecuniary loss; and an award of $60,000 as pecuniary loss to Pamela Goodlett, the adult daughter of the decedent.

The jury further awarded the estate $250,000 for damages incurred by the decedent for his conscious physical pain and mental anguish, as well as $20,243 as reasonable medical expenses and $2,678.01 as reasonable funeral and burial expenses.

At a hearing on Hobrecht's motion to enter judgment on the verdict, the trial court disregarded the jury's answer awarding Mrs. Hobrecht $250,000 as damages for the loss of consortium after death and entered judgment in the amount of $667,921.49. The trial court denied Malone's prayer to limit the judgment to $500,000 plus reasonable medical expenses pursuant to Tex. Rev. Civ. Stat. Ann. Art. 4590i and further refused to suggest a remittitur.

Malone appeals the damages assessed.

Case Holding: Malone challenges the $250,000 awarded to the decedent for pecuniary damages. The court did not agree with the challenge since the $250,000 was for the physical pain and mental anguish suffered by the decedent for a 30-day period before his death. From the date of the first overdose until his death, the decedent's condition worsened continuously. The decedent developed congestive heart failure, shortness of breath, and water in his lungs. The decedent's appetite lapsed and his bladder lost its ability to void normally. He eventually developed acute tubular necrosis of the kidneys, which eventually led to dialysis.

Based upon all the facts adduced, the jury was authorized to draw a reasonable inference of the pain and mental anguish experienced by the decedent during the last month of his life. The appeal court concluded that the jury's amount awarded is supported by factually sufficient evidence.

Malone also challenges the $250,000 awarded as damages suffered by Mrs. Hobrecht as pecuniary loss. The appeals court argued that when taking into account the care, maintenance, support, services, advice, counsel, and reasonable contributions of pecuniary value that Mrs. Hobrecht would, in reasonable probability, receive from the decedent, the amount awarded is appropriated. The appeals court goes further to explain the close relationship of Mrs. Hobrecht to her husband and her dependence on his income to sustain the day-to-day activities of the family.

> In cases where recovery of pecuniary damages is sought on behalf of a surviving spouse, the law rarely, if ever, furnishes a precise legal measure of recovery. Thus, the amount to be awarded rests primarily within the discretion of the jury, and unless the award is so large as to indicate that it was the result of passion, prejudice, partiality, or corruption, or that the evidence had been disregarded, the verdict of the jury is conclusive and will not be set aside as excessive, either by the trial court or on appeal.

Malone further challenges the pecuniary loss award assessed to Hobrecht's children. The appeals court found that the $30,000 pecuniary loss award to the decedent's son Richard was not founded based upon the evidence, but the other pecuniary awards to the other two children were justified.

Regarding the loss of consortium suffered by Mrs. Hobrecht prior to the death of Mr. Hobrecht, Malone challenges the $25,000 award. The appeals court noted that the loss of consortium and its constituent elements (affection, solace, comfort, companionship, society, assistance, and sexual relations are components to consider with regard to a successful marriage and are items constituting consortium) were present. The duty of resolving the monetary value to be placed on the loss falls upon the jury and its impartial conscience and judgment acting reasonably, intelligently, and in harmony with the evidence. The appeals court found the award somewhat excessive, and reassessed the loss of consortium to be valued at $2500 for the period from September 8, 1980 to October 10, 1980 during the time of the decedent's final hospitalization prior to his death.

Punitive Damage Awards

Punitive damage awards are considered when the defendant acted with intent in causing the injury or harm to the plaintiff. In addition, they can be awarded when the defendant is found to be grossly negligent—where it is found and proven that the defendant acted recklessly and/or with wanton disregard for human life. Punitive damage awards are intended to punish the defendant for his or her reckless or uncaring behavior, and are generally awarded in higher dollar amounts than compensatory damage awards.

MCCLURE V. WALGREEN

Supreme Court of Iowa 613 N.W.2nd 225 (2000)

Desired Remedy: The plaintiff seeks punitive damages in a gross negligence claim against the defendant pharmacy for receiving the wrong drug, causing injury.

Issues: Is a plaintiff who is injured by receiving the wrong drug entitled to punitive damages from a defendant who has shown a pattern of providing the wrong drug to other patients, and the defendant company has done little to correct this situation?

Facts of Case: Walgreen appeals from a jury verdict and judgment for punitive damages because of injuries Shari McClure suffered resulting from a prescription misfill error. In 1995, doctors diagnosed Ms. McClure with pancreatic cancer. She underwent a surgical procedure in which doctors removed a substantial portion of her stomach, small intestine, and pancreas.

In 1997, the plaintiff's cancer recurred. She underwent a second surgical procedure. Later, her doctors placed her on a fluorouracil chemotherapy and radiation regimen. On July 31, 1997 after hospitalization, and being sent home, she received three prescriptions that she had filled at the defendant pharmacy: Diflucan (for yeast infection caused by chemotherapy and radiation), Kytril (an antinausea medication), and Pepcid (to control production of stomach acid).

Upon filling the prescription at Walgreen Pharmacy, Ms. McClure was mistakenly given paroxetine (Paxil) 20 mg tablets instead of Pepcid tablets. When the plaintiff started taking the Paxil twice daily as noted on the label from July 31, 1997 to August 28, 1997, she started exhibiting increased irritability, weakness, confusion, and inattention to hygiene.

On August 18, 1997, her physician, Dr. Buroker, unaware of the medication error, prescribed Zoloft to control the plaintiff's behavior. On August 22, 1997, the doctor suspended the use of the Zoloft because Ms. McClure was exhibiting very low blood pressure.

On August 23, 1997, Ms. McClure had gotten up to go to the bathroom, became dizzy, and fell. As a result of the fall, she suffered fractures in her right leg and left foot. Medical testimony attributed the fall to the changes in her mental status and equilibrium brought on by her ingestion of Paxil.

Because of her injuries, she was admitted to a retirement care facility on August 26, 1997. The medications she received previously were brought with her to the facility. The nurses at the facility continued to administer the Paxil until one of the nurses finally discovered the error on August 28, 1997. The facility physician was immediately notified, and the Paxil medication was immediately stopped.

Walgreen was notified of the error, and at no time did Walgreen discuss the side effects of the Paxil medication with the plaintiff's family or warn of potential withdrawal problems associated with the abrupt discontinuance of the drug.

On September 9, 1997, the day Ms. McClure was released from the retirement care facility, she fell again because of dizziness. This time she suffered injuries to her head, back, and pelvis. Medical testimony attributed this fall to symptoms of a withdrawal syndrome associated with the abrupt discontinuance of the Paxil.

On October 2, 1997, the plaintiff sued Walgreen for compensatory and punitive damages. A jury returned a verdict for compensatory damages against the defendants in the amount of $100,000, and $150,000 in punitive damages. The punitive damages were based upon a repetitive history of dispensing incorrect medications to other patients, and the corporate officers doing little either to review why these errors were occurring or to make changes in the workplace to lessen them from happening in the future, thus acting in a manner that suggested a wanton disregard for human well-being.

Case Analysis: Punitive damages serve "as a form of punishment and to deter others from conduct that is sufficiently egregious to call for the remedy."[1] The evidence in this case was not limited to one innocent misfill. The pharmacist was the sole pharmacist on duty at the time the plaintiff's prescriptions were filled and at a time the pharmacy was exceptionally busy. The pharmacist admitted that she needed extra technicians to help staff during this rush hour at the pharmacy.

Additionally, there were 34 incident reports in evidence. These reports indicated dispensing errors nearly identical to the dispensing error in this case. The errors all occurred within a three-year period before the incident in question. Viewing the evidence in the light most favorable to the plaintiff, the court concluded the jury could reasonably infer that Walgreen had a serious problem in this regard, knew it had the problem, but did not take adequate steps to correct it. What made Walgreen's conduct particularly egregious, however, was its failure to warn the plaintiff or her doctors of the serious adverse side effects associated with Paxil and the abrupt discontinuance of the drug. Walgreen learned of the error 12 days before the plaintiff's second fall. Viewing the evidence in the light most favorable to the plaintiff, the court concluded that such a warning would have prevented the injury.

Case Holding: The trial court's decision is confirmed in favor of the plaintiff.

BAAS V. HOYE SUPER REXALL DRUG

766 F.2d 1190 (1985), Iowa

Desired Remedy: Defendant Hoye Super Rexall Drug appeals from a jury verdict awarding damages in favor of the Jessica Baas estate and Jessica's parents based upon the plaintiff's claim that the defendant violated a consumer product safety law requiring the dispensing of drugs in childproof containers. The plaintiff, however, cross-appeals the lower court's decision denying the plaintiff recovery on a claim for negligent infliction of emotional distress. The lower court also awarded punitive damages, which were reversed by the appeals court.

Issue: What circumstances limit the appeals court in granting a recovery for negligent-infliction-of-emotional distress and punitive damages?

Facts of Case: On July 12, 1981, the pharmacist at Hoye Super Rexall Drug filled a prescription for 50 Tedral SA tablets in a non-childproof container, and on August 10, 1981 a refill for the same drug was provided in a non-childproof container.

On August 21, 1981, young Jessica Baas opened the non-childproof container and consumed a number of the Tedral SA tablets. Medical efforts to save young Jessica failed and she died on September 4, 1981 from complications associated with an overdose of the Tedral SA tablets.

The Baas family filed suit against defendant Hoye Super Rexall Drug in a district court pleading federal jurisdiction under 15 USC Sec. 2072, which provides that "any person who shall sustain injury by reason of any knowing (including willful) violation of a consumer product safety rule shall recover damages sustained." Regarding this cause of action, both compensatory and punitive damages were requested. In addition, the Baas family filled a claim for negligent infliction of emotional distress.

On appeal, the defendant argued that it did not violate the consumer product safety law since the drug was attainable over the counter (OTC) without a prescription, and therefore does not require that it be placed in a childproof container. The defendant also contends that a non-childproof container was requested (15 USC Sec. 1473[b] allows for non-childproof containers if requested by the purchaser). It is the plaintiff's contention that upon the refill of the drug, a non-childproof container was not requested. The defendant argues that when the plaintiff provided the old container to the pharmacist, because it was not in a childproof container, one could infer that the drug should be provided on the refill in the same manner as previously provided. The appeals court on this issue noted that Ricky Baas in fact testified that when he came in for the refill, although he did not say anything about the type of container to be used, he expected the prescription to be placed in a childproof container. The appeals court agreed with Mr. Baas.[2]

Case Analysis: The appeals court, in accordance with submitted evidence that the United States Pharmacopeia lists Tedral SA as a prescription drug, did not accept the argument that it was an OTC drug. As a prescription drug, it therefore required childproof containers upon being dispensed by the pharmacy.[3]

Regarding the plaintiff's entitlement to punitive damages that was allowed in the lower court decision, the appeals court disagreed based upon a finding that "Congress did not intend for punitive damages to be recoverable under 15 USC, Sec. 2072(a)."[4] Therefore, the decision by the lower court to award punitive damages was reversed by the appeals court. The compensatory damages were allowed and not challenged by the appeals court.

The appeals court upheld the decision of the lower court in denying the plaintiff negligent-infliction-of-emotional-distress damages based upon two cases.[5] The *Barnhill v. Davis* case allowed a bystander to recover damages for emotional distress resulting from witnessing the negligent infliction of harm on another person. The *Barnhill* court noted that there must be a "sensory and contemporaneous observance of the accident, as contrasted with learning of the accident from others after its occurrence."[6] The *Oberreuter v. Orion Industries* case stated in pertinent part that "while observing the 'event,' there must be a reasonable and actual belief that the victim would be seriously injured or killed."[7]

In applying the previous two cases, Jessica's father did not actually observe his daughter ingesting the Tedral SA tablets. He was not aware of what was happening until he heard his wife screaming and yelling that "Jessica had gotten into the pills." The mother attempted to induce vomiting and summoned help to get Jessica to the doctor's office. The plaintiffs, neither the mother nor the father, had a "sensory and contemporaneous observation of the accident" as was required under *Barnhill.* Therefore, the lower court properly decided in not awarding damages for negligent infliction of emotional distress.

Case Holding: The appeals court held that the plaintiff was only entitled to compensatory damages (and not punitive damages) for the pharmacy not placing the Tedral SA prescription drug in a childproof container, and reversed the decision of the lower court in its finding that there was negligent infliction of emotional distress on Jessica's parents as a result of Jessica's death.

REFERENCES

1. *Coster v. Crookham,* 468 N.W.2d 802, 810 (Iowa 1991).
2. *Baas v. Hoye,* 766 F.2d 1194.
3. *Ibid.* at page 1193.
4. 15 USC, Sec. 2072(a) and Baas v. Hoyle, 766 F.2d 1195.
5. *Barnhill v. Davis,* 300 N.W.2d 104 (Iowa 1981) and *Oberreuter v. Orion Industries, Inc.,* 342 N.W.2d 492, 494 (Iowa 1984).
6. *Barnhill v. Davis* at page 108.
7. *Oberreuter v. Orion Industries, Inc.,* at page 494.

QUESTIONS

1. In *Pressler v. Irvine Drugs,* do you believe all elements of negligence were satisfied?
2. Do you agree with the damages that were awarded?
3. In the case of *Malone & Hyde, Inc. v. Hobrecht,* was the appeals court correct in reducing the loss of consortium prior to the death of Mr. Hobrecht from $25,000 to $2500?
4. What is the take-away message of this case as it pertains to the practice of pharmacy?

5. In *McClure v. Walgreen*, should the pharmacist be held responsible for failing to warn about the dangerous side effects of discontinuing a drug?
6. What other causes of action could be brought on behalf of the plaintiff, and against whom?
7. When, and only when, can punitive damages be awarded in a civil court case involving a tort action?
8. Bill and Mary are not married, but have lived together for 10 years in the same house they bought together. Bill is killed in a terrible traffic accident caused by the negligence of the other driver ("the defendant"). Just before the accident, Bill gave Mary an engagement ring, and both were planning to be married the following month. Because Bill and Mary lived so long together in the same house, all the neighbors thought they were already married. It was recently discovered that Mary is four months pregnant and Bill is the unquestionable father. Since Bill has no other living family members, Mary sues the other party who caused the accident for compensatory damages due to the defendant's negligence, and for loss of consortium. With regard to this suit, answer the following questions:
   a. What type of damages would Mary be able to claim under her request for compensatory damages?
   b. Regarding her request for "loss of consortium damages," what arguments could you pose to support this claim on Mary's behalf?
   c. Would a negligent infliction of emotional distress claim brought by Mary also be a viable claim? Explain why or why not.
   d. If Mary, in her claim, proposes a $1,000,000 amount for pain and suffering, would this be reasonable, and are there any formulas to determine what the award to Mary under this claim would or should be if she were to be entitled to an award under this claim?
9. While it is true that a plaintiff can request future medical expenses be assessed to his or her injury that results from a negligent act on the part of a defendant, what is your thought regarding how those future medical expenses should be assessed and supported?
10. In *Baas v. Hoye Super Rexall Drug*, are you convinced the parents (plaintiffs) of Jessica Baas, who died, were properly denied punitive damages and damages for negligent infliction for emotional distress by the appeals court? If you disagree with the appeals court decision regarding the denial of these two awards, can you construct arguments contrary to the appeals court arguments?

CHAPTER 9

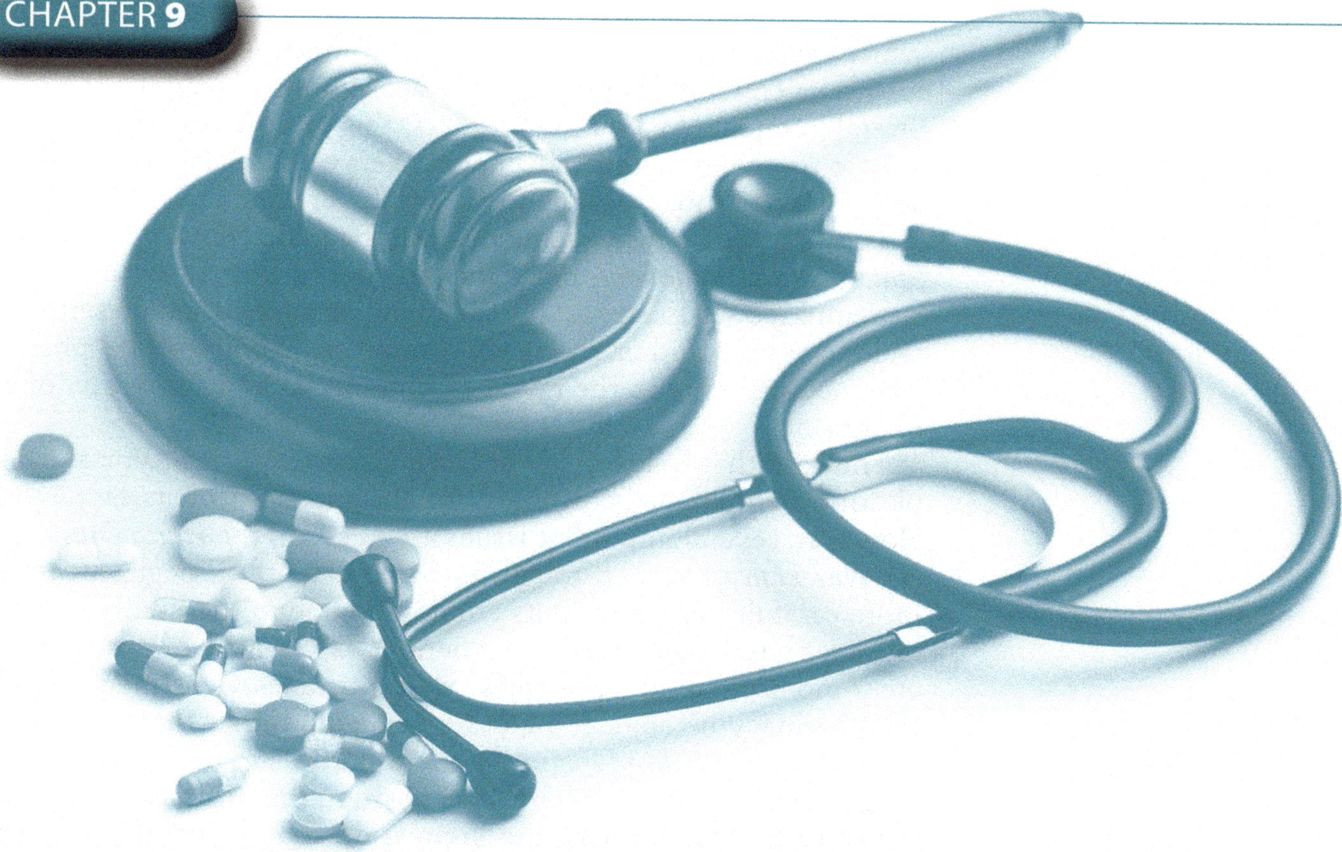

Negligence (Part V) Miscellaneous Categories: Vicarious Liability and Premises Liability

Included in this chapter are discussions and case presentations dealing with two additional areas of importance associated with the topic of negligence. *Vicarious liability* and *premises liability* cases represent a relatively high proportion of lawsuits brought against businesses, including pharmacies.

VICARIOUS LIABILITY

When a pharmacist employee makes a mistake on a prescription that causes injury to a patient who then takes legal action because of the error, usually both the pharmacist who was responsible for the error and the employer will be named in the filed lawsuit. Thus, any action taken against the employer for the liability created by the employee is referred to as *vicarious liability*. Another term specifically associated with employer-employee liability issues is the term *respondeat superior,* which means that the employer is jointly and severally liable with the tortfeasor employee for the tortious acts committed within the scope of employment. As you might guess, this gives a plaintiff a right of way to reach the so-called deeper pockets or the party that holds the larger sums of money, namely, the employer company.

The first case presented under this heading, *Randle v. California State Board of Pharmacy*, deals mainly with an intent by a pharmacist employee to misrepresent the filling of methedrine prescriptions and the State Board of Pharmacy's imputing liability of this pharmacist's actions on both the involved pharmacist and the owner of the pharmacy.

The case that follows, *Harco Drugs v. Holloway,* is a typical example of an employer being sued for the mistakes of its employees. However, several important issues are raised in the *Harco Drugs* case: (1) Was *Harco Drugs*, through its corporate office, negligent in not more carefully supervising its employees due to the number of mistakes reported over a three-year period? (2) Because of not appropriately monitoring its employees when mistakes were made, should the pharmacy be adjudged grossly negligent rather than just simply negligent? The *Harco Drugs* case represents a situation in which the employer places the employee in a position that increases the potential of error, thus creating the impression that total liability should be imputed to the employer. The minority dissenting opinion is also included to suggest that *Harco Drugs* was doing everything in its power to prevent errors of the type represented in the case, and that the number of errors over the three years was proportionally small and possibly insignificant based upon the number of total prescriptions filled over this period of time.

RANDLE V. CALIFORNIA STATE BOARD OF PHARMACY

Court of Appeal of California, 240 Cal. App.2d 254: 49 Cal. Rptr. 485; 1966 Cal. App.

Desired Remedy: Defendant pharmacy owners issue an appeal from the decision rendered by the administrative law judge to revoke their pharmacy license, and the license of pharmacist Lloyd Randle.

Issues: Does the Board of Pharmacy have the right to revoke a pharmacy and owner-pharmacist license if evidence shows that there is no record of prescriptions for over 38,000 methedrine ampules, that there were prescriptions forged for this drug, and the owner-pharmacist has been found guilty in the past of other criminal actions?

Facts of Case: A finding by the State Board of Pharmacy that defendants sold 38,441 methedrine ampules without prescriptions in violation of Bus. & Prof. Code, Sec. 4227, was against the weight of the evidence where one defendant testified unequivocally that he never sold methedrine without a prescription, though 38,441 ampules were unaccounted for when the amount on hand plus the amount for which prescriptions were filled was subtracted from the amount sold and delivered to the defendant's pharmacy.

Appellants, husband and wife, brought this mandate proceeding to set aside the decision of the respondent board revoking appellant Lloyd R. Randle's license to practice pharmacy and appellant Cecil Randle's permit to maintain and conduct a pharmacy.

The wife's responsibility for the claimed misconduct is vicarious, being based upon *respondeat superior*. She employed her husband to manage and operate the pharmacy. The other employees were one full-time pharmacist (Bohm) and two part-time pharmacists.

There is no dispute that the 38,441 ampules of methedrine are missing and unaccounted for. The proof shows that 132,000 ampules were sold and delivered to the pharmacy during the specified period, that only 2640 ampules were on hand at the end of such period, and that the prescriptions on file for methedrine during said period totaled only 90,919 ampules, thus leaving 38,441 ampules unaccounted for. Also, it was noted that a number of the prescriptions for the ampules were forged.

In opposition to this evidence, Randle testified unequivocally that he had never sold a methedrine capsule or ampule without a prescription.

Further, Randle's license to practice pharmacy was revoked by the board on November 23, 1951. This revocation was based upon Randle's conviction on September 20, 1951 of a violation of Penal Code, Sec. 274 (abortion), a felony. Also, on August 12, 1959, Randle was convicted in the superior court in San Francisco of violating Health and Safety Code, Sec. 11170, subdivision (4), an offense involving affixing false or forged labels to packages of narcotics. This offense was reduced to a misdemeanor by the court at the time of the sentencing.

Turning to Mrs. Randle, there is no evidence that she had any actual knowledge of the misconduct charged in the first four counts of the accusation. As stated before, the disciplinary action taken by the board with respect to her permit to conduct and maintain a pharmacy is based upon the doctrine of *respondeat superior.*

Case Analysis: The decision of the board to revoke the licenses of the pharmacy and the pharmacist based upon not being able to account for the missing methedrine ampules, the forging of prescriptions for this drug, and prior criminal acts of the pharmacist-owner, is sufficient to both protect the public and ensure that drugs of this nature are appropriately accounted for.

Holding: The superior court saw no abuse of the board's discretion as to the disciplinary action taken and, therefore, did not remand the case to the board for a reconsideration of the penalty to be imposed. Therefore, the judgment of the administrative law judge is affirmed.

HARCO DRUGS V. HOLLOWAY

Supreme Court of Alabama, 669 So.2d 878, 1995

Desired Remedy: Defendant Harco Drug Company appeals from a judgment entered on a $225,000 jury verdict in favor of plaintiffs based on the defendant misfilling a prescription for the plaintiff, and having a history of 233 similar types of misfilled prescriptions over the last three years. The plaintiff at trial was awarded both compensatory (in the amount of $100,000) and punitive damages (in the amount of $150,000). Mr. Holloway was awarded $5000 on his derivative claim for loss of consortium.

Issues: Did the trial court abuse its discretion in admitting evidence of certain incident reports prepared by Harco employees in connection with drug errors that had occurred previously?

Facts of Case: The Holloways alleged that one of Harco's pharmacists had negligently or wantonly misfilled Ms. Holloway's prescription for a breast cancer medication. The Holloways' complaint also alleged that Harco had failed to initiate sufficient institutional controls over the manner in which prescriptions were filled and that, as a result, Ms. Holloway's prescription was misfilled.

Harco admitted negligence in misfilling Ms. Holloway's prescription. In doing so, it admitted that it had a duty to the Holloways, that it breached that duty, and that the breach of that duty had proximately caused Ms. Holloway's damage. Ms. Holloway's prescription for tamoxifen was filled incorrectly with Tambocor (a heart medication used by cardiologists to treat arrhythmias).

Case Analysis: The jury was informed of 233 incident reports that had been prepared by Harco employees during the three years preceding the incident involving Ms. Holloway. Those reports dealt in some way or another with customer complaints of errors on the part of Harco employees in filling prescriptions, and the vast majority of them indicated that Harco employees had committed errors in filling prescriptions. This evidence, in addition to the evidence of complaints filed with the State Board of Pharmacy, and the evidence of lawsuits filed alleging that Harco employees had misfilled prescriptions, was relevant to show Harco's knowledge of problems within its pharmacies and, thus, was admissible in connection with the wantonness claim, predicated upon Harco's having failed to initiate sufficient institutional controls over the manner in which prescriptions were filled.

Case Holding: The trial court's decision affirmed in favor of plaintiff Holloway.

Dissent: This holding of admissibility may tend to stifle self-review and efforts to improve a company's safety for fear that the very process of considering alternatives will make the failure to adopt them present a jury question on wantonness.

The testimony was uncontroverted that Harco had filled between 15 and 16 million prescriptions during the three-year period in which there were the 233 incidents of misfilled prescriptions. This translates into a 16/10,000th of a 1% chance (0.0016%) that a prescription might be misfilled. The 233 incident reports were generated by Harco employees when a customer, for any reason, received medicine other than the medicine prescribed by the physician. Most of these incidents were not shown to be similar to the misfilling of Ms. Holloway's prescription, and, to the extent they may have been similar, they tended to show that Harco had in place procedures for catching and correcting errors, not that Harco wantonly disregarded incidents of misfilled prescriptions.

Harco offered testimony that the incident reports upon which the plaintiffs relied were generated by Harco employees and were sent to the director of pharmacy operations for review. The director of pharmacy operations testified that he reviewed each report and counseled the pharmacist who misfilled the prescription. Occasionally, a pharmacist would be transferred to a store with less volume if Harco believed that the pharmacist could perform better in a lower-volume store. Harco had relieved some pharmacists who could not adequately perform their duties. The Holloways offered no testimony to contradict the testimony of the Harco executives regarding the precautions that Harco took, and they offered no testimony that any other pharmacy employed clerical help to verify a trained professional pharmacist's work for accuracy.

PREMISES LIABILITY

There are three classifications of an individual entering the premises of a given location:

1. *As an* ***invitee***: An individual, such as a customer entering a retail store, who has been expressly or impliedly invited onto the premises. The duty owed to an invitee is to both warn and correct any dangerous circumstances that might exist (eg, a bottle of shampoo that falls to the floor from the store shelves and spills over an area traveled upon by customers—the customers must be warned of the hazard before and during its cleanup).
2. *As a* ***licensee***: An individual whose presence on the premises is allowed and is owed a reduced duty of care. If the premises have areas of danger, the licensee need only be warned of those areas of danger (they do not usually have to be repaired for the licensee). Example: A delivery person delivering drug products from a wholesaler.
3. *As a* ***trespasser***: An individual who is not invited to enter the premises, but enters anyway. Examples: A store is closed, and a burglar breaks into the store through the roof; or an invitee goes into an area of the store that is declared off-limits, as noted on a sign, "For Employees Only." The only duty owed to a trespasser is for the owner to exercise reasonable care and to keep the area in a safe condition. The owner must only give notice of any traps used or concealed dangers (eg, "beware of dog") that the owner knows about.

Generally, consumers who enter a business zone such as a community pharmacy (which can also include the parking lot area as well as the premises of the pharmacy) are referred to as *business invitees* who are owed a duty of being warned of any dangers, and to have such dangers repaired as reasonably as possible.

The majority of premises liability cases involve "slip and fall" claims. A landowner or occupier of land or premises owes a duty of due care to invitees to ensure that the conditions associated with the premises are reasonably safe. The occupier of a premise may have the responsibility of either conducting reasonable inspections of the premises to ensure that they are kept safe, or to at least provide warning of possible dangers associated with the premises.

In the following *Sokolowski v. Medi-Mart* case, issues are presented as to the admissibility of statements made by the store's manager to settle or compromise, and whether the item that the plaintiff slipped on was there for a sufficient period of time to provide the defendant with constructive notice of its presence. The *Sokolowski* case is very typical of the classic "slip and fall" category of business invitee cases. *Rodgers v. SuperX* is another such business invitee case, although it deals primarily with the question of liability in situations when a business invitee is harmed from dangerous circumstances immediately outside the occupier's premises (which may still be considered to be a part of or within the zone of the occupier's premises).

SOKOLOWSKI V. MEDI-MART

Appeals Court of Conn., 587 A.2d 1056, 1991

Desired Remedy: The defendant, Medi-Mart, Inc., appeals from the judgment rendered after a jury trial decides in favor of the plaintiff. The plaintiff brought the underlying action to recover damages for injuries and losses she allegedly sustained as a result of a fall at the defendant's store on December 30, 1985. On February 28, 1990, the jury returned a verdict of $45,000 in favor of the plaintiff and further determined that there was no comparative negligence involved in the case. On March 5, 1990, the defendant moved to set aside the verdict. The trial court denied the defendant's motion on April 4, 1990.

Issues: In a slip-and-fall case occurring in the defendant's pharmacy, what is the level of responsibility owed to an invitee regarding a product that falls from the shelf, breaks open, and can potentially cause an innocent party to slip and fall as a result of it not being cleaned up within a timely manner? Further, regarding a situation like this, what duty is owed to a customer or invitee who enters business premises? What is considered to be a reasonable period of time for an item that breaks open on the floor of business premises to be cleaned up? Also, are offers to pay medical bills for an injury admissible evidence in courts of law to be used as an admission of wrongdoing by a defendant?

Facts of Case: On December 30, 1985, the plaintiff, a business invitee of the defendant, slipped on a foreign substance and fell to the floor inside the defendant's store. The offending substance was located about 8 to 10 feet from a counter where three of the defendant's employees were working and within a similar distance from at least five customers who had been standing there for a period of approximately 15 min prior to the plaintiff's fall. No witness testified to having heard a bottle break during this time period.

As a result of the fall, the plaintiff sustained a 5% permanent partial disability of her cervical spine and incurred $1100 in medical expenses and $500 in lost wages.... The store's assistant manager allegedly told the plaintiff, "Anything you need or want, you know, just let us know," and "if you have any medical bills, bring them in, and we'll take care of them."

Case Analysis: "To promote the settling of disputes, offers of compromise, if made to buy peace, are not admissible against the party making them as an admission of liability." The assistant manager's comments in this case, however, are ambiguous. "Where it is not clear whether the statement is an offer of compromise or an admission of liability and the motive of the declarant is subject to speculation and conjecture, the statement must be excluded as evidence." Thus, the trial court should have excluded the assistant manager's hearsay statements, which could have easily been construed as an offer to settle or compromise. Federal Rule of Evidence 409 similarly provides, "Evidence of furnishing or offering or promising to pay medical, hospital, or similar expenses occasioned by an injury is not admissible to prove liability for the injury."

Viewed in the light most favorable to the plaintiff, the record reveals that the plaintiff, after standing near a counter for approximately 15 min, moved a few paces toward the store's pharmacy area, where she slipped and fell. No one heard the bottle break during that 15-min period. The jury could have reasonably found from the evidence that there was a substance on the floor and that the substance was aftershave lotion. Furthermore, the evidence revealed that the floors of the store were swept nightly and that the accident occurred around 5:00 PM. Finally, the evidence showed that the store had no formal policy for periodic checks for breakages or spills.

The determinative question is whether the defective condition existed for such a length of time that the defendant, in the exercise of reasonable care, should have discovered it and remedied it. The jury could have concluded from the totality of the evidence that the spilled aftershave lotion had remained on the floor for more than 15 min. From this fact, the jurors could have inferred that the defendant, in the exercise of reasonable care, should have detected and remedied the condition. This suggests the inference to support a finding of constructive notice, and the reasonable assumption that the store's management should have done more frequent surveillance to determine if items had fallen on the aisles of the store, and needed to be cleaned up.

Case Holding: The judgment of the trial court in favor of the plaintiff is affirmed.

RODGERS V. HOOK-SUPERX

Appellate Court of Illinois, 4th Dist., 562 N.E.2d 358, 1990

Desired Remedy: Plaintiff Mary Rodgers appeals the trial court's order granting defendants', Hook-SuperX, Inc., and Hook Drugs, Inc., motion for summary judgment that indicated the defendants were not responsible for the plaintiff's robbery that occurred directly outside the store's premises on the sidewalk entrance area leading to the defendants' pharmacy.

Issues: Is the defendant negligent in not providing sufficient protection of a plaintiff that may be subjected to a robbery in an area immediately outside of the defendant's store on the sidewalk entrance area to the defendant's premises?

Facts of Case: The plaintiff brought a negligence action against defendants as a result of an April 25, 1986 robbery outside their store. It is undisputed that the plaintiff entered the Hook's store in order to make a purchase. When leaving, the plaintiff exited through the front entrance and onto a private sidewalk that surrounded a portion of the front of the store. Here, the plaintiff was confronted by two men who took her purse and knocked her to the ground.

The plaintiff's complaint alleged the defendants had a duty to protect her from criminal attacks by third persons that, the defendants knew or should have known, were reasonably likely to occur. The plaintiff stated that the defendants should have known that it was reasonably likely she would be attacked since, just prior to the attack, the two men had been inside the store harassing a customer. The plaintiff additionally cited the rumor that approximately two months earlier, a similar robbery had occurred in the area. Last, the plaintiff stated that the defendants were negligent in failing to provide adequate lighting.

The defendants filed a motion for summary judgment. The trial court granted the motion, finding no material issue of fact existed and, as a matter of law, defendants had no duty to protect plaintiffs from the actions of third parties. The trial court stated that to impose upon defendants such a duty would be tantamount to making a business of this nature an absolute guarantor for the safety from being robbed of every individual who walks into the store.

Generally, there is no duty to protect another against the criminal attacks of third persons. However, an owner or occupier of land in Illinois owes a duty to invitees on his premises to reasonably guard against acts of third parties when such attacks are reasonably foreseeable. The question here then is whether the attack upon the plaintiff, an invitee of the defendants, was reasonably foreseeable.

The plaintiff stated in her deposition that, while she was in the store, she had not seen the two men who later robbed her. While exiting the store, she saw the men through the store window. The plaintiff walked by the two men and thought they were merely visiting or getting ready to go into the store. She lived across from the store and had visited the store at their location since 1947. She had not previously been aware of any problem with criminal activity in the area. The plaintiff stated that the night of the incident, she heard the cashier at Hook's tell a police officer a similar incident had happened about two months earlier.

The plaintiff could not remember whether an outside overhead light was on at Hook's. She did recall there was some sort of light but could not remember whether it was coming from inside the store. She recalled that when the store was Harding's, it had fluorescent lights along the edge of the roof. The plaintiff stated that the night of the robbery, these lights on the edge of the roof were not on.

In Bipin Desai's deposition, he stated that he was the pharmacist and assistant manager at Hook's in the evening hours on April 25, 1986. Desai recalled on that evening two men had been in the store harassing a customer. The cashier at the front register asked the two men to leave and they had complied. The plaintiff had been in the store at the same time as these two men, and Desai estimated she left the store about five minutes after they did. Desai stated that it is Hook's store policy to ask troublemakers to leave. Desai stated the front lighting and lighting around the building were on that evening. Desai had checked the lights at 5:00 PM that day as part of his routine inspection schedule.

Case Analysis: The circumstances here are such that the attack upon a plaintiff by a third party was not reasonably foreseeable. The allegations regarding a previous purse snatching and the actions of the two men while inside the store are insufficient to make the attack upon the plaintiff reasonably foreseeable.

The fact a dispute exists between the plaintiff and defendants' employees regarding the exterior lighting does not alter the result in this case. The plaintiff stated in her deposition she saw the two men through the store window before exiting the store. She thought the men were merely visiting or entering the store. The claimed lighting inadequacy does not appear to be a cause or factor of the criminal attack.

Case Holding: The trial court did not err in finding defendants owed no duty to the plaintiff in this matter. The judgment of the trial court is affirmed.

QUESTIONS

1. In *Randle v. California State Board of Pharmacy*, should the wife be held vicariously liable for the actions of her husband?
2. How would you weigh the evidence of Randle stating he never sold methedrine without a prescription against the undisputed 38,441 missing ampules of the drug?
3. In *Harco Drugs v. Holloway*, what is the difference between compensatory and punitive damages?
4. How would you describe the error rate of Harco Pharmacy when comparing the number of errors (or complaints of errors) against the number of prescriptions filled for a given period of time?
5. Do you agree with the dissenting argument about stifling self-review of errors?
6. In *Sokolowski v. Medi-Mart*, should the plaintiff's award of damages have been reduced because of comparative negligence?
7. How quickly should store staff be required to respond to a spill in order to avoid an accusation of failing to correct a defective condition?
8. In *Rogers v. Hook-SuperX*, did the court come to the correct conclusion?
9. What other measures could the pharmacy have taken to protect its customers?
10. What other measures could the plaintiff have taken to protect herself?

CHAPTER 10

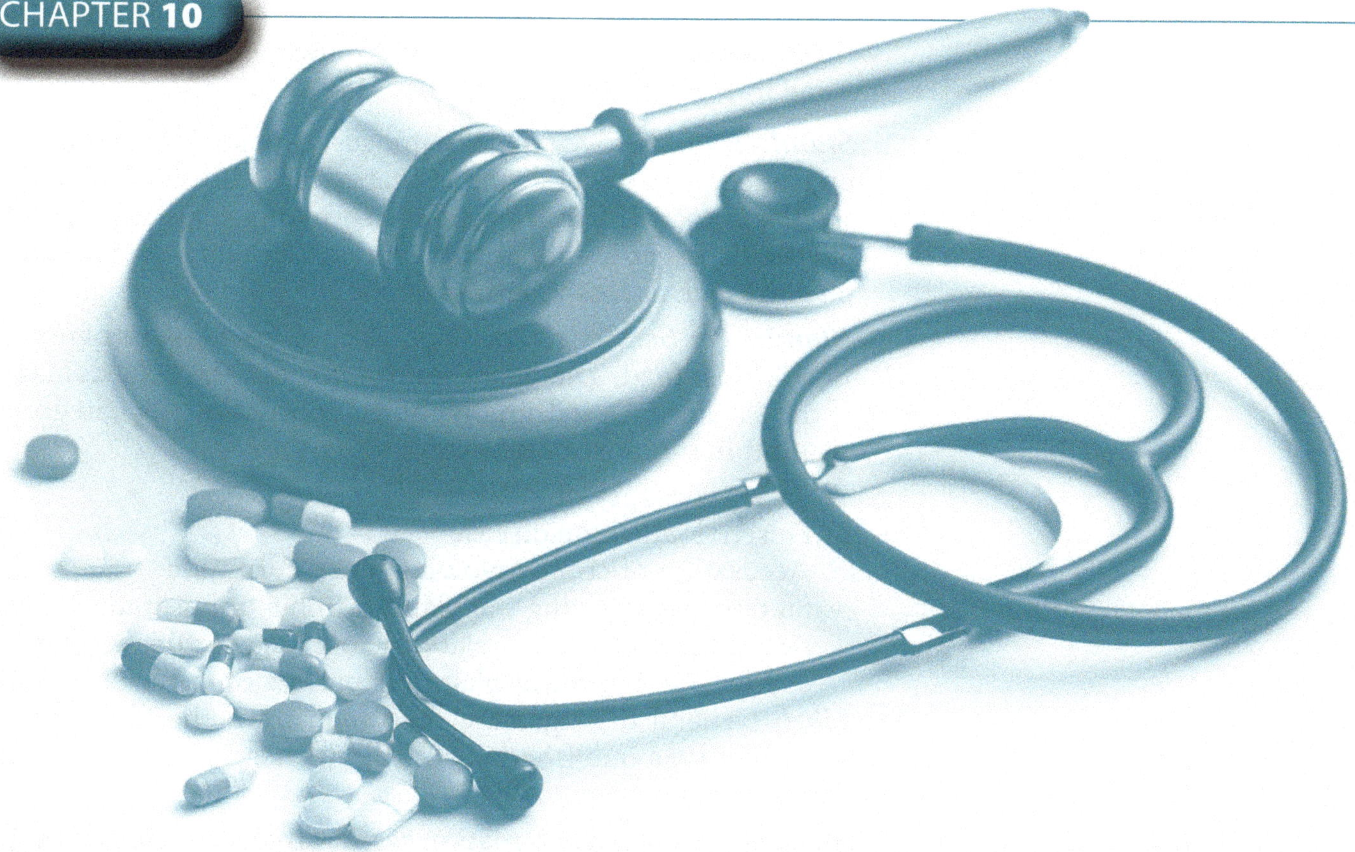

Defamation

WHAT CONSTITUTES A DEFAMATION ACTION?

In order for the tort of defamation to exist, it requires a *defamatory statement of and concerning the plaintiff that is published to third persons, is false, and causes damage to the plaintiff's reputation.* The elements involving this tort can be broken down in the following manner:

1. What is a ***defamatory statement***?: A statement that tends to lower the plaintiff's reputation with at least a substantial minority of the community.
2. ***Of and concerning the plaintiff:*** Must prove that the defamatory statement referred to the plaintiff.
3. ***Publication to third persons:*** The plaintiff must show that the statement was published to a third person and who understands the statement to be defamatory. Publications can be intentional or negligent.
4. ***Falsity:*** The statement in fact must be false.
5. ***Damages:*** The statement must be damaging to one's reputation. Here, the damages depend on whether the defamation is ***libel***

(written defamatory statement) or ***slander*** (spoken defamatory statement).

a. ***Slander:*** Must prove special damages; general damages are not presumed. The general rule is that defamation in the form of slander is not actionable without a showing of special damages. Special damages are identifiable losses actually suffered by the plaintiff such as loss of employment and medical expenses.

b. ***Slander Per Se:*** General damages are presumed—loss of reputation is presumed. The plaintiff need not show special damages. If the slander falls within one of the four following categories, plaintiff has a cause of action for *slander per se.*

   i. Lack of chastity of a woman
   ii. Present loathsome disease
   iii. Accusation of crime involving moral turpitude
   iv. Statements affecting the plaintiff in his or her trade or business (statement must relate to some characteristic that has special significance to plaintiff's profession)

c. ***Libel:*** General damages are presumed from the fact that the statement was published. The plaintiff need not show special damages to recover.

A liable defendant in a defamation case is anyone taking part in the publication, including the originator, republicator (person involved in repeating the defamatory remark started by the originator), and the disseminator (anyone who circulates the physical embodiment of the defamation and who may be acting unreasonably).

There are a number of defenses that can be employed by the defendant to counter a defamation claim:

1. ***Consent***. Proving that the plaintiff agreed to the release of the alleged defamatory statement.
2. ***Truth*** of the statement being made.
3. ***Status*** of the person who is the subject of the defamatory statement.

   a. ***Non-public figures:*** The statement made was a fair comment, or honest opinion (the publication was for a non-vindictive purpose). Where the defamatory statement is regarding a non-public person, there is less concern for freedom of speech and press. Further, private individuals are more vulnerable to injury from defamation because they do not have an opportunity for public access for rebuttal.

   b. ***Public figures:*** Applies a constitutional privilege. A defamatory statement made by the news media is privileged unless the statement is published with actual malice. Actual malice is knowledge of the falsity or reckless disregard for the truth. If the public figure plaintiff can show knowledge of falsity or reckless disregard for the truth, he or she can recover general common-law damages and punitive damages without affirmative showing of injury. Sometimes, a difficult matter is to establish whether or not a targeted individual who is the subject of being defamed is a public figure or not.

SOUTHWEST DRUG STORES V. MRS. W.H. GARNER

Supreme Court of Miss., 195 So. 837, 1967

Desired Remedy: The plaintiff, Mrs. W. H. Garner, recovered a judgment for $8,000 against defendants, Southwest Drug Stores and Wilroy Ratcliff, as damages for slander and unlawful detention. The defendants appeal the trial court decision.

Issues: In this case, did the elements of slander meet the requirements for defamation?

Facts of Case: On November 19, 1963, while on a family visit, Mrs. Garner and her sister stopped at the Southwest Drug Store. They went into the drug store, leaving their father, who was ill, in the car in the parking lot in front of the drug store.

While Mrs. Garner was at the cosmetic counter looking at soap, Ratcliff, the store manager, approached her and asked if he could help her. She told him she wanted a bar of soap, and he said he would have one of the clerks wait on her. With the assistance of the saleslady, Mrs. Garner found the soap, and with the saleslady, she went to the cashier and paid for it. She received a sales ticket and the soap was placed in a small paper bag.

Mrs. Garner's sister continued to shop, since she also wanted some soap. Mrs. Garner told her that she would go to the car to see about their father and would take some of the sister's packages with her. She walked out of the store, and before she reached the car, Ratcliff hurried after her, calling in a loud voice to stop. She testified that he said to her in a rude and loud manner, "Hey, wait there. You stop there, I want to see what you got in that little bag. You stole a bar of soap." Mrs. Garner said further, "And I looked at him, I said, 'You mean you're accusing me of stealing this soap.' I pulled the soap out of the bag, and Ratcliff responded, 'Yes, you stole the soap, and let's prove it, let's go back to the store.'"

Mrs. Garner said that a number of people were close by and heard the exchange of words, but that she did not know any of them. Ratcliff did not put a hand on her or her belongings, but he did demand that she return with him to the store.

When they got back in the store, Mrs. Garner asked the cashier if she had bought the soap, and the cashier told her that she had paid for the soap. She told the cashier that Ratcliff was accusing her of stealing the soap. She then began to cry and was extremely embarrassed.

Ratcliff apologized and did not ask her to remain in the store. Mrs. Garner said the incident made her sick and she had to go to the family doctor twice. Her father, whose hearing is not that good, testified that he heard Ratcliff yell at his daughter to stop in the parking lot, but that he did not hear the rest of the conversation.

Ratcliff testified that he saw Mrs. Garner handling a bar of Lowilla soap at the soap counter, and saw her put a bar of the soap in her bag and walk out. He asked the cashier if she had paid for a bar of Lowilla soap. The cashier told him "no," and he went out after Mrs. Garner. He denied he accused her of stealing. He said that she opened the bag and showed him the soap, and that when he saw it was not Lowilla soap, he apologized, and that it was Mrs. Garner who insisted on going back to the store.

Case Analysis: The defendant argued that the proof shows a *qualified privilege* existed and it was not exceeded; that he investigated what he believed to be a case of shoplifting upon probable cause in a reasonable manner; and therefore that, under the laws of Mississippi, such an investigation was privileged and no action was maintainable thereon . The statute relied upon is Mississippi Code, Sec. 2374-04, which reads as follows:

> If any person shall commit or attempt to commit the offense of shoplifting, as defined herein, or if any person shall willfully conceal upon his person or otherwise any unpurchased goods, wares or merchandise held or owned by any store or mercantile establishment, the merchant or any employee thereof or any peace or police officer, acting in good faith and upon probable cause based upon reasonable grounds therefore, may question such person, in a reasonable manner for the purpose of ascertaining whether or not such person is guilty of shoplifting as defined herein. Such questioning of a person by a merchant, merchant's employee or peace or police officer shall not render such merchant, merchant's employee or peace or police officer civilly liable for slander, false arrest, false imprisonment, malicious prosecution, unlawful detention or otherwise in any case where such merchant, merchant's employee, or peace or police officer acts in good faith and upon

> reasonable grounds to believe that the person questioned is committing or attempting to commit the crime of shoplifting as defined in this act.

Defendant Ratcliff argued that he had observed Mrs. Garner and believed by her actions that she was committing an act of shoplifting, that her actions gave him probable cause to investigate, and that he acted in good faith and upon an occasion of privilege in carrying out his duties to protect his employer's property.

Although the occasion was one of *qualified privilege*, the privilege was lost by the manner in which it was exercised. Mrs. Garner testified, and the jury found, that she was wrongfully accused of stealing in a rude and loud voice in the presence of other people outside the place of business. The jury found that Ratcliff had reason to believe that Mrs. Garner had put a bar of soap in her purse and left the store without paying for it, and that he had probable cause to make an inquiry, but still he was careless and negligent in his method of ascertaining whether Mrs. Garner had paid for the soap.

Had Ratcliff asked the cashier if Mrs. Garner had paid for a bar of soap, he would have ascertained that she had. Instead, he asked if she had paid for a bar of Lowilla soap. Then, instead of making an inquiry in a reasonable manner, he accused Mrs. Garner of stealing a bar of soap. When he did so, he exceeded the *qualified privilege*. In order for a communication to be privileged, the person making it must be careful to go no further than his or her interest or duties require.

The South Carolina Supreme Court, in a more recent case, summarized when an individual may exceed the *qualified privilege*:

> The publisher of the statement must not wander beyond the scope of the occasion. The privilege does not protect any unnecessary defamation. In order for a communication to be privileged, the person making it must be careful to go no further than his interests or his duties require. Where the speaker exceeds his privilege and the communication complained of goes beyond what the occasion demands that he should publish, and is unnecessarily defamatory of the plaintiff, he will not be protected.

Defendants urge that although the jury found that Ratcliff made the slanderous statements, the proof does not show a sufficient publication of the statements. This argument is based on the fact that none of the people who were nearby and heard the statements testified in this case. Involving actions of slander, it has not been deemed requisite to introduce the customers in a store, or bystanders in the place of business, to testify as to their understanding of the meaning of the words complained of. It has only been necessary to prove that such persons, or some of them, heard the charges, or that the facts and circumstances would entitle the jury to believe that they heard and understood the same. The evidence in this case is sufficient to support a finding by the jury that there was publication. Accordingly, such publication, whether or not the persons hearing the slanderous statements knew the person who was the recipient of the slanderous remarks, is not necessary and is deemed to be damaging to the plaintiff's reputation nonetheless.

The jury by its verdict found that Ratcliff exceeded the privilege and thus malice could be inferred from the words spoken, which are actionable per se. The jury could have found, and no doubt deem that the action of Ratcliff in failing to make a sufficient inquiry as to whether Mrs. Garner had paid for a bar of soap and then falsely accusing her of being a thief exhibited that he was in a frame of mind indicating that he did not care whether the words spoken were true or not. Malice in fact relates to the state or condition of mind of a person who speaks defamatory words. In this case, it appears that Ratcliff's words were spoken recklessly without knowing or caring whether they were true.

Case Holding: Each case of slander must be settled on its facts and circumstances, and since we find no reversible error, the decision of the lower court is affirmed.

WHITEHURST V. MARTIN MEDICAL CENTER, ET AL.

Tenn. Court of Appeals, 2003

Desired Remedy: The plaintiff seeks damages from defendant Martin Medical Center and others in a defamation action.

Issues: While a plaintiff may appear to have a viable case in defamation against a defendant, are there intervening circumstances that would otherwise cause the discharge of a defamation suit against the defendant?

Facts of Case: Dr. Johnson and Dr. Whitehurst are husband and wife; both are physicians, and Dr. Johnson specializes in Ob-Gyn. A rumor that Dr. Johnson was HIV positive began to circulate—thought to be started by Dr. Johnson's daughter around the time both Dr. Johnson and Dr. Whitehurst had separated. Other doctors where Dr. Johnson practiced got wind of the rumor and passed it on to the pharmacist at Martin Medical Center Pharmacy. The pharmacist told other pharmacists at Martin Medical Center of Dr. Johnson's HIV-positive status. In short course, everyone in the pharmacy and at other pharmacies in the town knew of Dr. Johnson's alleged condition. A pharmacist on duty at the local Wal-Mart pharmacy, while filling a prescription for a patient of Dr. Johnson, asked the patient if she had received a letter from Dr. Johnson's office regarding Dr. Johnson's HIV status. This patient called Dr. Johnson's office after telling other people to find out if the information was true. Dr. Johnson stated that it was untrue. Dr. Johnson brought a defamation suit against the other physicians she worked with, and the pharmacies where this information was disseminated to both patients and employees of the pharmacies. Dr. Johnson claimed that the story was defamatory and that her reputation in the community had been damaged so severely that she could no longer practice medicine. The trial court found for the defendants.

Case Analysis: At trial, the defendants testified that the information received from Dr. Johnson's other physician colleagues was true and that they had a duty to inform the patient of Dr. Johnson, and that the other employees in the pharmacy needed to know the information as well. The trial court jury ruled in favor of the defendants.

The appeals court analyzed the case and facts from the rule for defamation:

- "Publication" of a statement—undisputed.
- "Knowledge that the statement is false and defaming to another"—it was noted that the information regarding Dr. Johnson was false and would be defamatory to Dr. Johnson.
- "Showing a reckless regard for the truth or being negligent in failing to ascertain the truth regarding the defamatory statement made"—the appellate court noted that the defendants were entitled to assert a defense of a "qualified privilege" if the allegedly defamatory statement was "made in good faith" where there may be a necessity to transmit such information. The privilege usually applies in defamation cases where the duty is not a legal one, but where it is of a moral or social character of imperfect obligation. When a statement is qualifiedly privileged, it is not actionable unless the plaintiff can show that it was made with actual or express malice. The fact that the information transmitted came from a trusted physician provides weight to the statement being more true than not.

Case Holding: The court concluded—" Testimony about circumstances surrounding the publication of the false information 'from reliable sources,' such as the reason defendants published the information and the reason they relied on the information from the physicians, was admissible to put the defendants' conduct in context, and the admission of that evidence does not constitute reversible error. The decision of the trial court was affirmed.

CONSIDERING HYPOTHETICAL DEFAMATION CASE SCENARIOS

The following case scenarios are based upon actual cases that involve issues associated with defamation:

Scenario 1: Refusing to Fill Patient Prescriptions from a Specific Physician

A patient comes into a chain pharmacy with a Vicodin prescription from a physician who has a reputation in the pharmacy community for writing these types of prescriptions for addicts. The pharmacist who receives this physician's prescription tells the patient he does not have the drug in stock, and proceeds to contact the chain pharmacy pharmacist supervisor in order to determine how to handle similar situations involving prescriptions from this physician. The supervisor contacts the DEA offices and is told that this particular physician is being investigated. The supervisor then sends out an e-mail to 14 stores that he supervises, advising the pharmacists not to fill any prescriptions for this particular doctor since he is under investigation by the DEA. At one of the chain's pharmacies, the pharmacist tells a patient who brings in two prescriptions—one is for Vicodin and the other is for Lotensin (for treatment of hypertension)—that she is unable to fill these prescriptions because this doctor's license is under suspicion for abuse. The patient calls the doctor to tell him what happened and what was said. The doctor, quite upset regarding this conveyed message to his patient, brings a suit against the pharmacist and the chain pharmacy.

Does defamation regarding the physician appear to exist based upon the facts presented?

What different actions might have been taken by either the pharmacist or the pharmacist supervisor?

Scenario 2: A Chain Pharmacy Firing Its Pharmacist Based on a Claim That the Pharmacist Did Not Follow Company Policies and Failed to Secure the Pharmacy

The woman pharmacist has been working for the chain pharmacy for 10 years and received reasonably good annual employee reviews from her supervisors.

On a number of occasions during her employment, she complained that as a pharmacy manager and being a female, the chain operation refused to pay her a comparable salary paid to males in the same job capacity. She also complained about controlled substance drugs disappearing from the pharmacy. One day, management approached her with an immediate termination letter indicating that she had violated company policy and failed to properly secure the pharmacy. The pharmacist, offended by the allegation in the letter that suggested she was involved in drug theft, felt she was being both discriminated (gender) and defamed. As a result, she filed a lawsuit claiming that the chain operation fired her because of the illegal actions of the pharmacy technician who worked at the pharmacy she managed, and that management made statements that she did not receive excellent reviews during the course of her employment.

Evidence was presented that the chain allegedly was upset with the pharmacist's legitimate complaints, and that gender discrimination appeared evident. The court considered the issue of her being fired for the statement in the termination report that she managed the pharmacy in a manner that made it easy to steal controlled substances, thus denigrating her and making it appear that she was totally responsible for the lack of security in the pharmacy. This latter point, if true, and the subject of her termination, would have made it impossible for her to find a new position as a pharmacist employee.

While a pharmacy employer can fire a pharmacist for not abiding by its policies, if the breach of those policies was done by another employee (a pharmacy technician in this case) and not known by the supervising pharmacist, should that supervising pharmacist be held to a rule of termination for the inappropriate acts of others?

When does a termination for a specific stated reason appear to be for an entirely different reason (eg, the employee complains too much)? In addition, how can one prove that the termination was in fact for the other reason (applied to the facts in this case scenario)?

Can a pharmacist employee who has a good work record (supported by annual reviews) be terminated without a stated reason for the discharge (a "termination without cause")?

How does the element of defamation come to surface in this case, and does the pharmacist have a good argument that she has been defamed, especially if she is being told why she is being terminated and the consequences that it will have on her employability?

QUESTIONS

1. In *Southwest Drug Stores v. Mrs. W.H. Garner*, did the accusations of stealing that were shouted in the parking lot constitute "publication"?
2. Was Mrs. Garner's claim of embarrassment reasonable?
3. In *Whitehurst v. Martin Medical Center*, how much malice did the defendants show when disseminating the information about the HIV-positive physician?

4. If you found out a physician was HIV positive, would you tell anyone? If so, whom, and would there be any protections (by law) afforded you for telling another person about this physician?
5. If someone expresses his or her opinion regarding another—for example, "In my opinion, the pharmacist who has been filling my prescriptions is incompetent"—could or would that opinion rise to the level of a defamatory remark if the statement was not entirely true? Explain.
6. What are your thoughts as to why general damages are presumed in a case of libel, and not in a case of slander?

CHAPTER 11

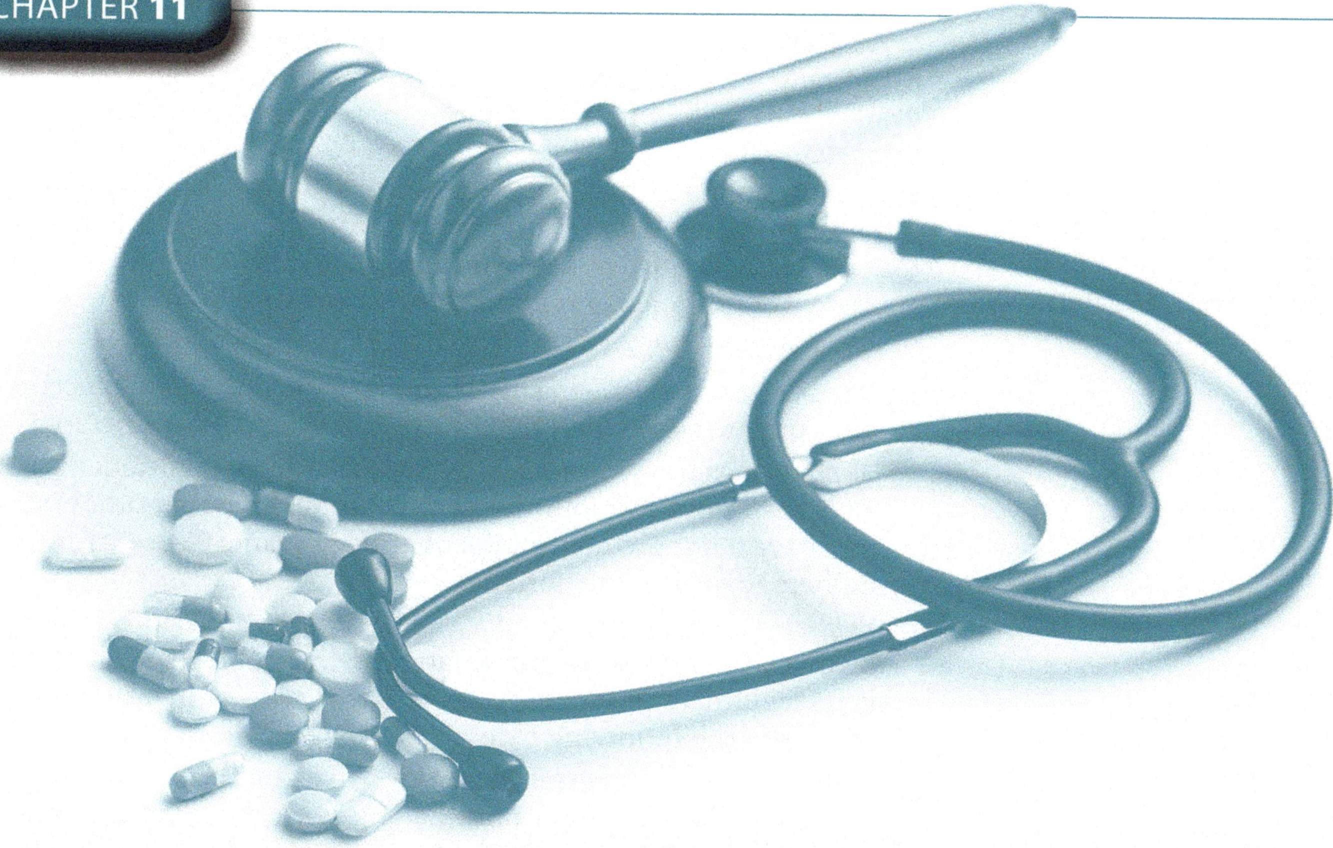

Invasion of Privacy and Issues Pertaining to Confidentiality

ISSUES OF CONFIDENTIALITY AND INVASION OF PRIVACY

In 1996, the federal Health Insurance Portability and Accountability Act (HIPAA) came into existence and dealt with protecting patients from having their medical information inappropriately disseminated, providing greater security of an individual's health care information. Prior to this Act, many of the states had relatively stringent health care privacy laws. As an example, California had and still has four such laws:

- *Confidentiality of Medical Information Act (CMIA)*
- *Patient Access to Medical Records Act (PAMRA)*
- *Medical California Family Codes & Regulations—Protection of the sharing of family members' medical information, especially information pertaining to children*
- *Lanterman-Petris-Short Act (LPSA)—Protection of the information related to the care and treatment of mentally ill patients*

All these laws together provide substantial protection for patients, preventing their health care information from being easily made available to individuals or entities not having the right to such information.

The tort of invasion of privacy takes on a bit of a different approach, more general than simply being limited to patient health issues. This tort generally involves someone intruding into the private life of another where there is no legitimate reason. There are several types of invasion of privacy:

1. *Intrusion upon seclusion*. This involves someone gaining access to your private space such as placing a camera in your bedroom.
2. *Appropriation of name or likeness*. This is similar to a trademark for a company but for your own name and likeness. In other words, you have a right to control if a pharmacy wants to use your photo in their advertising materials.
3. *Publicity given to a private life*. This type of invasion of privacy involves your personal information being published where there is no legitimate public concern. It is this type of invasion we will discuss in the following case.
4. *Placing someone in a false light publicly*. An example would be including an innocent person's photo along with the photos of known criminals on a published website.

In general, a private citizen is afforded much more privacy than a public figure or celebrity. It is assumed that public figures (like politician or celebrities) have placed themselves in the public eye, and thus matters that private citizens would normally keep private are considered newsworthy and publishable for public figures.

The following two cases represent the view on the part of many courts prior to the twenty-first century that the pharmacist was not a true health care professional. As a result, many of the state's confidentiality laws would not necessarily view the pharmacist as one who would strictly be responsible for keeping a patient's medical prescription records confidential. The first of the two cases (*Washburn*) struggles somewhat with patient prescription drug record security, but yields to protect the plaintiff patient on the basis of a technicality in the issuance of a subpoena for such records. The second case (*Suarez),* by the court's determination, does not hold the pharmacist to the same confidentiality in the releasing of a patient's medical prescription information based upon what is stated in the state's confidentiality laws. Today, both the federal and state laws provide the security protection on patient prescription information.

The two cases are purposely presented to show you how the courts generally decided before 2000, and the basis for those decisions. Today, patient medication prescription information is protected because of such laws as HIPAA and the states' reconsideration of their confidentiality laws, making them stricter and involving all parties that handle this type of information.

WASHBURN V. RITE AID CORP.

Supreme Court of Rhode Island, 695 A.2d. 495; 1997 R.I.

Desired Remedy: The plaintiff wife, in a divorce proceeding, seeks damages from defendant Rite Aid Pharmacy, Inc. for providing her pharmacy medication records to her husband pursuant to the husband's attorney issuing a subpoena directly to Rite Aid requesting the plaintiff's records without any notification to her that such a request for her medication records was being made, and without any judge-ordered subpoena for such records.

Issue: Can one spouse, through a separate attorney, order by subpoena medication records from a pharmacy and receive such records regarding the other spouse without going through the court system to have a judge sign off on the subpoena, and without such issuance of this information constituting a breach of the plaintiff wife's privacy rights?

Facts of Case: The plaintiff's husband filed a court motion seeking to restrain his wife from ingesting prescription drugs during her pregnancy without first obtaining the court's consent. To accomplish this, the husband's attorney prepared a subpoena *duces tecum* and had it served on Rite Aid Pharmacy, where the plaintiff had her prescriptions filled. The subpoena requested that Rite Aid bring to court all prescription drug records for both the plaintiff and her husband for a five-year period (from June 1987 through June 1992). The plaintiff did not receive a copy of this subpoena from either her husband or Rite Aid.

Rite Aid forwarded the subpoena to its corporate office. Rite Aid then mailed the plaintiff's prescription drug records directly to the husband's attorney, believing that this action would probably obviate any need for Rite Aid to have one of its employees attend the court hearing and testify about the records.

The plaintiff sued Rite Aid contending that by disclosing her prescription drug records to her husband's attorney without complying with the subpoena, Rite Aid violated both the state's Confidentiality Health Care Information Act and her statutory privacy rights. The trial court granted summary judgment in favor of Rite Aid on the plaintiff's claims based upon Rhode Island law at the time that did not recognize pharmacies as health care providers even if they were responsible for the filling of prescriptions and the keeping of those records. (Thus the technicality of pharmacies not being considered health care providers appeared to be the determining factor as to why the trial court issued a summary judgment in favor of the defendant pharmacy.) The plaintiff appeals the lower court's decision.

Case Analysis: The subpoena required that the defendant pharmacy bring the records to the court. Had it done so, it could only then disclose the records when and in what manner the court may direct. Otherwise, the plaintiff would have to authorize her consent to allow her medication records to go directly to her husband's attorney. "Only after the privilege holder has been notified of the subpoena and has had the opportunity to review the information in the subpoenaed records, to object to the requested disclosure, and, if needed, to request possible protective limitations from the court on the nature and the extent of the requested disclosure and use of these records should such privileged information be turned over to the subpoenaing party."

At the time of this case, the court noted according to the state statute that a pharmacy such as Rite Aid is not licensed to perform "health care services" as defined by the Confidentiality Act since they do not perform "acts of diagnosis, treatment, medical evaluation or counseling, or other such acts as may be permissible under the health care licensing statutes of the state of Rhode Island." Under the act at this time, "the dispensing of medicines pursuant to prescriptions ordered by licensed health care providers does not fall within the definition of the existing act." However, "... third parties such as Rite Aid that receive and retain a person's confidential healthcare information must establish security procedures to prevent unauthorized disclosure, including limiting authorized access to this information."

By the plaintiff stating a "right to privacy" claim that is in accordance with a state statute, by the defendant disclosing the plaintiff's confidential health care records to an unauthorized person representing an adverse party, Rite Aid violated the plaintiff's "right to be secure from unreasonable intrusion." By the defendant pharmacy disclosing this information to the husband's attorney who subpoenaed the records, Rite Aid committed "an invasion of a matter that is entitled to be private or would be expected to be private".

Rite Aid was obligated to follow the directions noted on the subpoena by bringing those records to the court, and not providing them to the husband's attorney.

Case Holding: By providing the plaintiff's prescription records directly to the husband's attorney when the subpoena required that the records be brought to the court, Rite Aid violated the plaintiff's confidentiality and privacy rights.

The appellate court reversed the trial court's decision on its issuance of summary judgment in favor of Rite Aid and finding for the plaintiff, and remands back to the trial court to determine damages.

The following case, *Suarez v. James Pierard & K-Mart Corp.*, is an example of the court only considering the existing law in 1996, months before the law had changed regarding the status of a pharmacist as being recognized as a health care provider or not being recognized as a health care provider. Unfortunately, at the time this case was heard (1992), as was the situation in the previous case presented, the court went by the strict letter of the law as stated in the Illinois Mental Health and Developmental Disabilities Confidentiality Act and decided in favor of defendant K-Mart. The plaintiff also added wording in her complaint from the Illinois Pharmacy Act (which was later amended after this decision) that may have drawn an inference of confidentiality on the patient's information as being held confidential.

It is important, as you read this case, to acknowledge that the decision was based upon the meaning given to specific words, and the appeals court's decision not to accept the wording of the Illinois Pharmacy Act essentially because it does not incorporate the subject provisions of the state's Confidentiality Act. Nevertheless, because of newer laws and developing practice standards for pharmacist, this case would more than likely be decided differently today.

SUAREZ V. JAMES PIERARD & K-MART CORP.

Appellate Court of Illinois, Third District, 278 Ill. App.3d 767; 663 N.E.2d 1039; 1996 Ill. App.

Desired Remedy: The plaintiff brings a civil suit for damages as a result of James Pierard and K-Mart Corp. (as defendants) discussing confidential information at a bar with several individuals about the patient's mental medical problem and medications she was receiving.

Issue: Does a plaintiff patient who has a defendant pharmacist publicize information about her health and the drugs that she is taking to others at a public setting (such as a bar) have legal recourse in bringing an action against the defendant for breach of confidentiality?

Facts of Case: On December 13, 1992, the plaintiff went to the K-Mart pharmacy to have a prescription filled. The prescription was for a drug used to treat a mental health disorder. Defendant Pierard, the pharmacist on duty, questioned the plaintiff about her treatment and condition and the plaintiff disclosed confidential information to Pierard. The plaintiff, on one occasion, met Pierard while at a local bar. According to the plaintiff's complaint, Pierard began talking about confidential information concerning the plaintiff's condition and drug treatment in the presence of several other people, thereby embarrassing and humiliating the plaintiff.

In the plaintiff's complaint, she contends that the defendant and K-Mart had a duty not to disclose information concerning the plaintiff's medical treatment under the State of Illinois' Mental Health and Development Disabilities Confidentiality Act (hereafter referred to as the "Confidentiality Act"). Based upon wording in the act, the plaintiff likened defendant Pierard to a "therapist" that is defined "as any person who provides mental health services."

The plaintiff also imports language from the state's Pharmacy Act, which provides that the practice of pharmacy includes "advising or counseling patients on the use of drugs or devices." The plaintiff further notes that the Pharmacy Act was amended after her cause of action accrued to include a definition of confidential information as "information, maintained by the pharmacist in the patient's records, released only to the patient or, as the patient directs, to other practitioners and other pharmacists or to any other person or governmental agency authorized by law to receive the information."

Case Analysis: The appellate court notes that the plaintiff ignores the distinction between prescribing drugs and merely dispensing them. Thus, the pharmacist's function is essentially that of providing a product to a customer, not providing mental health services to a patient. Further, the Pharmacy Act does not incorporate the provisions in the Confidentiality Act. The court found nothing in the Pharmacy Act indicating that the legislature intended to make pharmacists subject to the Confidentiality Act.

Case Holding: For the two reasons stated previously by the appellate court, the judgment of the lower court is affirmed and the causes of action stated by the plaintiff are dismissed in favor of the defendant.

ANONYMOUS V. CVS CORP.

Supreme Court of New York, New York County, 188 Misc.2d 616; 728 N.Y.S.2d 333; 2001 N.Y.

Desired Remedy: As a result of Trio Drugs in 1999 selling its operation to CVS, all patient prescription information was transferred to CVS. CVS only notified patients who had received their prescription medications from Trio Drugs after the sale to CVS. The anonymous patient plaintiff diagnosed with HIV in 1986 and AIDS in 1989 states that he selected Trio Drugs as his pharmacy based upon an expectation of privacy. For nearly 20 years, the plaintiff used Trio Drugs, expecting it would keep all personal medical and prescription information confidential and not disclose it without his prior knowledge and consent. The plaintiff was only told about the sale after it occurred and that all of his prescription records were transferred to CVS.

The plaintiff commenced this action claiming that now all of his prescription drug information is in the computer network system of CVS. According to the plaintiff, the data base is networked and accessible by CVS pharmacies nationwide. He further contends that his confidential information is accessible to tens of thousands of CVS store employees and the health care plans and managed care providers that contract with CVS. Having known of this sale before it occurred, the plaintiff would have removed all of his prescription record information and found another smaller, more private pharmacy operation to help service his prescription needs.

Issue: Should CVS or Trio Drugs, as fiduciaries, have contacted patients who use the prescription services of the Trio Drugs operation prior to the transfer sale so that patients like the plaintiff could have moved their prescription records to a pharmacy that, they would feel, could better ensure the confidentiality of their prescription information?

Facts of Case: The facts of the case are noted in the "Desired Remedy" section. Essentially, the plaintiff claims that the defendant pharmacies had a fiduciary responsibility in notifying him prior to transferring the pharmacy to CVS so that the plaintiff could have transferred his prescription records to a small pharmacy where he would feel confident that those records would be secure and kept private. Because he now has AIDS, he did not want his prescription and medical information to be provided throughout the entire CVS network.

Case Analysis: The plaintiff claims that the transfer of his medical and prescription information to CVS without his permission is a violation of Sec. 2782(1) of New York's Public Health Law.

Defendant pharmacies claim that Trio Drugs has a right to sell its pharmacy and CVS has a right to buy that pharmacy and all information such as prescription files that are contained therein, without the notice to Trio Drug customers. Defendants contend that because the statutory framework requires a discontinuing pharmacy to sell its records, the Trio Drugs transaction was not done in breach of any duty or in violation of the law.

Because customers place trust in pharmacists to provide them with their medical and prescription drug information, and because pharmacists counsel customers about medications and answer health-related questions, the transaction between customers and pharmacists involves the principal characteristics of a fiduciary relationship. The fact that the defendant pharmacies did not notify their patients about the transfer was a deceptive practice causing the plaintiff to suffer a loss of his right to privacy. If defendants owed customers a duty of confidentiality, if prior notice had been given, the plaintiff might have had an opportunity to fill or refill his prescriptions elsewhere. The New York statutes are not necessarily helpful in recognizing the pharmacist as a health care provider, but simply as a provider of a product. However, withholding information from a patient, such as the transfer of the pharmacy to another when the plaintiff depended upon his original pharmacy not to disclose his prescription records, is deceptive and prevents the plaintiff from making other arrangements prior to the transfer.

Holding: On appeal, the court held that the practice of withholding notice of transfer of information to the plaintiff was deceptive, thus preventing the plaintiff from exercising his right to take action to prevent or minimize the disclosure of his medical information.

SHEPARD'S PHARMACY V. STOP & SHOP COMPANIES

Appeals Court of Mass., 640 N.E.2d 1112, 1994

Desired Remedy: The plaintiff, Shepard's Pharmacy, filed suit against the defendant, Stop & Shop Companies, for

(1) tortiously interfering with the plaintiff's business relations, (2) invasion of privacy, and (3) intentional infliction of emotional distress.

Issues: If the defendant takes a picture of the plaintiff to use in an ad showing that the plaintiff was selling his pharmacy operation to the plaintiff when in fact the contract to sell was based upon certain conditions that needed to be met, but were not met, and the picture is published suggesting the sale took place, has the defendant violated the plaintiff's right to privacy?

Facts of Case: In March 1990, a representative of Stop & Shop approached Shepard and inquired if Shepard would be interested in selling his pharmacy to Stop & Shop and becoming a staff pharmacist at the Stop & Shop. Shepard indicated his interest.

During the course of the negotiations, Stop & Shop offered to pay Shepard the sum of $25,000 for the prescription portion of his business, to purchase his inventory except certain items, and to employ Shepard for two years as a staff pharmacist at a salary of $47,000 to $48,000 per year. Shepard responded that he was willing to sell to Stop & Shop but wanted enough money from the sale of the inventory to pay all his debts and "to come out whole." The judge found that Shepard never disagreed with the offer of $25,000, and there was no real disagreement as to the salary he would receive.

Negotiations reached the point where on August 15, 1990, the parties discussed a September 27, 1990 closing date for the transaction. Also around August 15, Shepard notified his attorney that he had been negotiating with Stop & Shop. On September 17, 1990, Shepard's attorney received a purchase and sale agreement from Stop & Shop. The agreement included a clause providing that Shepard would not compete within a 10-mile radius of the West Springfield Stop & Shop for a period of three years from the date of the closing of the transaction. (Two clearly erroneous findings by the judge must be noted here. The judge's finding that the purchase and sale agreement was not sent to Shepard and his lawyer until around September 19 or 20 is at odds with the undisputed evidence that Shepard's attorney received it on September 17. The judge also concluded that the noncompetition clause stated that "Shepard would not compete for a period of three years after any termination whether by Stop & Shop or Shepard but [his employment with Stop & Shop] was for only two years." The judge misread the clause. The period of time is from the date of the closing of the transaction, not the date of Shepard's termination.)

On September 18, 1990, a representative from another company, Maxi Drug, met with Shepard and discussed the possibility of purchasing Shepard's Pharmacy for $125,000 plus his inventory and hiring him as a pharmacist on terms comparable to those offered by Stop & Shop. Maxi Drug knew nothing of Shepard's negotiations with Stop & Shop until September 18, 1990, when Shepard told Maxi Drug that he had met with other people about a possible sale. (The judge did not make any finding as to when Stop & Shop discovered that Maxi Drug was interested in purchasing the pharmacy, but Shepard testified he did not tell Stop & Shop about Maxi Drug's interest until September 28.)

On or about September 24, 1990, Shepard learned that Stop & Shop intended to announce in a circular to be included in the September 30 edition of the *Sunday Republican* that it had purchased the pharmacy and to invite Shepard's customers to shop at its pharmacy located in its supermarket in West Springfield where Shepard would be employed. Shepard's photograph was to accompany the announcement.

On September 26, Shepard indicated to Stop & Shop that their deal was off.

Shepard and his attorney met with representatives of Stop & Shop on September 28 in an attempt to have Stop & Shop withdraw its circular from the Sunday newspaper. Stop & Shop stated it would be too expensive and refused, but it increased its offer for the prescription portion of the business from $25,000 to $50,000. A representative of Stop & Shop acknowledged that it had "botched" the transaction. Shepard refused the increased offer and insisted that Stop & Shop withdraw its circular. Stop & Shop did not do so but did print a quarter-page statement in the same edition of the newspaper, stating that the circular was in error regarding the purchase of Shepard's pharmacy. Sometime after the circular was published, Maxi Drug withdrew from its negotiations with Shepard, claiming it was doing so because the negotiations had become public knowledge and because it had the impression that Shepard and Stop & Shop "were substantially further along in … conversations than was represented."

Case Analysis: The trial court judge made the following findings of fact concerning the taking of Shepard's photograph. "In late August, Stop & Shop was pressing Shepard to have his picture taken for any advertisement relative to the opening of the new acquisition, which Stop & Shop was hoping would be September 27, 1990. Mr. Shepard was not agreeable as he told them they did not have a deal. The Stop & Shop representatives told him the lack of a firm deal would not matter as the photographer was coming to the Riverdale store on a certain date and would not be back for a long time." The judge then stated, "I believe this was just a ruse to get his picture for the circular they were planning to print up as his picture certainly could have been taken on short notice once the agreement was finalized." As noted, in his ultimate finding on this point, the judge stated that Stop & Shop made "the less than credible statement the photographer could only come to the Riverdale store once a year ...." There is simply no evidence that supports the judge's findings concerning the circumstances surrounding the taking of Shepard's photograph or, specifically, that conduct by Stop & Shop constituted a ruse.

Shepard testified that he agreed to have his photograph taken but told Stop & Shop that it could not be used unless both parties agreed to the sale of the pharmacy. There was no evidence whatsoever that Stop & Shop told Shepard that the photographer had to take the photograph on a particular date because, as the judge found, he "would not be back for a long time" or that Stop & Shop told Shepard that "the photographer could only come to the Riverdale store once a year."

The invasion of privacy claim states, in relevant part, "A person shall have a right against unreasonable, substantial or serious interference with his privacy ...." The trial judge found that "Stop & Shop never had permission, oral or written, to announce the purchase and sale or to print Shepard's picture with the announcement he had joined Stop & Shop and all his customers should now get their prescriptions filled at Stop & Shop." The trial judge concluded that Stop & Shop's action was "an unreasonable, substantial and serious interference with [Shepard's] privacy."

Information about the negotiations, and what Stop & Shop thought was the state of the transaction, was in the common possession of both Shepard and Stop & Shop. Shepard did not produce any evidence that there was an agreement with Stop & Shop to keep the negotiations confidential. In fact, Shepard testified that he told Maxi Drug that he had met with other people about a sale of his pharmacy. Further, Shepard admitted that he was agreeable to the publication of his photograph, in the event the sale was consummated.

There was sufficient evidence to support the judge's finding that by means of its circular, Stop & Shop unreasonably, substantially, and seriously misappropriated Shepard's name and likeness.

While the finding of an invasion of privacy was warranted, we are not able to conclude that the separate damages awarded by the judge for that tort were supported by the evidence.

The judge concluded that Stop & Shop was "guilty of an unfair and deceptive business practice in that [it] applied economic coercion beyond what would be proper in the market place, [was] unethical, overbearing and unscrupulous and [its] conduct was a substantial departure from the fair dealing of the market place." However, the award of damages in the amount the trial court allowed is questionable.

Case Holding: The judgment for damages awarded by the trial court for invasion of privacy is vacated.

RUSSO V. CVS PHARMACY

Superior Ct. of Conn., 2005

Facts of Case: Mr. Russo, a City of Hartford, Connecticut Police Dept. detective, brings action for invasion of privacy based on CVS's release of his pharmacy records to requesting law enforcement personnel with the DEA. He alleges that no valid warrant was issued or other legitimate legal process undertaken to achieve such records. Russo claims he had a privacy interest in the records at CVS, and did not authorize or give consent to release those records. As a result, Russo also claims that due to CVS's conduct, he has been subjected to ridicule, embarrassment, vexation, and humiliation, and suffers from severe emotional distress.

Court's Analysis: Connecticut Law regarding release of pharmacy records provides, "prescriptions, orders and records … shall be open for inspection only to federal, state, county and municipal officers, whose duty it is to enforce the laws of this state or of the United States relating to controlled substances …." "While an individual using prescription drugs has a right to expect that prescription records will customarily remain private … such a right is not absolute, however. While individuals have a legitimate expectation of privacy in their prescription purchases of controlled substances, such right must be weighed against the state's interest in monitoring the use of dangerously addictive drugs."

As a matter of law, since Russo had no objectively reasonable expectation that his pharmacy records would not be disclosed by CVS to the officers, he has no legally sufficient claim for invasion of privacy as a result of CVS' voluntary provisions of the records in response to the requests.

QUESTIONS

1. How does the Health Insurance Portability and Accountability Act (HIPAA) regarding a patient's information being protected pursuant to a right to privacy differ from the tort law as it applies to a person's right to privacy?
2. What is meant by a *subpoena duces tecum*, and what is its purpose?
3. In *Washburn v. Rite Aid Corp.*, the trial court issued an order of summary judgment dismissing the case and claiming that the defendant pharmacy had a right to release Mrs. Washburn's prescription records pursuant to the submission of a subpoena directly to the pharmacy by Mr. Washburn's attorney. The appeals court reversed this decision allowing this subpoena issued by Mr. Washburn's attorney to be acted upon, but only if acted upon in a certain manner. What was the condition by which these records could be released upon the issuance of a subpoena by Mr. Washburn's attorney?
4. In *Suarez v. James Pierard & K-Mart Corp.*, the defendant pharmacist, while off duty and at a bar, discussed medical information (Ms. Suarez's mental medical problem and medications she was receiving) pertaining to Ms. Suarez to several individuals who the pharmacist knew while socializing at the bar. The appeals court dismissed the plaintiff's claim of the defendant breaching Ms. Suarez's right to have this information kept confidential. What rationale did both the trial court and the appeals court present to decide to dismiss the case against the pharmacist and the pharmacy? Do you think that this case would be decided differently today in other jurisdictions?
5. In *Anonymous v. CVS Corp.*, the plaintiff (an HIV patient) was not asked his permission to have his prescription record information transferred to CVS from an independent pharmacy where he filled and purchased his prescriptions for nearly 20 years. What concern or concerns did the plaintiff have with regard to having this transfer of his prescription record information to CVS? If this case had taken place in Illinois (where the *Suarez* case was heard), do you think the outcome of the case might have been different? Explain.
6. In reading the facts of the *Shepard's Pharmacy* case, aside from the appeals court decision, do you think that both sides dealt fairly with one another, or were the actions of one party to the lawsuit more inappropriate than the other? How would you have decided in this case? On the basis of the causes of action brought by the plaintiff, Shepard's Pharmacy, explain whether or not, in your opinion, the following tort violations brought by the plaintiff are viable causes of action:
   a. Interference with business relations
   b. Invasion of privacy
   c. Intentional infliction of emotional distress
7. Do you agree with the decision in the *Russo* case and the rationale of the court in coming to its decision? Explain.

CHAPTER 12

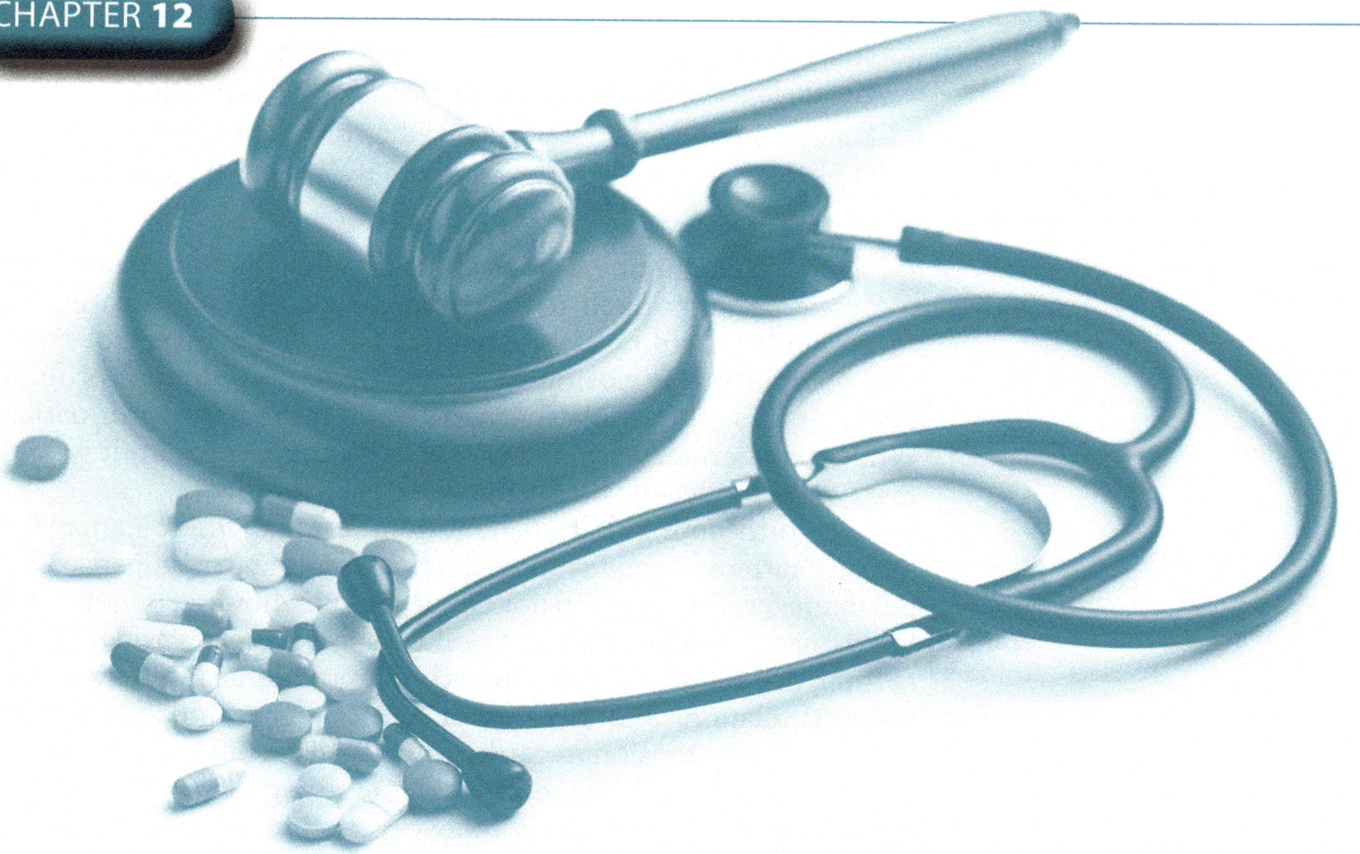

Intentional Interference with Business Relations

Interference with business relations is one type of tortious interference. The other type of tortious interference is interference with contracts. While both torts are similar, one involves a contract between parties and one does not. This chapter covers the type of tort where there is no contract in place but the interference allegedly causes harm between the plaintiff and another third party for which there is or could be a business relationship. In simple terms, this tort involves the plaintiff accusing the defendant of interfering with his or her business, resulting in damages (loss of revenue or potential revenue).

In most jurisdictions, there are five elements needed to be proven in order to show that there was an intentional interference with one's business relations.

1. There is a business relationship or prospective business relationship between the parties.
2. The defendant had knowledge of the business relationship or expected business relationship.

3. The defendant purposely caused one of the parties to terminate the business relationship or expected business relationship.
4. The defendant was not authorized to interfere.
5. There were damages suffered by the plaintiff because of the interference.

Regarding element number four, in what circumstance would someone be authorized to interfere with a business relationship? An example would be a state board of pharmacy inspector coming to a pharmacy and closing down the operation because of finding twenty-one serious violations that could ultimately harm patients. While the pharmacy will likely lose business as a result, it was necessary and proper for the inspector to interfere.

It is worth noting that element number five, where damages are actually suffered, is the same as the final element in negligence. Without damages, the case will not be successful. Showing or quantifying the damages can be tricky, as will be shown in the following case. Further, this following case covers both intentional interference with business relations and invasion of privacy. As you read this briefed case, note the tension regarding controlled substances. The prescriber is doing what she thinks is right (taking care of patients), and the pharmacists are correctly following their corresponding responsibility. Did the pharmacists take it too far?

BROWN V. CVS PHARMACY, L.L.C., ET AL.

___ F.Supp.2d ___, 2013 WL 5574486 (M.D. Tenn. Oct. 9, 2013)

Desired Remedy: Dr. Joyce Brown seeks relief from four pharmacies for intentional interference with business relations and invasion of privacy after the pharmacists at these pharmacies refused to fill prescriptions written by her and for telling patients that she was under investigation.

Issues: Did the pharmacists at the four pharmacies intentionally try to harm Dr. Joyce Brown's business relations and invade her privacy by refusing to fill prescriptions and by telling patients that Dr. Brown was under investigation?

Facts of Case: Dr. Joyce Brown, a pain-management physician, focused her practice on treating patients needing pain relief. Because of the focus of her practice, she prescribed many narcotic medications. The Smyrna, Tennessee Police Department and the DEA investigated Dr. Brown but never brought charges against her. Also, she was never the subject of professional discipline.

Pharmacists from four pharmacies refused to fill Dr. Brown's prescriptions and, on several occasions when patients asked why, they were told that Dr. Brown was under investigation. The plaintiff brought suit claiming intentional interference with business relations and invasion of privacy against the four pharmacies.

Reasoning: In order to be successful with a claim of intentional interference with business relations, Dr. Brown needed to prove all of the following: (1) there was a prospective or existing business relationship with identifiable third parties; (2) the pharmacies' knowledge of these relationships was more than a "mere awareness"; (3) the pharmacies intended to cause a termination or breach of the business relationship; (4) the pharmacies had improper means or motive; and (5) Dr. Brown must have sustained damages because of the interference.

Dr. Brown failed to prove most of the elements required. There was no improper motive or intent to harm Dr. Brown's business. In fact, the court found that the pharmacists were attempting to protect their patients from improper prescribing. There was also no evidence that Dr. Brown's business was harmed, or that future business was lost. Dr. Brown needed to show that business relationships with specific third parties were harmed and she could not. Thus, Dr. Brown was not able to show that she was damaged as a result of the pharmacies' actions.

In order to be successful with a claim of invasion of privacy, Dr. Brown needed to show that the actions of the pharmacists made public certain private facts that involved the private life of another, would be highly offensive to a reasonable person, and were not of legitimate concern to the public.

Dr. Brown failed because the investigation launched by the Smyrna Police Department and the DEA was not a private matter. The number of times the pharmacists disclosed the investigation information about Dr. Brown to patients was not sufficient to be considered "publicity." Furthermore, the disclosures were not considered "offensive" as they were not untrue or inflammatory. Finally, the court found that the disclosures were of legitimate concern to the public because they involved the prescribing of controlled substances that were lightly regulated and potentially dangerous.

Case Holding: The Federal District Court found in favor of the defendants on the basis that the plaintiff did not satisfactorily prove the necessary elements for intentional interference with business relations and invasion of privacy.

In summary, one can see that proving intentional interference with business relations and invasion of privacy is not easy.

The physician felt wronged by the pharmacists because they turned away her patients. But was she harmed? It couldn't be proven. While she was probably embarrassed that knowledge of the investigation against her was told to some patients, it was not sufficient to warrant legal action. It was, as the court put it, of legitimate public concern.

What is the take-away message for pharmacists? Your corresponding responsibility to make sure controlled substance prescriptions are for a legitimate medical purpose is imperative. And this includes refusing to fill the prescription if you see red flags. It might make you look like the bad guy to patients or prescribers when you refuse to fill a prescription, but it is a much safer alternative than filling everything that comes through the door and ultimately suffering the consequences of losing your license, or worse, hurting a patient.

What you tell a patient when you refuse to fill a prescription because you believe it is not for a legitimate medical purpose is worthy of discussion. Speak to your colleagues and ask your employer how they would like you to proceed. Being successful in a lawsuit as the defendant is important. However, avoiding the lawsuit altogether makes good business sense.

Another case that involves alleged interference with the business operations of a pharmacy is *Park Medical Pharmacy v. San Diego Orthopedic Associates Medical Group*. As we'll see in this case, the pharmacy was not happy that doctors were dispensing drugs to their own patients and taking away business.

Was this a fair business practice? Wasn't it a conflict of interest?

PARK MEDICAL PHARMACY V. SAN DIEGO ORTHOPEDIC ASSOCIATES MEDICAL GROUP

Court of Appeals, 99 Cal. App. 4th 247; 120 Cal. Rptr. 2d 858 – Calif. 2002

Desired Remedy: The plaintiff pharmacy sued the defendant Medical Group for dispensing drugs in violation of Cal. Bus. & Prof. Code, Sec. 4170, which basically states that no prescriber shall dispense drugs to patients in his or her office or place of practice unless certain conditions are met. Defendant doctors dispensed drugs on a for-profit basis to their workers' compensation patients. Since the Medical Group is in the same building as the pharmacy, the pharmacy claims that the Medical Group is in violation of Sec. 4170 and is interfering with the pharmacy's business interests.

Issues: Are there situations that a physician can dispense drugs that he or she orders for his or her office use, when only the physician is providing, using, or dispensing them to his or her patients who come for office visits?

Facts of Case: Park Medical Pharmacy's complaint states that the medical group in the same building as the pharmacy was dispensing drugs in violation of the Cal. Bus. & Prof. Code, Sec. 4170 and is essentially interfering with the pharmacy's business interest. The physicians in the Medical Group individually dispense drugs on a for-profit basis to their workers' compensation patients. When a workers' compensation patient first registers with the Medical Group, he or she is given a form entitled "Worker's Compensation Dispensing Disclosure." This form tells the patient that a Medical Group physician can dispense some prescribed medications and that the patient has a choice of between obtaining the medications from the Medical Group physicians or obtaining a prescription that may be filled at the pharmacy of the patient's choice. The Medical Group keeps drugs in a secure area and places appropriate labeling upon the container of a dispensed drug. The pharmacy alleges that the Medical Group is serving patients as a pharmacy and should be licensed by the Board of Pharmacy. The pharmacy claims that the Medical Group, while in violation of Sec. 4170, has acted in a manner that is intentional or negligent in interfering with the pharmacy's prospective economic advantage.

Case Analysis: While Sec. 4170 states that "no prescriber shall dispense drugs to patients in his or her office or place of practice," there are exceptions stated in this statute. If the prescription drugs are dispensed to the prescriber's own patients, the drugs dispensed are necessary in the treatment of the condition for which the prescriber is attending the patient, the prescriber does not keep a pharmacy or advertise for the retailing of prescription drugs, the prescriber fulfills the necessary labeling requirements and record keeping, and the prescriber offers to give a written prescription so the patient may elect to have it filled at any pharmacy, then the prescriber will be allowed to dispense the prescription drugs directly to the patient from his or her office practice.

Case Holding: A prescriber may dispense drugs for profit that he or she purchases for his or her office as long as the patients are patients of the prescriber, and the prescriber does not dispense drugs beyond the boundaries of his or her professional practice to persons who are not patients of that prescriber and who may come in off the street to receive prescription drugs as they would do in a typical pharmacy.

From a pharmacist's perspective, it would be a conflict of interest for a doctor to diagnose the patient, recommend a drug therapy, and sell the patient the prescribed medication. There would be no independent third party to verify the prescription and offer counseling. However, California law allows for this to happen with certain restrictions.

From a patient's perspective, it would be very convenient to see your doctor and have your prescriptions filled all in one visit. Instead of suing the doctors, the pharmacy could have considered being competitive on price or offering a discount to those patients.

As one can see, there was no interference with business interests as far as the law was concerned in this case.

QUESTIONS

1. Should the pharmacists have suffered some consequences for "outing" the physician for being investigated by the local police department and the DEA?
2. How would you have handled the patients who came to your pharmacy with suspicious prescriptions from Dr. Brown?
3. What would be an appropriate response to a pharmacy manager who insisted you fill Dr. Brown's prescriptions even if there were red flags?
4. If it turned out the prescriptions were completely legitimate and you still refused to fill them, what other legal actions might be taken against you?
5. If you were losing business in your pharmacy because of doctors dispensing their own medication, what alternatives would you have? What are the laws in your state regarding this type of situation?
6. When the defendant pharmacists raised their concerns to law enforcement, which were later found to be baseless, about the use of certain pain medications by the plaintiff physician in *Brown v. CVS*, what facts in this case caused Dr. Brown's claim for interference with business perspective to also be baseless?

CHAPTER **13**

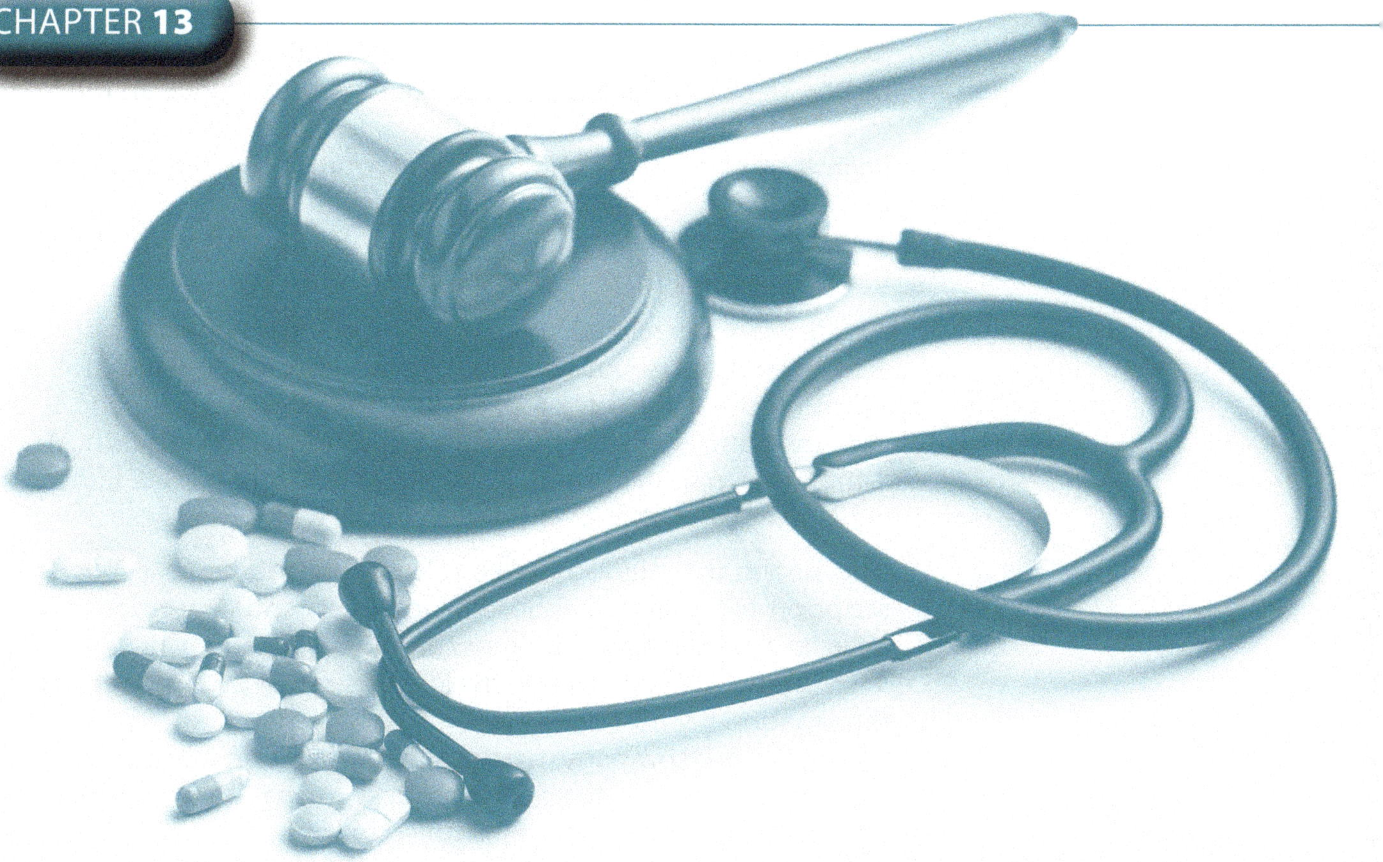

Fraud and Negligent Misrepresentation

INTRODUCTION TO FRAUD

The tort of fraud can go beyond a civil action and, in a number of cases, can have criminal implications. A general definition for *fraud* is the following:

> *An intentional misrepresentation of a material fact that induces a party to act to his or her detriment.*

Like all the other tort actions that have been presented, the tort of *fraud* is bounded by the rule described earlier. Thus, each of the elements of the tort must be established:

- *Intent:* The party committing the act of fraud must have the so-called *mens rea* element, or state of mind knowing that it is committing the fraudulent act.
- *Misrepresentation of a material fact:* The information or fact being misrepresented must be a significant piece of information or fact that somehow demonstrates importance to the party being

exposed to that fact or information. In other words, the material fact "is of substantial importance that may influence an individual to act."

- *Inducing a party to act*: The misrepresentation prompts the party to take an action from which it hopes to benefit.
- *Detriment*: However, instead of benefiting, the party is in some way harmed *to its detriment* by acting on the misrepresentation.

As an example related to pharmacy practice, consider a case in which a pharmacist knowingly bills an insurance company for a medication order filled for a patient who does not exist, and is paid by the insurance company for filling the bogus prescription. Applying the *fraud rule* described previously, the following elements of fraud appear to exist:

- The pharmacist had knowledge that he was filling a bogus prescription for a patient who did not exist, and charging the insurance company for the filling of that bogus prescription.
- The phony or bogus prescription serves as the material fact or information.
- The insurance company, trusting that the pharmacist is acting honestly, acts upon the receipt or request for payment, and pays the pharmacy for filling the bogus prescription.
- The insurance company, paying the pharmacy for the bogus prescription, is acting to its detriment since no real patient is benefiting from the payment to the pharmacy for filling the bogus prescription.

Once the party acting to its detriment—like the insurance company described earlier—realizes that it has been taken advantage of, it can bring a civil action against a defendant for both compensatory damages as well as punitive damages (the latter damages based upon the fact that there was intent to commit the act of fraud). In addition, if a report is filed with law enforcement, a criminal action may also be initiated against a defendant who commits a fraudulent act since most criminal fraud offenses are considered felonies.

The areas where fraudulent acts occur in high abundance are those in which credit cards or banking loans are involved.

THE FALSE CLAIMS ACT

The False Claims Act is a federal law, also referred to as the "Lincoln law," that imposes liability on persons and companies who defraud governmental programs. When an action is taken under this act, it automatically becomes a criminal action since a law has been violated. Therefore, if our previous scenario involved a fraudulent act in the bogus filling of a *Medicaid* prescription, the government would step in and file a violation under the False Claims Act.

Sometimes, the government finds out on its own about a fraudulent act against it instituted by a company or organization, or sometimes, it is reported to the government by an individual citizen or group of citizens. If it is reported by an individual or a group of individuals, these persons are referred to as *whistleblowers* (also referred to as *relators*, who are the parties filing the suit on behalf of the government).

Of interest, whistleblowers or relators cannot bring a fraud action themselves against a company or organization if a government entity is being defrauded. They must report the fraudulent misconduct to the government entity. The government then brings the action against the company or organization that has acted fraudulently in the name of the individual relators. This allows for citizens to then sue on behalf of the government. This procedure is referred to as *qui tam*. Further, if the government should prevail in its suit against a company or organization, the relator(s) is to receive a percentage of the financial recovery.

The False Claims Act also contains an anti-retaliation provision, which allows a relator to recover, in addition to his or her award as a relator for reporting fraud, double damages (twice the amount awarded) plus attorney fees for any acts of retaliation for reporting fraud against the government.

NEGLIGENT MISREPRESENTATION

The definition for *negligent misrepresentation* has the same key elements that are contained in the definition for *fraud,* with the exception of the term *intentional.* Thus, the definition for negligent misrepresentation is:

> *A non-intentional misrepresentation of a material fact that induces a party to act to his or her detriment.*

Usually the person making a false statement or claim is unaware that it is false. For example, a pharmacist filling a prescription notes on the label that the prescription is for 100 tablets. When he prepares the prescription, he uses a Baker-type counting machine that only yields 90 tablets of the prescribed drug. The pharmacist believes he is providing 100 tablets to the patient, when in fact the patient is only getting 90 tablets. In this example, there is no "intent" to give the patient only 90 tablets, but nevertheless by virtue of the label indicating that there are 100 tablets contained in the vial, this is a mistaken misrepresentation.

Negligent misrepresentation cases are generally civil in nature, and many are resolved outside of the courtroom since the mistaken party who recognizes its mistake will usually attempt to make things right. If legal action were to ensue regarding a negligent misrepresentation action, the tort of negligence would be raised with the usual remedies sought under this cause of action.

FRAUD CASES

ZWERIN V. MACCABEES MUTUAL LIFE INS. CO.

111 F.3d 140 (10th Cir. 1997)

Desired Remedy: Plaintiff Mark Zwerin sued defendant Maccabees Mutual Life Insurance Company based upon the insurance company's decision to stop paying plaintiff disability benefits.

Issue: Can an insurance company stop payments on a disability claim if the party who filed the claim has acted in a manner judged fraudulent by the insurance company?

Facts of Case: The plaintiff, Mark Zwerin, a pharmacist and owner of a pharmacy, had hit hard times in his business from 1978 to 1983 since his pharmacy was not doing well and was robbed five times during this period. In 1982, the plaintiff purchased an insurance policy from the defendant company, Maccabees Mutual Life Insurance. The plaintiff also had another life and disability insurance with another company. The plaintiff filed a disability claim with the insurance companies in 1985, indicating that he could no longer work as a pharmacist because he was unable to stand as the result of a blocked artery. The claim was supported by his physician.

The plaintiff in 1985 began receiving $10,000 per month from the two insurance companies due to his disability until his benefits were stopped in 1993. During this time, the plaintiff was examined by several of the defendant's physicians who claimed that the plaintiff was not disabled, finding no evidence of vascular disease. Further, during this time, the plaintiff's physician changed his diagnosis to a torn ligament and back injuries from being kicked while in the pharmacy during a robbery, and that the disability would last indefinitely. The plaintiff stated that he could not walk more than two blocks at a time, that it was difficult for him to drive, that he could not stand for more than 20 min, and that he could not tolerate lifting any weight. A second physician (orthopedic surgeon) for the plaintiff rendered an opinion in September 1992 that the plaintiff remained totally disabled because of a post-traumatic stress syndrome. This physician later changed his opinion after the insurance company showed surveillance videos that the plaintiff was engaged in strenuous physical activities. By September 1993, both insurance companies terminated the plaintiff's coverage.

The plaintiff sued the insurance companies, claiming that they terminated his benefits in "bad faith." One of the insurance companies filed a countersuit claiming that the plaintiff had committed fraud in obtaining the disability benefits.

During trial, the pharmacist plaintiff admitted that he had filled out the majority of the physician statements supporting his disability and that the physicians just signed the reports. The plaintiff further admitted that he engaged in hiking, horseback riding, tennis, football, walking, and jogging while he claimed he was disabled. Both the plaintiff's wife and son provided testimony that the plaintiff was not really disabled by making statements in court that the plaintiff kept a cane in the closet to use in case an investigator came to the door, that he never complained of pain or discomfort, and that he would not play basketball with his son if he thought anyone was watching.

Case Analysis: In this case, the admission by the plaintiff that he engaged in activities that would suggest he was not disabled made it reasonably easy for the trial court to find for the defendants.

Case Holding: The trial court jury found in favor of the defendant insurance companies, and granted a judgment in restitution to the insurance companies. The jury assessed a financial judgment in favor of the insurance companies for $971,299, and the judge added prejudgment interest and fees that increased the judgment to $1,349,067. The jury verdict was upheld on appeal.

RNH, INC., et al. V. BILLY M. BEATTY

571 So. 2d 1039, Alabama 1990

Desired Remedy: Plaintiffs, a group of investors who arranged for the purchase of the defendant seller's pharmacy, found that the seller breached his agreement (a stock purchase) not to purchase another pharmacy that would be in competition with the plaintiffs' purchase. The plaintiffs' claim was that the other purchase by the defendant was a fraudulent act and a misrepresentation based upon the purchase agreement.

Issue: Did there exist clear wording in the buy-sell agreement that would disallow the defendant seller from relocating to another pharmacy owned by the defendant in the area of the purchased pharmacy, thus becoming a competing entity?

Facts of Case: This case involves the sale of stock in a corporation operating a drugstore, Price Drug, in downtown Montgomery, Alabama. On November 7, 1988, the plaintiff, RNH, Inc., and the defendants entered into an agreement whereby RNH, Inc. bought and the defendants sold all of the outstanding shares of stock of Price Drug Company, Inc., an Alabama corporation.

The 91-page stock purchase agreement between plaintiff RNH, Inc. and defendant Beatty had several clauses that attempted to prevent future competition with the newly acquired Price Drug and the defendant. The clauses in the stock purchase agreement that raised concerns were (1) the sellers agreed not to solicit the customers of Price Drug in any area within a 50-mile radius of Montgomery County for a period of five years; (2) the sellers agreed that they would not solicit any employee of Price Drug to leave his or her employment relationship for five years; and (3) the sellers agreed to exercise their reasonable best efforts to preserve the goodwill of the suppliers, customers, and others having a business relationship with Price Drug so that they would continue to do business with the company.

Shortly after the agreement was signed, Beatty moved his other pharmacy, City Drug, to a new location in downtown Montgomery only a few blocks away from Price Drug. The reason given for this move was that the original building City Drug was in was deteriorating, and the landlord refused to renovate that building. When Beatty moved to the new location, the plaintiffs, RNH, immediately issued a court action that Beatty was in breach of his agreement and acted fraudulently and misrepresented his position. However, according to the plaintiff's testimony at trial, Beatty had not solicited customers, nor had he harmed the goodwill of Price Drug.

On December 13, 1988, the plaintiffs became aware that the defendant, Billy Beatty, breached the agreement when he relocated another pharmacy in the same downtown area of Montgomery. The plaintiffs sought to enjoin Beatty from operating that relocated pharmacy and further wanted to rescind the purchase they made of the other pharmacy.

Case Analysis: The trial court found that at the time the agreement was signed, the plaintiff was aware for at least two years that the defendant had another pharmacy in reasonably close proximity and that direct competition already existed between the two pharmacies. While this appeared to be a concern of the plaintiffs even before signing the agreement, it was not a fact that changed their minds or had them reconsider the terms of the agreement.

The plaintiffs argued that Beatty had a duty to disclose, prior to the signing of the agreement, that he was planning to move his pharmacy. The trial court, however, concluded that Beatty had no such duty since both parties were knowledgeable businessmen dealing at arm's length and acting upon the advice of competent attorneys. The agreement was negotiated and signed, with both sides inquiring as to the competition aspect of the contract. At no time was the question of relocation presented as a concern, nor was there any restriction on it in the agreement. Additionally, throughout the negotiations, Beatty and his lawyer made it clear to the plaintiffs that he planned to continue in competition with Price Drug.

Case Holding: In that the trial court found no fraud nor misrepresentation of business purpose associated with the agreement between the parties, it granted summary judgment in favor of the defendant. On appeal, the appellate court agreed that the elements of fraud or misrepresentation were not present based upon the facts of the case and, notably, the agreement that was signed by both parties.

CASE SCENARIO 1: MARYLAND PHARMACY OWNER SENTENCED TO 57 MONTHS IN PRISON

The defendant pled guilty to health care fraud, aggravated identity theft, and conspiracy to misbrand pharmaceuticals.

On July 1, 2008, the U.S. District Court sentenced the defendant to 57 months in prison followed by three years of supervised release for health care fraud, aggravated identity theft, and conspiracy to misbrand pharmaceuticals. The defendant, a licensed pharmacist, will also be required to forfeit her home and pay restitution of $505,745.89.

According to the defendant's guilty plea, she owned and operated two pharmacies located in Baltimore. From January 2003 to July 2008, the defendant identified patients who had filled prescriptions at her pharmacies and for whom the physician authorized refills that had never been requested. She then claimed reimbursement from health care benefit programs, using patients' personal identifying information, for refills of those prescriptions, although no drugs were ever dispensed to customers. The defendant's pharmacies fraudulently obtained more than $500,000 through this scheme, and the proceeds were deposited into one of her pharmacy's bank accounts.

In her plea, the defendant also admitted to misbranding and re-labeling prescription drugs purchased in large drums from an unlicensed supplier for resale in her pharmacies. She then filled prescription orders for pharmacy customers with misbranded pharmaceuticals including metformin and gabapentin.

On July 7, 2008, the Maryland Board of Pharmacy conducted a surprise inspection of one of the two pharmacies that the defendant owned and recovered 11 drums of misbranded pharmaceuticals containing more than 200,000 misbranded pills. Later that month, federal agents searched the pharmacies and the defendant's home. They recovered drugs from the pharmacies with expiration dates removed and others with altered labels and seized expired controlled substances from the defendant's home, including oxycodone, fentanyl, amphetamine, and morphine.

CASE SCENARIO 2: ANOTHER BLATANT ACT OF PHARMACY FRAUD

Pharmacist Smith has been experiencing a steady drop in his prescription business over the last year. As a result, he begins to falsify the filling of prescriptions for patients who have recently gone to other pharmacies. In the process of his fraudulent activity, he bills the third party insurance payors for prescriptions that he writes up for the prescription record files, but never fills, and for medications that patients have not received in the past. In an attempt not to be too obvious about this fraudulent activity, he only falsifies non-schedule drug prescriptions and submits such claims on the average of 20 per week. The claims are for relatively expensive drugs for which he gets paid. One of his prior patients gets a record from her insurance company, noting prescription drugs she has never received. An investigation of pharmacist Smith by the third party payor is presently under way.

If any of these prescriptions were issued under the Medicaid or Medicare Program, this pharmacist would also, most probably, be facing charges under the False Claims Act, especially if the patient who got a record from the government program showing medicines that she did not receive, and was willing to serve as a "relator (whistleblower)" in filing a court claim on behalf of the government.

CASE SCENARIO 3: A POSSIBLE CASE OF NEGLIGENT MISREPRESENTATION, BUT COURT MIGHT FIND FRAUD

ABC Pharmacy does approximately 60% of its prescription business by filling Medicaid prescriptions. What often happens is that a Medicaid patient goes to his or her doctor, receives from one to four prescriptions, then goes to ABC Pharmacy to have the prescriptions filled, but never comes back to pick them up. In the meantime, ABC Pharmacy fills the prescriptions, bills the Medicaid program, and puts them in "Patient Will-Call." It is the store's policy that after 30 days, if a filled prescription is not picked up by the patient, it is to be returned to stock. Almost in every case where a filled Medicaid prescription is not picked up and is returned to stock within 30 days, the pharmacy does not call Medicaid to reverse the charges on the prescription.

QUESTIONS

1. Describe what is meant by the term *qui tam.*
2. In what ways can a fraud case become a civil, criminal, and administrative matter?
3. A patient brings in a prescription to a pharmacy to be filled for 100 tablets of Percodan (a Schedule II controlled substance). Upon counting the number of tablets of Percodan in the vial after arriving home, the patient only accounts for 90 tablets being dispensed in the prescription vial. This error could have been the result of either a fraudulent act or a simple negligent misrepresentation. Since the only element in dispute is whether or not there was "intent," what thoughts do you have as a plaintiff that would suggest there was intent by the pharmacist or pharmacy? On the other hand, what arguments would the pharmacy or pharmacist pose and hopefully prove that it was simply a negligent misrepresentation without intent? Based upon another case in a preceding chapter, how would you prove or argue that there was gross negligence, rather than pure fraud or a simple act of negligent misrepresentation?
4. In the *Zwerin* case, it appears fairly straightforward that Mr. Zwerin lied about his disabled condition sometime between 1985 and 1993, perhaps while having some level of disability during 1985 up to an unknown period. However, it appears that the insurance company wanted every dollar paid to Mr. Zwerin back during the eight plus years he was collecting $10,000 per month. In your opinion, was requesting every dollar back plus interest the proper verdict by both the trial court and the appeals court? Would you have decided differently, and if so, what would be your determination as to how much money was owed back to the insurance company due to the apparent fraud by Mr. Zwerin?
5. In *Case Scenario* 3, the element of intent may be questionable. If the placement back in stock without reversing the charge was an occasional happening, might the situation just be labeled a simple mistake or a "simple misrepresentation" where there was never an intent not to reverse the charge on the prescription that was not picked up? However, if this were a common occurrence where many of the filled Medicaid prescriptions that were not picked up were placed back on the shelf without reversing the charge, could you then make a case of fraudulent conduct on the part of the pharmacy and its staff? Could fraud be found if the argument is made that even if the pharmacy staff did not

know of the need to reverse the charge, should they have known to take that action as a matter of common sense? Then, if they "should have known," can a case for fraud be argued?

6. Regarding the *RNH v. Billy M. Beatty* case, although we do not have all of the specific contract wording between RNH and Mr. Beatty in consideration of the sale of his pharmacy, Price Drug, there appear to be several clauses that attempt to prevent future competition with RNH's purchase of Price Drug, and prevent Mr. Beatty from soliciting customers of Price Drug within a 50-mile radius for a period of five years. Another pharmacy owned by Mr. Beatty, City Drug, existed before the signing of the contract, and the plaintiffs appear to be aware that it existed within the 50-mile radius. Evidently, this preexisting pharmacy, over time, managed to attract customers doing business with Price Drug. The appeals court found no wrongdoing on the part of Beatty since RNH had sufficient opportunity to make necessary inquiries of the intentions and goals of Mr. Beatty in the operation of his other pharmacy. Do you agree or disagree with the court's decision? What is the basis for your agreement or disagreement with the appeals court decision?
7. In the *RNH v. Billy M. Beatty* case, if RNH were to prevail in its claim against Mr. Beatty for committing fraud, what arguments could you make that Mr. Beatty acted fraudulently using the elements that comprise the tort of fraud?
8. In *Case Scenario 3*, the pharmacy fills and bills the Medicaid provider for all the prescriptions that are filled, and then places the prescriptions in a "will-call" area of the pharmacy. The store's policy is that if the patient does not pick up the prescriptions within a 30-day period, the drugs are to be returned to stock. If the Medicaid provider is not called to reverse the charges after 30 days, or any time thereafter, and the charges to Medicaid remain, in your opinion would this be a case of fraud or negligent misrepresentation?

CHAPTER 14

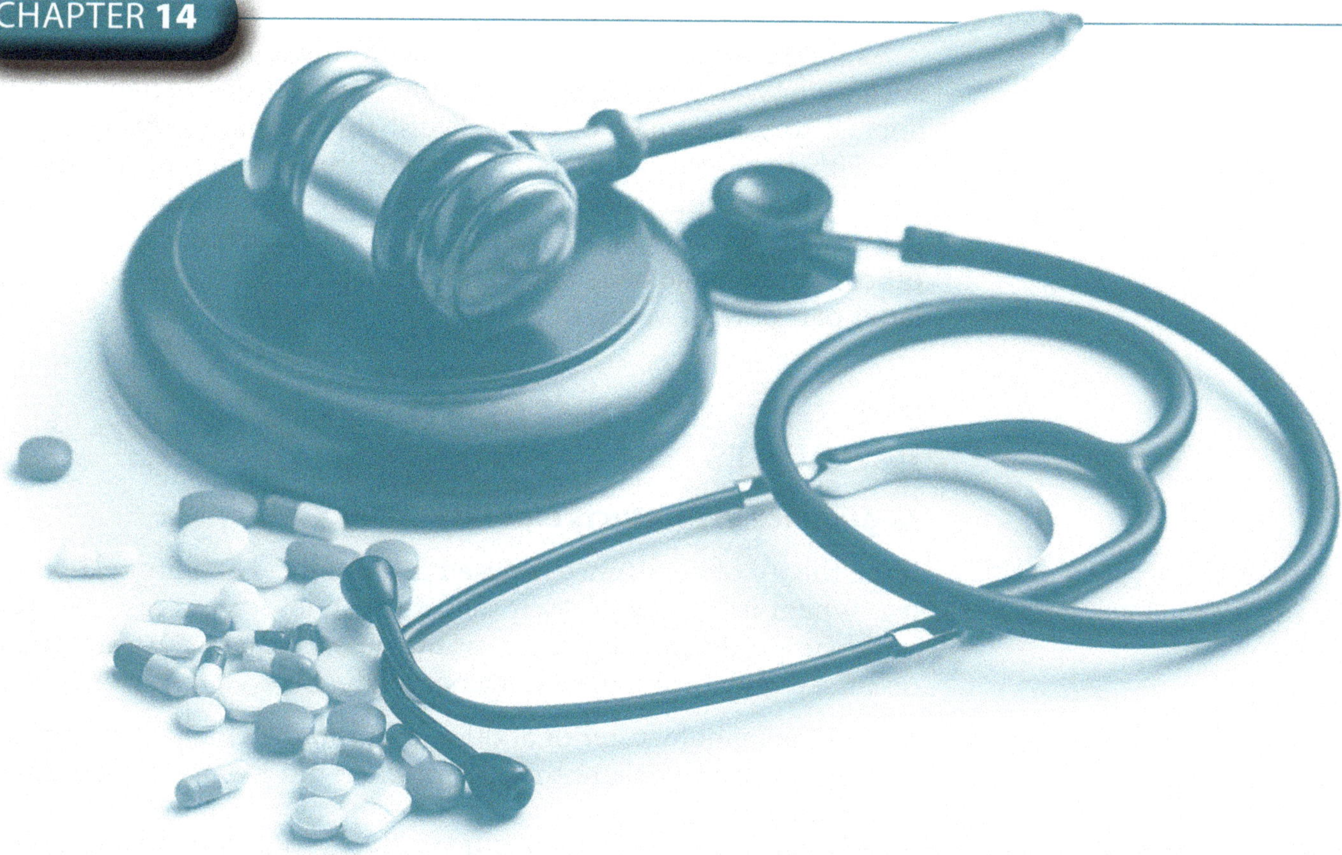

Products Liability (Part I): General Principles

BACKGROUND

The principle of *caveat emptor* ("the buyer beware") existed prior to the mid-1900s regarding the consumer's acquisition and purchasing of a manufacturer's product. Since the mid-1900s, the principle of *strict liability* has been one of several theories that has been applied to products liability claims. Essentially, strict liability does not cast fault on a defendant, but rather attempts to attach liability to the product that caused the alleged injury or harm due to some defective characteristic that could only have been made safer by that product's manufacturer.

Besides strict liability, other major theories that plaintiffs could sue on if they are injured by a manufacturer's product are *negligence* and *breach of warranty*. These different theories will be discussed in reasonable detail so they can be understood within the context of products liability issues for drug products and the pharmaceutical industry.

As products liability cases have been litigated, issues have arisen such as: how are the three or possibly four theories of liability to be applied to these types of cases? Must the injured party be in privity with the manufacturer? What constitutes a defective product? Does the plaintiff or the manufacturer have the burden of proving the product was or was not defective? These questions and a host of other matters have been addressed through court decisions over the latter part of the twentieth century.

THE THEORIES OF LIABILITY APPLIED TO PRODUCTS

Negligence in Products Liability Cases

If the theory of negligence is raised in a products liability related case (eg, where it may be shown that a possible defect was associated with the product), then the plaintiff must address the same issues discussed previously in a negligence analysis:

1. Did the manufacturer or another party in the chain of distribution have a duty to ensure that the product did not have the defect it possessed?
2. Did the manufacturer or another party in the chain of distribution breach its duty in allowing the defective product to come onto the market and into the hands of the plaintiff?
3. Was the defective product the actual or proximate cause of the plaintiff's injury?
4. Was the plaintiff's injury caused by the defective product?

The creation of a negligently unsafe product may be the result of a design flaw; the method in which the product was put together during the manufacturing process; or insufficient or incorrect information concerning warnings or directions for use. The latter situation—labeling information—is often the problem associated with drug products in products liability cases.

There is also consideration beyond the manufacturer's involvement with the product. Often, in products liability cases, all those involved in the chain of distribution may in some way be responsible for negligence. Involved in that chain of distribution, other than the manufacturer, are the provider of raw materials to the manufacturer, wholesalers, distributors, and retailers of the potentially unsafe product. These other entities may have acted in a negligent manner for their failure to discover or their failure to warn of the product's unsafe condition.[1]

As a general rule, manufacturers and designers of a product generally have a duty to inspect a product that they produce in order to discover and correct any noted defects that would be found during an inspection. If there are dangers associated with the use of the product, then the manufacturer has a duty to properly warn the consumer if the product is unavoidably unsafe. Wholesalers and retailers, on the other hand, do not generally have a duty to inspect unless there is reason to know that the product may have some dangerous element associated with it.

In products liability cases, the facts may not be apparent in how the manufacturer or product designer may have breached its duty of due care. Thus, in proving a breach of duty, the theory of *res ipsa loquitur* must be applied, with the following elements satisfied: (1) the injury would not have occurred in the absence of someone's negligence; (2) the product's production was within the exclusive control of the defendant; and (3) the plaintiff did not contribute to his or her own injury.

Strict Liability in Products Liability Cases

Strict liability, as applied to potentially unsafe products, has not always been a concept rooted as a major attack in products liability cases. It was a California Supreme Court justice, Justice J. Traynor, who in the mid-1900s imposed strict liability thinking with regard to unsafe products in at least two major cases: *Escola v. Coca Cola Bottling Co.* and *Greenman v. Yuba Power Products.*[2]

The *Escola* case involved a bottle of Coca Cola that exploded in the plaintiff's hand, causing injury. Of issue was the potential of a defect in the manufactured bottle that was aggravated by the buildup of pressure from the gases created by the carbonated drink contained inside. Justice Traynor's concurring statement in the case opinion helps set the direction for strict liability having a more predominant role than negligence in products liability cases since the elements of negligence may be difficult to prove.

> *"I believe the manufacturer's negligence should no longer be singled out as the basis of plaintiff's right to recover in cases like the present one. In my opinion it should now be recognized that a manufacturer incurs an absolute liability when an article that he has placed on the market, knowing that it is to be used without inspection, proves to have a defect that causes injury to human beings .... If such products nevertheless find their way into the market, it is to the public interest to place the responsibility for whatever injury they may cause upon the manufacturer, who, even if he is not negligent in the manufacturing of the product, is reasonable for its reaching the market.*[3]"

In the *Greenman* case, the plaintiff purchased a power tool that could be used as a saw, drill, and wood lathe. While using it as a wood lathe, the wood disengaged from the tool, striking the plaintiff on the head. The plaintiff argued both negligence and breach of warranty. The *Traynor* court, however, viewed the circumstances as a case in strict liability.

> *"A manufacturer is strictly liable in tort when an article he places on the market, knowing that it is to be used without inspection for defects,*

proves to have a defect that causes injury to a human being .... Although strict liability of a manufacturer has usually been based on the theory of an express or implied warranty running from manufacturer to plaintiff, the abandonment of the requirement of contract between them, the recognition that the liability is not assumed by agreement but imposed by law, and the refusal to permit the manufacturer to define the scope of its own responsibility for defective products make clear that the liability is not one governed by the law of contract warranties but by the law of strict liability in tort .... The purpose of such liability is to insure that the costs of injuries resulting from defective products are borne by the manufacturers that put such products on the market rather than by the injured persons who are powerless to protect themselves."

Shortly after the *Greenman* case, guidelines were established in the American Law Institute's *Restatement (Second) of Torts* to support the adoption of strict liability in products liability cases. Section 402A of the *Restatement* reads as follows:[4]

> *(1) One who sells any product in a defective condition unreasonably dangerous to the user or consumer or to his property is subject to liability for physical harm thereby caused to the ultimate user or consumer, or to his property, if:*
>
> *(a) the seller is engaged in the business of selling such a product, and*
>
> *(b) it is expected to and does reach the user or consumer without substantial change in the condition in which it is sold.*
>
> *(2) The rule stated in Subsection (1) applies although*
>
> *(a) the seller has exercised all possible care in the preparation and sale of his product, and*
>
> *(b) the user or consumer has not bought the product from or entered into any contractual relation with the seller.*

Section 402 stood for the principle "that if a product was defective and the defect caused harm, liability would be imposed upon the manufacturer and distributors, whether or not they were at fault and whether or not they were in privity with the plaintiff."[5] According to Sec. 402, the plaintiff would have the burden to prove the following elements:[6]

- That the defendant was in the business of selling products
- That the defendant sold or provided the product in question to the plaintiff
- That the product was expected to and did reach the plaintiff without substantial change
- That the product was defective when it left the defendant's possession
- That the product's defect was the cause of the injury to the plaintiff

Historically, in the mid-1800s, the concept of strict liability had its early origin by holding the manufacturer liable only to the party who purchased the product and was considered to be in contractual privity with the product's manufacturer. If this so-called contractual privity did not exist, the injured party would have no claim.[7] Later, in the early 1900s, the privity rule lost favor, especially where the claim against the defendant was based in negligence.[8] At the same time, the theory of *breach of warranty* also began to take hold as a method of bringing suit against a manufacturer. The theory of breach of warranty is discussed later.

While strict liability during this time became more of the rule than the exception, negligence and breach of warranty actions still could be employed as causes of action in products liability suits.

From the mid-1900s, the application of strict liability in products liability cases appeared to concentrate on product flaws—products that were defective and unreasonably dangerous. This focus did not necessarily address product manufacturing, design, or warning defects. It still appeared that cases argued on the basis of negligence regarding these three specialized defect areas made more sense than using other theories of tort law.

In 1998, the American Law Institute published the *Restatement (Third) of Torts*. As a result of several decades of wondering whether strict liability was the most appropriate theory for recovery in products liability cases, there was a strong sentiment that negligence should serve as the standard in deciding design and warning defects. The recent *Restatement* strongly suggests that "strict liability be retained when it comes to product flaws, but negligence … is the test of liability when it comes to design and warning defects."[9] The newer *Restatement* essentially retains the same burden of proof elements discussed previously in Sec. 402, and further incorporates a provision for design and warning defects whereby any risk of harm from the product must be foreseeable.[10]

Breach of Warranty in Products Liability Cases

Products liability cases may involve claims other than simply a tort action. These cases often carry with them characteristics that attach to contractual concepts, such as warranties. Essentially, warranties are promises, both express or implied, that a product shall do what it is intended to be used for, and shall be safe when used. As a result, when there is a breach of warranty regarding a product, a consumer plaintiff is provided even more grounds on which to claim a product may be unsafe.

There are three types of warranties to be considered under this heading: (1) express warranty, (2) implied warranty of merchantability, and (3) implied warranty of fitness for a particular purpose. These warranty areas are codified within the Uniform Commercial Code (UCC) with respect to the transaction of goods.

An *express warranty* (usually provided in writing) is a promise or guarantee that the product should work for the purpose it is intended for, is safe, and should serve the buyer's needs for a reasonably good period of time before normal wear and tear begin to minimize its effect. Manufacturers may provide limited express warranties realizing that common wear and tear will eventually render some products ineffective over time. A good example is an express warranty associated with the sale of a new automobile—"All parts and labor costs will not be charged to the purchaser if such parts should fail to function under normal wear and tear circumstances within five years or 50,000 miles." There are generally no similar express warranties associated with drug products per se.

An *implied warranty of merchantability* requires that the product be fit for the ordinary purpose for which it was sold. There is an expectation that the product must be reasonably safe. Remember, there are products that may have inherent underlying dangers associated with their use, especially if used in an inappropriate manner, or carelessly. A sharp carving knife or an electric saw—while inherently dangerous objects—if used properly for their intended purpose, any danger to the user should be minimized or hopefully eliminated . Of course, it is the responsibility of the manufacturer to ensure that otherwise inherently unsafe objects placed in the stream of commerce will be safe when used for the intended purpose by the consumer. For example, a knife must have a well-structured handle that allows consumers to get a firm grip on it so that their hands will not slide down to the blade and cut their fingers; or, an electric saw, besides having a firm handle, also has a proper guard over the top to prevent the rotating blade from being exposed at the top so that wood fragments aren't thrown in the direction of one's face.

An *implied warranty of fitness for a particular purpose* is usually where customers depend upon the expertise of the seller who may give them advice on what and why a given product is best for their needs, and how to properly use it. The consumer here relies on the advice given as to why the product will fit the consumer's particular needs. Pharmacists are generally participants in an implied warranty in that consumers will often ask their advice on a given drug product that is being sold as an over-the-counter medication.

A breach of any of the warranties described earlier related to a given product shares both the elements of tort law and contract law. If a claim in breach of warranty is made by a plaintiff, it is its own cause of action and neither negligence nor fault needs to be proven. There is, however, a privity requirement in that only the direct purchaser has the right to bring a breach of warranty claim, and not some ultimate consumer down the line (eg, the purchaser lends the product to a friend who is subsequently injured by the product).

In that warranty issues are contract related, contract defenses may be imposed by the defendant such as (1) the seller must receive reasonably prompt notice of the breach from the purchaser; (2)

the purchaser must show proof of relying upon the warranty; or (3) the seller his limited or disclaimed the implied warranties.[11] These defenses tend to be more favored in commercial loss (eg, a retailer brings a breach of warranty claim against a manufacturer) as compared to an individual filing a breach of warranty claim against a manufacturer. Individuals more commonly claim negligence in products liability actions.

The *Uniform Commercial Code* has tended to expand the breach of warranty allowance beyond the purchaser in privity with the seller of a defective product. Here, the privity rule was dropped if members of the purchaser's immediate family were to use the defective product and were injured by it, allowing them to file a breach of warranty claim if they might be expected to use the product.[12]

Misrepresentation in Products Liability Cases

Somewhat aligned to *implied warranty of fitness for a particular purpose* and *strict liability* is when a consumer is led to believe—often through advertising or by the word of a person who is thought to be an expert regarding the use of a product—that a particular product is safe or appropriate for a consumer's needs, but is subsequently found to be neither safe nor appropriate. In pharmacy practice, if a pharmacist recommends or warrants the use of a particular over-the-counter product as serving the needs of a customer, and the recommended product, when used, causes harm to the customer because it was not correctly represented, that customer may bring a products liability suit against the pharmacist and possibly the product's manufacturer for any misinformation presented that induces the customer to use that product to their detriment.

TYPES OF PRODUCT DEFECTS: MANUFACTURING, DESIGN, AND WARNING

Today, a product is considered defective if it has a manufacturing, design, or warning flaw. If a product falls apart when there is an expectation by the consumer that that should not happen under normal use and according to the manufacturer's instructions, then it can be inferred that there is some defect in the manufacturing process. If such is the case and the consumer is injured as a result of the manufacturing defect, the manufacturer will be strictly liable to the consumer for the resulting injury.

Design defects pose a different issue when compared to manufacturing defects. When the manufacturer designs a given product and places it on the market, there may be some aspect about the product that renders it unsafe. As an example, some brands of reclining chairs a few years ago did not contain a guard when the footrest portion was extended. A small child could place his or her head between the upright-positioned chair and footrest portion, and upon inclining the seat, the child's neck could be broken by the reconfiguration of the two moving parts. While there was no manufacturing flaw, there was a definite problem in design that could be improved by placing a guard across the opening so that a child could not get caught in this otherwise-open space.

Even in the area of drug products, design defects may exist. In a given category of drugs used for a specific purpose, where one or more of those drugs pose serious adverse consequences—and there are morphologically similar drugs that can be used in the same or similar condition but pose substantially less of a risk to the patient—then on a comparative basis, the use of the potentially dangerous drug may be considered to be design defective.[13]

A warning defect occurs when a potentially dangerous product must be used in a specific way or has possible bad effects when used and such information known to the manufacturer is not conveyed to the consumer as a packaging insert, as an FDA medication guide, or as part of the product's labeling. Warning of dangers by the manufacturer can be a big issue for the pharmaceutical industry and for those involved in supplying a drug product to the consumer. The next chapter will present products liability cases that demonstrate how warning defects find their way to become consumer lawsuits against drug manufacturers, prescribers, and pharmacists.

THE APPLICATION OF THE "COST-BENEFIT ANALYSIS TEST" IN PRODUCTS LIABILITY CASES

In the "cost-benefit analysis test," a court will balance what it would cost to market the product as it is against what it would have cost to market the product free of the danger. If a safer product would require unreasonably high costs, the product is not defective and is simply required to have sufficient warnings describing the nature of the danger. If a safer product could be produced at a reasonable cost, the product is defective because there was a "reasonable alternative" and the defendant failed to allow for it. Thus, in using the electrical saw example, in order to prevent wood from flying in the face of the user, a guard would be placed over the top of the rotating saw blade. In addition, the electrical saw company could provide plastic eye covering or goggles with labeling that warns the consumer not to use the electric saw without wearing the goggles. This arrangement in making the product safer would not be suggestive of additional unreasonable costs.

Some products are inherently dangerous, like dynamite, and there is not much you can add to the product to make it safer other than to inform the user in the instructions and labeling to stay a given distance away from the dynamite prior to igniting.

With regard to drug products, the product, especially if it is a tablet, capsule, or liquid, should be contained in a child-resistant container along with labeling that informs the user of the risks versus benefits in taking the drug. The use of child-resistant containers and appropriate labeling provides reasonable safety measures at a reasonable cost for products purchased by consumers.

COMMON DEFENSES TO PRODUCTS LIABILITY CLAIMS

A defendant such as a manufacturer, distributor, or retailer who is sued on a products liability claim has several defenses that may be brought:

- The plaintiff may have substantially altered the product after it left the control of the manufacturer, distributor, or retailer. Example: The plaintiff removed the guard from the circular saw.
- The plaintiff may have inappropriately used the product. Example: The plaintiff, who weighs 250 pounds, stands on an aluminum folding table that has instructions posted on it that the table should not be climbed on since it cannot bear weight of over 40 pounds, and could easily collapse if more than 40 pounds is placed upon it. This defense may also be labeled an "assumption of the risk" as a result of misusing the product.
- The plaintiff files his or her suit well after the statute of limitations period.
- The plaintiff is unable to identify who manufactured the product or supplied it to him or her. However, there is an exception to this rule based upon a California case, *Murphy v. E.R. Squibb*, where a pregnant female received a prescription drug (diethylstilbestrol) that, some 20 years later, was found to cause vaginal carcinomas in females born to mothers receiving this drug. Some years later when it was established that this drug caused these forms of cancer, the record of which manufacturer was responsible for this was not available. But what was known was the number of drug manufacturers some 20 years earlier that were responsible for manufacturing this drug product, and the amount of market share they had at the time. Thus, in the *Murphy* case, the California Supreme Court assigned a market share percentage of liability to each of the some six companies that manufactured diethylstilbestrol at the time that the plaintiff's mother took the drug.[14] The *Murphy* case will be discussed in the next chapter in more detail.
- If the plaintiff brings a products liability claim arguing negligence, and if any of the elements of the negligence formula are missing, as previously discussed in the chapters on negligence, then all four elements of the negligence formula must be proven.
- In cases of design defects, manufacturers may be able to escape liability on the basis of a "state of the art" defense, which asserts that the manufacturer has used the best available technology and design to make the product as safe as possible. If there is no safer known design, a manufacturer might not be liable for design defects.[15]

Examples of this "state of the art defense" situation come up in a few cases. The *Elsroth v. Johnson & Johnson Co.* case involved several bottles of Tylenol that were tampered with, allowing the contents to be laced with cyanide. The bottles containing the Tylenol capsules had their seals opened, but were resealed carefully to ensure that the person opening the bottle would believe that the seal had not been tampered with. When the family of Elsroth brought suit, their claim was that the bottle seals could have been more secure and better methods of sealing could have been employed. The defendant pharmaceutical company argued that the sealing methods used were state of the art and nothing better could have been used to show that the product was tampered with. The defendants won on that argument. The *Elsroth* case is discussed in more detail in the next chapter.

REFERENCES

1. Kionka EJ. *Torts—Injury to Persons and Property.* St. Paul, MN: Nutshell Series of West Publishing Co.; 1983.
2. *Escola v. Coca Cola Bottling Co.* 24 Cal.2d 453: 150 P.2d 436; 1944 Cal. and *Greenman v. Yuba Power Products,* 59 Cal.2d 57, 27 Cal. Rptr. 697, 377 P.2d 897 (1963).
3. *Escola v. Coca Cola Bottling Co.* 24 Cal.2d 462.
4. *Restatement (Second) of Torts,* Section 402A, p. 713.
5. Dobbs DB. *The Law of Torts.* Hornbook Series. St. Paul, MN: West Group Publishing; (2000), p. 975.
6. *Ibid.* at p. 978.
7. *Winterbottom v. Wright,* 10 M&W 109, 152 Eng. Rep. 402 (Exch. Pl. 1842).
8. *MacPherson v. Buick Motor Co.* 217 N.Y. 382, 390, 111 N.E. 1050, 1053 (1916)—in the *MacPherson* case, the plaintiff was injured by his car he purchased from the retailer, not from the manufacturer; thus, there was no privity with the manufacturer. The *MacPherson* court allowed the plaintiff to go forward with his suite claiming, "If the manufacturer is negligent where danger is to be foreseen, a liability will follow." This case placed defective products within the realm of a negligence analysis.
9. Dobbs DB. *The Law of Torts.* Hornbook Series. St. Paul, MN: West Group Publishing; (2000), p. 977.
10. *Ibid.* at p. 978 and Restatement of Products Liability, Sections 2(b)(c) and 360.
11. Kionka EJ. *Torts – Injury to Persons and Property*. St. Paull, MN; Nutshell Series of West Publishing Co.; (1983), p. 262.
12. UCC §2-318.
13. *Brochu v. Ortho Pharm. Corp.* 642 F.2d 652 (1st Cir. 1981).
14. *Murphy v. E.R. Squibb,* 40 Cal.3d. 672, 221 Cal. Rptr. 447 (Calif. 1985).
15. *Common Defenses to Product Liability Claims*, prepared by the Schweril, Goetz & Sieben Law Firm, Minnesota Personal Injury Powerhouse, March 2007.

QUESTIONS

1. What are the possible theories that a plaintiff in a products liability case can raise?
2. Regarding the different theories that can be employed in bringing a products liability suit, explain how each can be applied to the product being sued on (hint: show how the rule for each of

the theories can be applied to a defective product placed upon the market).

3. With regard to a drug product defect, often the most common defect causing harm or injury is related to which one of the three defects noted under a strict liability claim?
4. If a products liability claim were to be brought under the theory of negligence because the product had a design flaw, what four elements would have to be proven with regard to that design flaw?
5. The products liability law does not require that the party who is injured must be in privity with the manufacturer or seller of that product. What does it specifically mean that the purchaser of the product be in privity with the manufacturer or the seller of the product? If the "privity" rule is no longer applied, to what extent would other parties injured by a product who are not in privity be allowed to file a products liability lawsuit? Give examples of who these other classes of persons, not in privity, might be.
6. What is the fundamental difference between an *implied warranty of merchantability* and an *implied warranty of fitness for a particular purpose*?
7. Provide one or two examples of what would constitute a breach of the implied warranty of fitness for a particular purpose by a pharmacist using over-the-counter drug products that are intended to be sold to a consumer based upon the consumer's inquiry on what product would be the best for his or her medical condition.
8. What is the major reason why a breach of the *implied warranty of fitness* for a particular purpose will only be afforded to the purchaser of a product, and not to some second or third party who is given the product by the purchaser and is injured by that product? Are there any exceptions to this rule?
9. Considering a specific product for each of the strict liability defects, provide an example when:
   a. The product presents a manufacturing defect.
   b. The product presents a design defect.
   c. The product presents a warning defect.
10. If a product is inherently dangerous but has utility for an intended purpose and after the application of the "cost-benefit analysis test," it is found that to make the product safer, an extensive amount of money must be spent for that purpose, can the product still be placed on the market without expending an unreasonable amount of money to make it safer? If it is placed on the market as such, what other methods need to be employed to ensure the product, without any corrections, is used safely?

CHAPTER 15

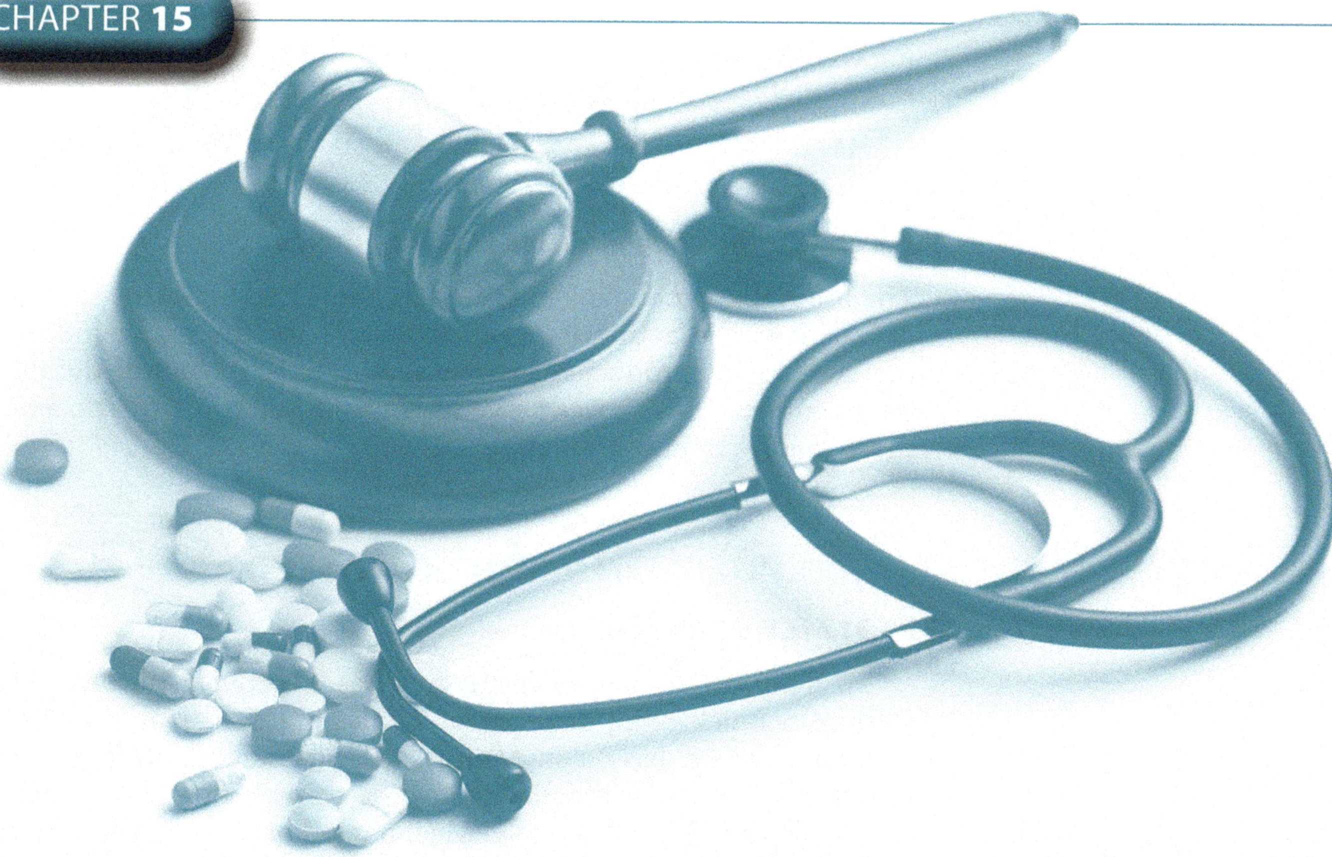

Products Liability (Part II): Case Presentations

The number of cases that involve products liability claims is extensive. The purpose of this chapter is to provide the reader with an overview of the products liability so-called playing field; thus the cases will not follow the same construction of previous cases from previous chapters, but will briefly state the facts, provide a concise case analysis, and provide a statement of the court's ruling. Also, there will be a series of case discussions in the beginning of this chapter that are not based in pharmacy or pharmaceutical industry claims. Most of these original products liability cases were aimed at the early developments in the automotive industry and the different types of injuries or mishaps that were occurring in this industry as it was rapidly advancing. These introductory cases set the stage of how the tort of products liability began in the early part of the 1900s and evolved to include claims that involve pharmaceutical products.

REVIEW OF NON-PHARMACY-RELATED CASES OF IMPORTANCE THAT SET THE STAGE FOR LATER CASES DEALING WITH PHARMACEUTICALS

Early Automobile Products Liability Cases

The following products liability cases addressed concerns that were prevalent in the automobile industry—one of the major industries associated with products liability cases in the first half of the twentieth century. These cases serve as some of the most classic among those involving automobiles.

MACPHERSON V. BUICK MOTOR CO.

217 N.Y. 382 1916

MacPherson, as the plaintiff, purchased a Buick automobile from a Buick retail dealership. While driving the automobile manufactured by Buick Motor Co., the defendant, a wheel collapsed, causing MacPherson to be thrown out of the automobile and injured severely. MacPherson brought a negligence suit against the Buick Motor Co., claiming that the automobile sold to him was an inherently or imminently dangerous product placed in the marketplace. The Buick Motor Co., applying a contract theory, insisted that the responsible party for the injury caused to MacPherson was the retailer who sold MacPherson the car based upon a privity of contract argument. The court, however, abolished the privity of contract requirement in negligence cases, allowing MacPherson to prevail against the Buick Motor Co.

BAXTER V. FORD MOTOR CO.

168 Wash. 456 1932

The plaintiff, Baxter, was driving a Ford Motor automobile whose windshield that the defendant, Ford Motor Co., expressly stated in writing to Baxter, was shatter-proof. Baxter suffered injuries when a pebble struck the windshield, causing small pieces of glass to fly into Baxter's eyes. Baxter sued Ford Motor Co., on a theory of misrepresentation. Again, even though Baxter was not the direct purchaser of the Ford vehicle, the court ruled that a manufacturer or retailer of a product is responsible for all representations made upon which the consumer must rely, regardless of a contractual relationship between the plaintiff and the defendant.

HENNINGSEN V. BLOOMFIELD MOTORS

161 A.2d 69 N.J. 1960

The plaintiff, Mrs. Henningsen, was severely injured when her steering gear malfunctioned and caused her car to crash into a wall. She sued Chrysler, the manufacturer of the car, and Bloomfield Motors, the dealer, from whom her husband purchased the car. The court ruled that when a manufacturer and a dealer put a new car in the stream of commerce and promote its purchase, an implied warranty is created that it is reasonably suitable for use as expected by the consumer. This implied warranty applies to the ultimate user despite any contractual provisions to the contrary.

Automobiles were obviously not the only targets for products liability suits. Any product manufactured that had a manufacturing, design, or labeling flaw could be subject to a products liability suit if the consumer was injured, barring any reasonable defenses that could be raised by the defendant. The following two product cases deal with a manufacturing and a design defect.

ESCOLA V. COCA COLA BOTTLING CO.

24 Cal.2d 453, Calif. 1944

A bottle of Coca Cola exploded in the plaintiff's hand, causing severe injury. Of issue was the potential of a defect in the manufactured bottle that was aggravated by the buildup of pressure from the gases created by the carbonated drink contained inside. This case led to justifying "strict liability" as a major theory to be employed since the theory of negligence was often too difficult to prove in these types of cases. "The manufacturer is in best position to either prevent harm or insure or spread the cost of risk; and the manufacturer of a product induces consumer reliance on the expectation of the product's safety and should be made to stand behind the product." While the manufacturer may believe that it has placed a safe product on the market—such as in this case, where it has contained a carbonated drink in a glass bottle—the manufacturer has to take into account what will happen if the carbonated liquid contained within can be prevented from causing the glass container to explode under the building up of pressure from the gases should they expand. The court opined that the manufacturer needs to consider the use of thicker glass containers or other types of containers to withstand the buildup of pressure from the potentially expanding gases within, especially when the product is shaken up. This case, under a theory of strict liability, represented a manufacturer's flaw in manufacturing and possible inappropriate design of the container.

GREENMAN V. YUBA POWER PRODUCTS

59 Cal.2d 57, Calif. 1963

The plaintiff, Mr. Greenman, was injured when a piece of wood flew out of a power tool (used as a saw, drill, and wood lathe) that he had purchased and was using struck him in the forehead. He sued both the manufacturer and the retailer for the injury he received. The court found that the manufacturer was strictly liable when a product it places on the market, knowing that it is to be used without inspection for defects, proves to have a defect that causes injury .... "The purpose of such liability is to insure that the costs of injuries resulting from defective products are borne by the manufacturers that put such products on the market rather than by the injured persons who are powerless to protect themselves."

In the previous chapter, we discussed the "cost-benefit analysis test"—could the product be made safer at very little expense by adding some component that would prevent an injury that might be classed as "foreseeable"? If the answer is "yes," the product is deemed flawed until the safety component is added. Remember, some products that are considered flawed or inherently dangerous may be too expensive to correct; if so, they are not really considered flawed, but require warning statements to ensure the consumer uses the product in a manner that will be safe once knowing the dangers associated with the product. In the *Greenman* case, the manufacturer of the saw would need to add a guard over the top of the rotating blade to prevent wood cuttings from moving in the direction of the consumer's face and eyes. The addition of a guard over the rotating blade would not be considered an excessive cost burden for the manufacturer, yet would be a valuable safety feature for protecting the consumer from being injured from flying wood cuttings.

THE APPLICATION OF PRODUCTS LIABILITY TO PHARMACEUTICAL PRODUCTS

Many of the drug cases that are associated with a products liability claim are often brought under the theory of strict liability. "Strict liability makes the manufacturer or seller of a defective product responsible for all injuries occurring from the use of the product. The victim must show that the product was defective and that the defect was the cause of the personal injury. If so proven, then strict liability holds the manufacturer or seller responsible, regardless of fault or intent."[1]

When a pharmaceutical product injures an individual—and such injury may be the result of an undiscoverable side effect at the time the drug was taken—should the pharmaceutical company that produced the drug still be held liable for the injury incurred? If the company is to be held liable, should there be a time period in which that liability should attach? The following California case, *Murphy v. Squibb Pharmaceutical Co.*, represents a case where an unknown side effect was not discovered for some 20 years after the taking of the drug. It is a unique case in that much of the information regarding which pharmaceutical company may have been responsible for causing an adverse effect that showed up 20 years later was lost. The decision by the California Supreme Court in the *Murphy* case represents one of the more innovative decisions using the concept of market share assessment.

CHRISTINE MURPHY V. E.R. SQUIBB & SONS, INC.

Calif. Supreme Court, 40 Cal.3d 672 – 1985

Desired Remedy: The plaintiff, Christine Murphy, developed clear cell adenocarcinoma at the age of 23 years in 1975, allegedly as the result of her mother taking diethylstilbestrol in 1952 for the purpose of reducing the risk of a miscarriage. The plaintiff sought damages on the theory of strict liability, alleging that the drug was defectively designed.

Issue: Does a plaintiff who was allegedly injured as result of an adverse effect from a drug that her mother took some 23 years earlier have a case in strict liability against the pharmaceutical company that produced the drug?

Facts of Case: Christine Murphy, plaintiff, developed vaginal adenocarcinoma at the age of 23 years in 1975, some 23 years after her mother took diethylstilbestrol in 1952 to maintain her pregnancy. Other cases were also being reported at this time providing strong evidence of the potential hazard the drug posed to females born to mothers who were placed on diethylstilbestrol therapy. The plaintiff's mother acquired the diethylstilbestrol from Exclusive Prescription Pharmacy, with a claim that the drug was provided by the E.R. Squibb pharmaceutical company. The problem that existed for the plaintiff was that all records from 1952 existing at the subject pharmacy were no longer available to substantiate the claim that E.R. Squibb was the company that supplied the diethylstilbestrol to the plaintiff's mother. It was determined that E.R. Squibb in 1952 held 10% of the market share of supplying diethylstilbestrol. The trial court, finding that it was impossible to prove that E.R. Squibb was the provider of the drug to the plaintiff's mother, entered judgment in favor of defendants. The plaintiff appeals.

Case Analysis: While the market share for Squibb was only 10% for diethylstilbestrol, there were at least five other companies that produced the product. The appeals court turned to the doctrine established in the *Summers v. Tice* case.[2] In the *Summers* case, the plaintiff had suffered an injury to his eye after two defendants had each shot a gun in his direction. The plaintiff was unable to demonstrate which of the defendants was responsible for his injury. The court reasoned that not to provide the plaintiff with a remedy would be unfair and shifted the burden of proof to the two defendants to have them prove which one of them caused the injury to the plaintiff. In applying the *Summers* outcome to this case, there were approximately five major pharmaceutical companies that produced the bulk of diethylstilbestrol in 1975, each having a specific percentage share of the market. Therefore, the court concluded to let each of those companies be responsible to the plaintiff for its market share percentage of the total financial judgment awarded.

Case Holding: The appeals court reversed the trial court's decision, and required that each of the major pharmaceutical companies that produced diethylstilbestrol be held to pay the plaintiff its market share percentage of the total financial judgment awarded.

The following case is a drug products liability case that resulted from a shocking discovery that capsules of Tylenol had been laced with cyanide, creating concerns whether or not drug manufacturers were properly containing or sealing their drug products during the packaging process.

ELSROTH V. JOHNSON & JOHNSON

700 F. Supp. 151 (S.D.N.Y. 1988)

Desired Remedy: The family of the deceased plaintiff seeks damages from McNeil Pharmaceuticals for the death of Diane Elsroth—who took Tylenol capsules laced with potassium cyanide—in a strict liability claim that the manufacturer of the capsules had used defective packaging.

Issue: Was there a defect in the packaging of Tylenol capsules that allowed a criminal to remove the package seals in order to lace the capsules contained within the package with potassium cyanide that caused the death of Diane Elsroth?

Facts of Case: On February 4, 1986, Harriet Notarnicola purchased a box of Tylenol Extra-Strength capsules from a New York grocery store owned by The Great Atlantic & Pacific Tea Co., (A&P). The Tylenol was manufactured by McNeil Products Co.

Diane Elsroth was visiting her boyfriend, Michael Notarnicola, for a week at the home of Michael's parents. Late on the night of February 7, Diane complained of a headache. Michael went to the kitchen, opened the box and plastic container of Extra-Strength Tylenol purchased by his mother at the A&P store, and returned with two capsules and a glass of water for Diane. A short time after ingesting the capsules, Diane retired. Her dead body was found the next day. The medical examiner concluded that the Tylenol capsules ingested by Diane were contaminated by a lethal dose of potassium cyanide. The murder remains unsolved, but evidence shows that the Tylenol bottle had been tampered with after the product left the manufacturer's control.

An unknown third party purchased the Tylenol, breached the packaging, substituted cyanide for some of the medicine contained in several of the gelatin capsules, somehow resealed the container and box in such a way that the tampering was not readily detectable, and placed the contaminated box on the shelf of the A&P store. John Elsroth, administrator of Diane's estate, brought this strict liability action against McNeil and A&P seeking $1 million in compensatory damages and $92 million in punitive damages.

Case Analysis: As a result of this unfortunate happening due to possibly one mentally disturbed criminal, for manufacturers of over-the-counter drugs, such as Tylenol, the FDA issued a final rule on tamper-resistant packaging. The rule defines a tamper-resistant package as "one having an indicator or barrier to entry that, if breached or missing, can reasonably be expect to provide visible evidence to consumers that tampering has occurred."

Following issuance of the rule, the makers of Tylenol have marketed the product in tamper-resistant packaging with the following features: (1) a foil seal glued to the mouth of the container or bottle, (2) a "shrink seal" around the neck and cap of the container, and (3) a sealed box (the end flaps of which are glued shut) in which the product and the container are placed.

It was the opinion of the court that the existing packaging was adequate as "state of the art," with the FDA noting that no packaging could prevent this kind of criminal tampering act since the form of tampering was carefully engineered. The packaging alternative designed by McNeil employed not one, not two, but three of the tamper-resistant features listed as alternatives in the 1982 FDA regulations. When all of these factors are thrown into the mix, we find, as a matter of law, that under a utility-risk analysis, this packaging was in a condition reasonably contemplated by the ultimate consumer and was not unreasonably dangerous for its intended use. Moreover, the plaintiff has presented no evidence of what other steps might feasibly have been taken to ensure a higher degree of safety. If there are better tamper-resistant features available that would be feasible for use here, the plaintiff has not described them. We return, however, to the fundamental premise: no packaging can boast of being tamper-proof.

Case Holding: The court held that there was no defect in packaging. The defendants are not, therefore, strictly liable for Ms. Elsroth's death.

JOAQUIN HEREDIA V. JAMES JOHNSON, MD, PAYLESS DRUG STORES & BURROUGHS WELLCOME CO.

U.S. District Court. Nevada 827 F.Supp. 1522 (1993)

Desired Remedy: Mr. Heredia sues the defendants named previously in strict liability and negligence for not providing him with proper labeling that would have warned him to discontinue his Pediotic Otic Suspension prescribed for his acute otitis media if symptoms of tympanic membrane rupture appeared.

Issue: Which of the previous defendants would be liable to Mr. Heredia for not providing him with the appropriate warning that the Pediotic Otic Suspension can cause tympanic membrane rupture?

Facts of Case: One of the medications prescribed by Dr. Johnson for Mr. Heredia's severe pain and numbness in his left ear was Pediotic Otic Suspension. The plaintiff claims that he carefully took all the drugs as directed on the labeling. However, he contends that the Pediotic Otic Suspension was not properly labeled in that it did not contain a warning that the use or administration of Pediotic Otic Suspension should be discontinued and the prescribing physician promptly contacted in case of symptoms of tympanic membrane rupture. The plaintiff contends that due to the defective and unreasonably dangerous manner in which the drug was dispensed (without appropriate labeling and warning), he suffers from severe and permanent injuries, including brain damage.

Case Analysis: The plaintiff brought suit against Payless Drug based upon a theory of strict liability and negligence. The strict liability claim argues that Payless did not provide an appropriate warning label ("defective labeling"), and the negligence claim imposes that Payless had a duty to provide such cautionary labeling, and breached its duty.

Strict tort liability may be imposed upon sellers and those in the chain of distribution as well as manufacturers for their role in placing a defective product into the stream of commerce. For purposes of the strict liability claim, the allegation is not directed at the conduct of the pharmacist but rather the nature of the product as it made its way through the stream of commerce. Since the information regarding the caution statement of causing rupture to the tympanic membrane was a condition noted in the Burroughs and Wellcome package insert, this information needed to be displayed or discussed with the patient as a serious adverse effect of the drug.

In the added negligence claim, the plaintiff claims the defendant Payless failed to properly label the container that contained the Pediotic Otic Suspension with the appropriate warning to the user of the product.

Case Holding: Payless's motion for summary judgment fails since the defendant Payless failed to include a written warning with a prescription drug supplied by the manufacturer, extending judgment in favor of the plaintiff.

CAN A DRUG BE DEFECTIVE IF CERTAIN INFORMATION SUCH AS DISCOVERED ADVERSE EFFECTS IS MISSING FROM THE LABELING?

An issue that may face a pharmaceutical manufacturer when it first places its drug on the market after the required FDA testing that demonstrates that the newly marketed drug is safe and effective for the medical purpose it is intended for is that newer adverse effects from that drug may be discovered once the drug is being used by increased numbers of patients. In other words, when the drug company, after years of research on a drug, thinks it knows everything about that drug and after approval and market release to larger population use, there is always the possibility that some newer non-desirable effects may be noted. Some of those newer non-desirable effects may present serious outcomes such as death.

When a pharmaceutical company is faced with this new knowledge about a potential serious adverse effect, it may hesitate placing necessary warnings on its labeling, arguing that it will need to validate these findings with further research. This obviously delays information of this nature being placed on the labeling that accompanies the drug to possibly allow both prescribers and pharmacists to instruct patients on newly discovered adverse effects that they need to know about. A question that is sometimes raised is: did the pharmaceutical company already know or should have known about this unlabeled adverse effect, sufficient to place such information in its labeling? If this newer information needed to be added to the drug labeling, and it was not, and patients using the drug void of this information are injured, they will generally bring suit against the drug company under a drug liability claim. Often, if reasonably large numbers of patients are injured by the drug due to this non-labeled side effect, a class action lawsuit is usually undertaken involving a large number of plaintiffs bringing the same claim and represented by one attorney or one law firm.

A number of drug products have identified with this category of "defective labeling." Discussed in the following is a sampling of drugs that have been associated with defective labeling and the outcomes the manufacturers of those drugs had to face.

FOSAMAX (ALENDRONATE SODIUM)

Fosamax, a product of the Merck pharmaceutical company, was FDA approved for the market in 1995 to be prescribed to increase bone density in patients with osteoporosis. Since 2006, numerous lawsuits were filed against Merck with claims that rather than increasing bone density and strengthening bones, in some cases the drug actually caused deterioration of the jaw bone or contributed to femur factures. Around this time, the drug company came out with a statement questioning these adverse effects, stating "that there does not appear to be any causal link demonstrated between long-term use of Fosamax and the factures being described."[3] Many of the cases of the fractures described were not generally seen until after around four or five years of continuous use of the drug. Merck in 2010 released a statement acknowledging the link between Fosamax and the jaw bone deterioration and provided the information in its patient package information source. However, Merck was allegedly told by the FDA in 2007 that it needed to revise the Fosamax labeling with the inclusion of the information pertaining to jaw and/or femur bone deterioration.

In one Fosamax case, *Shirley Boles v. Merck Co.* (a 2010 New York Federal Court case), along with several other Fosamax cases, the court stated that the Merck company failed to adequately research the drug and warn about the risk of jaw problems.[4] As a result, the plaintiff in this case was awarded $8,000,000 that was later reduced by the court to $1,500,000. Ms. Boles, who was 72 years old at the time of the decision, had been taking the drug for approximately eight years.

Fosamax is just one example of a multitude of drugs that prompted recovery damages and were cited for adverse effects that were not adequately publicized because either the described effects were still not entirely known or the information may have been withheld by the manufacturer for any number of reasons. Keep in mind that a drug company may not know of a newer adverse effect until it actually occurs. However, once it does occur, the drug industry may be required to warn about that effect if it appears to be reported in more than a few instances. Among some of the drugs that caused serious adverse effects or even deaths to a significant population of patients on those drugs, and where the subject pharmaceutical company involved had to pay out large sums of money either in settlements or judgments rendered by the courts, the following are briefly discussed:

Avandia: Used as an antidiabetic drug, it caused breathing difficulties, chest pain, fluid retention, and potential heart attacks. It is still available with necessary warnings and parameters for monitoring.

Baycol: Used to lower cholesterol levels, it was later found to cause rhabdomyolysis (a breakdown of muscle cells). This drug was removed from the market in August 2008.

Bextra: An anti-inflammatory COX-2 inhibitor primarily used for arthritis relief, it was responsible for causing heart attacks, stroke, severe skin reactions, and blood clots.

Propusid: Used to treat chronic gastroesophageal reflux disorders; however, it was later discovered to cause life-threatening heartbeat arrhythmias. The drug was removed from the market on July 14, 2000.

Rezulin: Employed to treat type-2 diabetes, it was later associated with deaths from liver damage. The drug was withdrawn from the market in March 2000.

Vioxx: A non-steroidal anti-inflammatory drug used to treat osteoarthritis, it was found to involve serious cardiovascular conditions leading to heart attacks. This drug was withdrawn from the market in 2004.

SUMMARY

When a products liability lawsuit is instituted, it may claim one or more of the following types of causes of action: (1) negligence, (2) strict liability, (3) breach of warranty, and/or (4) misrepresentation. Generally, strict liability is perhaps the more common cause of action taken since it directs attention to the fault in the product as having a defect in the manufacturing of the product, a defect in the design of the product, and/or a defect in the labeling of the product.

REFERENCES

1. Defective Products and Product Liability. From *LawyersandSettlements.com,* a Legal News Source. Updated on Feb. 28, 2014.
2. *Summers v. Tice,* 33 Cal.2d 80 (1948).
3. Fosamax Lawsuits. From *LawyersandSettlements.com,* a Legal News Source. Updated on January 21, 2015.
4. *Boles v. Merck* Fosamax Trial Jury Verdict is $8 Million for Plaintiff in June 2010. Posted by Tom Lamb at DrugInjuryWatch.com, June 26, 2010.

QUESTIONS

1. Each of the products liability cases presented in this chapter is important in developing the law associated with this area of tort law and helps serve a rule of precedence for future products liability cases. With regard to the cases presented earlier, briefly identify the rule that is established in the development of this area of tort law.
   a. *MacPherson v. Buick Motor Co.*
   b. *Henningsen v. Bloomfield Motors*
   c. *Escola v. Coca Cola Bottling Co.*
   d. *Greenman v. Yuba Power Products*
   e. *Joaquin Heredia v. James Johnson, MD, Payless Drug Stores & Burroughs Wellcome Company*
2. If a new drug product is placed on the market and the manufacturer withholds from the literature information about serious adverse effects it can cause, what arguments can be made under each of the various causes of action in a products liability suit for an injured plaintiff to prevail in a lawsuit against the drug manufacturer?
   a. Under the legal theory of negligence
   b. Under the legal theory of strict liability
   c. Under the legal theory of an implied warranty of fitness for a particular purpose
   d. Under the legal theory of misrepresentation

Glossary of Legal Terms

Appellant: Someone who is unsatisfied with the result of his or her lawsuit and asks an appeals court to review the decision. Note: If the defendant at the trial court level loses the case (plaintiff v. defendant), then the defendant can bring the case to the appeals court and is labeled the appellant and is in the first position on the lawsuit (eg, appellant (defendant originally) v. appellee (plaintiff originally).

Appellee: The party who the action is being taken against in an appeal. This party can be either the plaintiff or the defendant and is the one who usually loses at the trial court level.

Assumption of risk: The risk a party takes while engaged in what might be considered a dangerous activity, for example, working with explosives in building a tunnel through a mountain, and standing to close to the explosive when it detonates.

Cause of action: A party suing another party will list the reasons for bringing the lawsuit in the form of specific claims and facts and/or laws supporting the claims filed. Listings of "negligence," "defamation," and "invasion of privacy" are examples of "cause of action" claims.

Comparative negligence: The amount an award for damages in a negligence case is reduced based on the degree of negligence imputed to the plaintiff. Example: If the plaintiff is found to be comparatively negligent to the order of 20% negligent, then the plaintiff will only be entitled to 80% of the court award granted.

Compensatory damages: The amount of money awarded by a court to replace what was lost because of the unlawful conduct of another. The two types are special and general damages.

Conjecture: Speculation or a conclusion possibly based on incomplete information.

Constructive notice: Even if one didn't know, he or she should have known based on the standard of a reasonable person.

Contributory damages: Some jurisdictions apply this rule of damages to be awarded rather than the comparative damages rule. Under this damage arrangement in some jurisdictions, if the plaintiff is found to have contributed to his or her own negligence to any degree, he or she may be denied compensation entirely.

Defamatory statement: A false statement that injuries someone's reputation or business interests.

Defendant: An individual or company/institution/other entity that is accused or sued in a court of law.

Dismissal of a court case: A judge may dismiss a case from going forward based on a number of reasons. In dismissing the case, it may be done with or without prejudice:

- **Dismissal with prejudice:** It has been decided by the judge that the case brought before the court may lack specific features, and cannot be brought back to court in the manner the case was presented.
- **Dismissal without prejudice:** The dismissal of the case by the court does not prevent the case from being tried based upon the same cause of action(s) claims.

Enjoin: To stop some action from happening, such as stopping an individual from engaging in an activity that may be injurious to another usually through obtaining a court order.

Fiduciary: A responsible party that is expected to act in the best interests of another party, where the first party has a special relationship to the second party. Example: An attorney has a fiduciary responsibility to act in the best interest of his or her client, or a pharmacist who is expected to act in the best interest of patients he or she is serving.

Foreseeability: Usually a term associated with a causation analysis that allows to link the breach of a duty to the injury or harm caused. It is considered a perceivable anticipation that harm or injury will occur as the result of one's action, or omission to act.

Guardian ad litem: A court-appointed person to represent the interests of an incapacitated, mentally handicapped, or minor in a court case.

General damages: The amount of money awarded by a court to compensate a plaintiff for pain and suffering.

Hearsay: Information that cannot be confirmed adequately. Even though a statement may be hearsay, under the rules of evidence, certain hearsay statements may be admissible in a court of law.

Intervening force: In a situation where the defendant may appear to be the cause of an injury to a plaintiff, but some separate factor outside of the defendant's action may relieve the defendant from being held liable for the injury incurred to the plaintiff. Example: A defendant driving a car hits and injures a plaintiff pedestrian who attempt to cross the street. However, as the defendant's car closely approaches the plaintiff, the defendant driver finds out that someone standing behind the plaintiff pushed her into the line of the moving vehicle driven by the defendant. The person pushing the plaintiff in the line of traffic becomes the intervening force that breaks the chain of causation that would otherwise be attributable to the defendant.

Not all intervening causes relieve a defendant of liability. An intervening cause relieves a defendant of liability only if it would not have been foreseeable to a reasonable person, and only if damage resulting from the defendant's own actions would not have been foreseeable to a reasonable person. (See Wikipedia, "The Free Dictionary" by Farlex as reference for this last sentence.)

Last clear chance doctrine: A doctrine usually applicable to jurisdictions that follow the contributory negligence standard. The doctrine suggests that a negligent plaintiff can still recover damages if he or she is able to prove that the defendant had the last chance to avoid an accident.

Good faith: Attempt by one party to act in the best interests of another party without any intent of that party to seek an unfair advantage of another party.

Joint and several liability: Where a plaintiff may hold one or more of a group of persons liable for the same injury or harm caused collectively by that group of persons. Thus, the plaintiff may sue one or a few people in a group that caused him or her harm, or sue all of them together.

Libel: A false statement that is published and harms someone's reputation.

Loss of consortium: A claim in a tort case by a family member of the victim for loss of relationship. Only a spouse or family member can bring this action against a defendant.

Malfeasance: The doing of a wrongful or unlawful act.

Minimal damages: Money is awarded to a defendant who proves he or she was wronged, but cannot adequately quantify the extent of the damages. The amount awarded could be one dollar just to indicate that the plaintiff has won the case.

Negligence per se: An action is considered negligent because it violates a regulation or statute. The regulation or statute will usually define a duty that the defendant neglected to perform, or performed incorrectly.

Non-sequitur: An action by one party that may not have any relationship whatsoever to the reason the other party wishes to engage in a lawsuit regarding that action.

Pari delicto: A term to describe that both parties are equally at fault.

Plaintiff: Opposite of defendant. This is the party who brings a court case against another (the defendant).

Prima facie case: A Latin phrase that means, based upon the facts of a given case, that those facts presented are sufficient to prove that the conduct of the defendant will support a given cause of action that will most likely allow the plaintiff to prevail in a court of law.

Punitive damages: Additional money awarded to the plaintiff as a deterrent or punishment of the defendant. This is in addition to the amount awarded to compensate for the actual loss. Usually punitive damages are awarded in intent tort cases, or where the defendant was grossly negligent.

Qui tam: An individual may find that an entity like a large corporation has committed an act of fraud as an example, but the individual may not sue on his or her own behalf because the law only allows the state or federal government to bring such suits. However, the government may allow the individual to sue on behalf of the government, and receive a portion of any award in favor of the government granted by the court.

Reasonable person: "A hypothetical person who exercises those qualities of attention, knowledge, intelligence, and judgment which society requires of its members for the protection of their own interest and the interests of others." (*Restatement (Second) of Torts, Section 283[b].)*

Remand: When the appellate court sends back a case to the original trial court or to another court for further action or proceedings.

Remittitur: A ruling by a judge that lowers the amount of damages being awarded by a jury.

Rescind: To take back, and to make no longer valid.

Res ipsa loquitar: By definition, this term means "the thing speaks for itself."

Respondeat superior: Legal term that means the employer is responsible for the actions of the employees if they are acting within the scope of their employment.

Slander: Making a false statement verbally that harms someone's reputation.

Special damages: Compensation that is sought to return the injured party back to the condition they were in before the injury, such as lost wages, damaged property, medical expenses.

Standard of care: The prudence and care a person must take toward others, especially if that person is a professional providing services to others. That duty of care must be reasonable as what would be expected of a prudent individual providing such a standard of care under similar circumstances to others.

Stare decisis: Courts in making their decisions are to follow the decisions of previous cases decided in a given jurisdiction. Previous cases serve as precedence for future court decisions.

Summary judgment: A ruling by a judge that determines that outcome of a civil case before the full trial is complete. This is usually undertaken by the defendant's attorney presenting a motion for summary judgment to the court if all factual issues are settled, are missing, or are one-sided and the outcome can be quickly determined with little dispute.

Subpoena: An order issued by a court or an authoritative government agency to compel a witness to offer testimony or to request the production of documents. There are two types of subpoenas:

1. **Subpoena ad testificandum:** Commonly a court order requiring that a person testify at any number of formal hearings such as at a courtroom proceeding or at a deposition.
2. **Subpoena duces tecum:** Commonly a court order requiring that a person or an entity provide physical evidence or documents usually pertinent to a formal hearing in a courtroom proceeding or for review at a deposition.

Vicarious liability: Has the same meaning as *respondeat superior*, where the employer will be held liable for the acts of an employee while the employee is acting within the scope of that employment.

Ward of the state: An individual placed under the protection a legal guardian usually issued by a court order.

Index

Lightning Source UK Ltd.
Milton Keynes UK
UKHW050835121019
351455UK00005B/55/P

9 781259 640957